Praise for *Honest to Greatness*

"*Honest to Greatness* is a timely read for anyone who wants to engage with consumers in today's market. Peter Kozodoy sheds light on why some companies soar and others falter—it is as fascinating as it is informative!"
—Barbara Corcoran, *Shark Tank* star and founder of The Corcoran Group

"*Honest to Greatness* should be required reading for any aspiring leader. Filled with jaw-dropping stories and packed with actionable business tips, this book forces you out of your comfort zone and inspires you to make huge changes in your life and business!"
    —Richie Norton, author of *The Power of Starting Something Stupid*

"This is honestly one of the best books I've read in quite some time!"
        —Marshall Goldsmith, *New York Times* #1 bestselling author of
            Triggers, Mojo, and *What Got You Here Won't Get You There*

"*Honest to Greatness* explains why leaders need to be honest with others, but most importantly, honest with themselves. The book is chock-full of examples from companies like Domino's, Quicken Loans, The Ritz-Carlton, and Netflix, where leader-led cultures, focused on 'honest' practices like learning from customers and frontline employees, led to transformative breakthroughs. These stories show not only how honesty leads to the best decisions, but also how honesty is critical to gaining the trust that is so crucial to long-term success."
        —Dan Hesse, former CEO of Sprint

"The old rules of business no longer work in today's complicated environment. Only the most honest, transparent leaders and organizations will thrive into the future—and that's where *Honest to Greatness* comes in. You can't afford to miss this book."
            —Dave Kerpen, *New York Times* bestselling
                author of *Likeable Social Media*

"So well written, so timely. This book is a refreshing deep dive into the transformative power of total transparency. A masterpiece!"
        —Gino Wickman, author of *Traction* and *Entrepreneurial Leap*

HONEST TO
GREATNESS

HONEST TO
GREATNESS

HOW TODAY'S GREATEST LEADERS
—— USE BRUTAL HONESTY ——
TO ACHIEVE MASSIVE SUCCESS

PETER KOZODOY

BenBella Books, Inc.
Dallas, Texas

BenBella Books, Inc.
10440 N. Central Expressway
Suite 800
Dallas, TX 75231
www.benbellabooks.com
Send feedback to feedback@benbellabooks.com

BenBella is a federally registered trademark.

Printed in the United States of America
10 9 8 7 6 5 4 3 2 1

Library of Congress Cataloging-in-Publication Data
Names: Kozodoy, Peter, 1986- author.
Title: Honest to greatness: how today's greatest leaders use brutal honesty to achieve
  massive success / by Peter Kozodoy.
Description: Dallas, Texas : BenBella Books, Inc., [2020] | Includes bibliographical
  references and index.
Identifiers: LCCN 2020006140 (print) | LCCN 2020006141 (ebook) | ISBN
  9781948836500 (hardback) |ISBN 9781948836753 (ebook)
Subjects: LCSH: Success in business. | Leadership. | Entrepreneurship.
Classification: LCC HF5386 .K7785 2020 (print) | LCC HF5386 (ebook) | DDC
  658.4/09—dc23
LC record available at https://lccn.loc.gov/2020006140
LC ebook record available at https://lccn.loc.gov/2020006141

Editing by Debbie Harmsen
Copyediting by Judy Myers
Interior graphics by Spencer Mahar
Proofreading by Jenny Bridges
  and Sarah Vostok
Printed by Lake Book Manufacturing

Text design and composition by
  PerfecType, Nashville, TN
Cover image © Shutterstock/
  Sarawut Aiemsinsuk
Indexing by WordCo Indexing
  Services, Inc.

Distributed to the trade by Two Rivers Distribution, an Ingram brand
www.tworiversdistribution.com

Special discounts for bulk sales are available.
Please contact bulkorders@benbellabooks.com.

CONTENTS

FOREWORD

What does honesty really mean to you?

Do you believe that honesty really is the best policy?

Do you believe that honesty can drive long-term success?

Are you fed up with dishonest people and dishonest businesses being successful and seemingly getting ahead while honest people and businesses lag behind?

In *Honest to Greatness: How Today's Greatest Leaders Use Brutal Honesty to Achieve Massive Success*, Peter Kozodoy takes a bold and refreshing look at the importance of honesty in today's business world.

You may react to the title with a roll of your eyes or an "If only that were true." If so, you highlight the need for Peter's message . . . now more than ever.

We live and work in a society where the phrase "Honesty is the best policy" is usually followed by "except when . . ."

Despite making excuses for dishonesty in the business world, a stark dichotomy exists in our personal lives. When a beloved friend or family member deceives us, we take grave personal offense, since honesty plays such a pivotal role in most of our personal values; yet we live in a business world that has created a system in which both public and private organizations can lie, cheat, and steal, all from behind an Oz-like curtain, and most of us shrug our shoulders in apathy as we chalk it up to "that's the way things are."

When it comes to deceit, no one can claim immunity. Lying, however horrible we deem it to be, is an innate human condition. Sometimes we actively stretch the truth through rationalization or exaggeration to the point that we even believe the embellished version of the truth ourselves.

I remember a main stage speaker who owned over $15 million in real estate and told his audience he owned $100 million. As he left the stage, I asked him why he felt the need to exaggerate (lie) when the truth was good enough and quite impressive in its own right. His answer was "to sell more to them."

Unfortunately, there are too many so-called experts who share this practice, to the point that I have lost faith in many of them and have chosen to not share the stage with them anymore. I look for people who "walk the talk," not "fake it 'til you make it!"

It seems each week we hear of another business being "outed" for corruption, fraud, or deceit—companies that thought the short-term rewards justified their actions and dishonesty but found out they created long-term devastation for themselves, their investors, and their customers. Peter reveals the inside stories of some of these failures.

Today, the internet, instant news, and social media increase the transparency and public awareness of public figures and companies. In addition, younger generations are demanding social responsibility in the companies they support. This contributed to a tremendous growth in Conscious Capitalism. In fact, I teach that the most successful businesses either *solve a problem* or *serve a need*. Their financial success is a direct result of their contribution to society.

This is why I am delighted to support Peter's work and share the message of bringing honesty back in all aspects of our lives. He shares business cases so you can learn from some of today's greatest leaders and how they used brutal honesty to achieve game-changing business outcomes for their organizations, massively outpacing their industries and creating huge financial rewards in the process.

Given that we've twisted the truth for so long, the simple concept of honesty has become harder to implement than it should be. This book will show you that honesty not only matters but is also the first step toward massive success. And you'll be able to explain what honesty means, because it represents so much more than simply telling the truth.

Open-mindedness, humility, compassion, empathy, and curiosity all play a role in defining and using honesty wisely and effectively.

First, you'll learn to get honest about what's going on in your community—including what's changing in your industry and what's happening in our evolving world.

Second, you'll learn to get honest about how you view others around you, whether those others are your team, your customers, your prospects, or something else entirely.

Third, you'll learn how to get honest with and about yourself, define your own core values, and spot the right opportunities for growth.

Make no mistake: this shift toward brutal honesty is already happening everywhere, and you have the choice right now to be part of this *Honest to Greatness* movement. You have the power *and* the obligation to embrace the new, honest way to achieve greatness in the twenty-first century.

The stories and strategies in this book show that honesty is *the* fundamental element that leads you to greatness; it unlocks your potential to live your best life and achieve your wildest dreams, both personally and professionally. Hiding your true self no longer makes sense in a world that rewards authenticity and heralds honesty. And with the business cases in this book, you're going to see how today's greatest leaders are truly changing the business environment to one of honesty and contribution.

—**Sharon Lechter CPA, CGMA**
Founder and CEO of Pay Your Family First
Author of *Think and Grow Rich for Women*
Coauthor of *New York Times* best seller *Rich Dad Poor Dad* and
fourteen other Rich Dad books, *Three Feet from Gold, Outwitting the
Devil, Success and Something Greater*, and *Exit Rich!*
www.sharonlechter.com

INTRODUCTION

"Hurry up!" RH said over his shoulder to his cofounder, Marc, and their new CFO, Barry. "This is going to make us or break us. We can't be late!" The three hurried out of the Dallas/Fort Worth International Airport and flagged down a cab, which would whisk them to the gleaming Renaissance Tower—a bastion of successful national corporations in the year 2000. Marc sported a worn leather briefcase slung over his right shoulder, while a bright red box filled with palm-sized plastic squares balanced precariously on his left arm. He could feel his biceps giving way under the weight and his entire left side slipping into numbness as they hurried into the lobby. Marc slowed just long enough to gaze up at the faceted transparent glass ceiling above their heads, and RH wondered if they'd be in a much loftier place when they returned to this same lobby in just one short hour.

"Hopefully the heavens are with us," Barry uttered under his breath, also caught, mesmerized, by the articulated dome overhead.

"No need to pray, guys," RH shot back. "This is it. Today's our day."

Their nerves betrayed RH's confidence; on the elevator ride up, Barry's hands began to quiver ever so slightly, gathering energy as they finally reached the twenty-third floor. The elevator door snapped open, and with the collective inhale of a symphony of trumpet players about to carry their first note of the evening, the three pressed onward to the corner boardroom.

After what seemed like hours, John finally strode in like a corporate knight, with an executive assistant busily rattling off scheduling changes in his ear and a whole cadre of well-suited executives in tow. RH bolted to his feet to shake each one's hand and hunkered down for his presentation on why his firm would be the perfect acquisition target. He had rehearsed his blocking, his phrasing, his insistence on the worthiness of the firm's asking price: a not-too-shabby $50 million. Surely, RH reasoned, their ask was a pittance for the national industry leader in whose glass-walled, oak-tabled boardroom they sat. But Barry, always with an eye to the numbers, knew that their ask was a fortune compared to their company's monthly net *loss*. Neither was it any secret that the entrepreneurial company had never made money—as these seasoned executives surely knew.

To those executives in their hard-won tower, the little start-up in question looked like a fairly indecent proposal. The start-up, bleeding cash and promising all the "innovation" in the world, posed no threat to John's industry juggernaut. *There was time*, John presumed, loads of time in which to think and act strategically. There were plenty of opportunities at hand that could carry his already successful corporation forward into the new millennium. That's precisely why John did not acquire the little start-up company that day; instead, John and his team of shrewd executives laughed poor RH, Marc, and Barry out of the room, out of Renaissance Tower, and right out of Dallas, Texas.

Retreating to their tiny start-up headquarters in California, the three might have quit right then and there. Fortunately for all of us, they didn't. Instead, they grew to become the fastest-growing media company in the world and put John's multibillion-dollar empire right out of business—because RH is Reed Hastings, the cofounder of Netflix, and John Antioco, the CEO of Blockbuster, had just made the biggest mistake of his life.

My dramatization of this account notwithstanding, it's so easy for us to judge the Blockbuster vs. Netflix story in hindsight. *Of course* Netflix would triumph! *What a fool* Antioco must have been for letting Netflix slip through his fingers! The disbelief we feel can only be addressed by assuming that Antioco was inept, his team was completely ineffective, and this entire situation was due to idiocy at the highest levels.

But is that entirely true? If that's the obvious conclusion we're to draw from this disheartening disaster, there's a burning question we must also answer if we're to believe the lesson: *If Antioco was just a big ol' dummy, then how could he have possibly risen to become one of the most powerful CEOs in the media business?*

It turns out that the answer to this question is the most telling of all, because, as we can all agree, it takes a tremendous amount of raw intelligence, analytical skills, and political acumen to become the chief executive officer of an $8.4 billion company.[1] So if Blockbuster's downfall wasn't caused by idiocy, then what exactly caused it? And how can we learn from its demise for the benefit of our own business pursuits?

The Blockbuster story's root cause analysis echoed a similar question I asked myself during the early part of my career running an international marketing agency: Why did some of our clients use our growth strategies to get a massive return on their investment, while others never even got out of the starting gate? What was it, I asked myself, that prevented otherwise well-meaning and intelligent executives from recognizing trends, innovating, dominating their industries, and crushing the competition, as in the case of Blockbuster?

The answer, you may have guessed, is buried in a lesson we all learned between birth and preschool, in that time of our lives when we assumed that everyone would obey it.

That lesson: *Honesty is the best policy.*

Somehow we've forgotten the lesson, and at our own peril. To see just how perilous, let's look at the numbers. In 1994, just before the ill-fated John Antioco took control of Blockbuster, the home-video giant was worth about $8.4 billion.[2] For those keeping track, that was even before Netflix was founded in 1997 (ironically, the year Antioco took office). By 2010—just thirteen short years later—Blockbuster was worth a paltry $24 *million*, losing a market cap of approximately $8.376 billion. Put into a slightly different perspective, Blockbuster's talented executives obliterated a few billion more than the entire GDP of the wealthy nation of Monaco.

Now, what does this have to do with honesty? After all, if we're talking about numbers and honesty, Netflix was not in great shape at the time. *But there's much more to the concept of honesty than meets the eye.* Here's what I propose: Antioco and his merry group of well-heeled executives didn't lose $8.376 billion because they were *inept*. They lost their net worths and the hard-earned money of their investors because Antioco and his team were *not honest with themselves* about what was going on around them—the massive shift we consumers were making from physical DVDs to online streaming services.

However, this being a book about honesty, it wouldn't be fair to end the story here, where most accounts leave off. In fact, Antioco did eventually come around to the truth about how consumers preferred to consume their in-home entertainment. By late 2006, Antioco had done away with Blockbuster's legendary late fees and created Total Access, a DVD-by-mail program that had attracted over two million customers.[3] In a harsh twist of fate, Hastings even offered to buy Blockbuster's online operations in 2007 at a secret meeting at the Sundance Film Festival, which would have united Netflix's online program with Blockbuster's brick-and-mortar footprint.[4]

Unfortunately for Antioco, it was too little, too late. Since Total Access was hemorrhaging cash playing catch-up to Netflix, the venerable Carl Icahn stepped in as an activist investor to put a stop to the innovative program.[5] Icahn removed Antioco and installed James Keyes as CEO. Keyes immediately rejected Hastings's proposal to join forces with Netflix, raised prices, and put a stop to the fast-growing Total Access program. Even the great Icahn failed to get honest about the trends going on around him and chose to stick to the status quo. Not long after, like the tapes that once graced its whitewashed walls, Blockbuster—with Icahn and Keyes at its helm—would vanish into the pop-culture collage that was 1980s and '90s Americana. Antioco walked away with a new moniker: the Blockbuster Buffoon.[6] And Netflix? Netflix went on to be worth a staggering $151 billion by 2020, roughly eighteen times more valuable than Blockbuster ever was.

It's extraordinary what a little dishonesty can do to your business. But for the sake of argument, let's say Antioco sat his team down in

2001—just after meeting with the up-and-coming Netflix—and said, "OK . . . let's make sure we aren't missing something big here. Maybe it's time we get honest about what's changing in our industry, what we've built here at Blockbuster, and what we need to change within ourselves to make sure we keep innovating."

What might have happened then?

It turns out that all the MBAs, cash flow analyses, marketing tactics, and complex consulting strategies in the world can't save an organization that is fundamentally dishonest in the first place. As Blockbuster shows, it is not idiocy but a lack of *honesty* that causes the stagnation felt by many organizations that claim to desire innovation and growth. No matter what business you're in, what your goals are, or what obstacles confront you, honesty must come *first* . . . because without it, you won't even see your enemy staring at you from across the table in your own boardroom, high in the Renaissance Tower in Dallas, Texas.

WHAT IS HONESTY?

Usually when we label someone as dishonest, our first thought is they're not telling the truth. They're fudging the numbers, perhaps, or hiding something. But outright lying to people is just one intentional act—one facet of honesty. Individuals and companies are dishonest out of neglect, too, particularly when they lie to themselves.

Honesty is a broad concept. It could mean *true, candid, direct, transparent, moral,* or *trustworthy.* But as you'll see with the incredible companies we'll look at in this book, honest can also mean *innovative, ethical, fair, open-minded, willing to be humble, able to admit wrongdoing, ready for change,* and much, much more. As you read through these words and think about their meanings, you might assume something that I wrongfully assumed many years ago: *Doesn't every leader naturally exemplify these traits?*

When I first started preaching about the connection between honesty and business success, an interviewer asked me if I believe everyone is naturally honest. At that point, I answered, "Yes . . . for the most part." Now, years later, my answer is "Certainly not!" If anything, I've learned that honesty is a complex monster that rears its head every time you consider an action, make a decision, influence another, or even think. Like mindfulness, honesty is a practice you undertake as a lifelong pursuit of *being*, rather than an ad hoc criterion weighing on a certain decision.

> Honesty is a practice you undertake as a lifelong pursuit of *being*, rather than an ad hoc criterion weighing on a certain decision.

Honest leaders are able to pivot on a dime, recruit the best talent in their industry, create innovative products and services, earn outsized profits, create raving-fan cultures, scale their revenues, and create drool-worthy market returns. By contrast, those who brush honesty aside as a nice-to-have soft skill or dandy core value are risking millions or billions of dollars, public disgrace, and even jail time, as we'll see in some high-profile cases of dishonesty. Yes, honesty is that important and that intrinsic to your success, especially in our newly transparent world, where everything you say and do can be plastered all over social media and the global news in a matter of seconds—and then live on for generations to come.

SHORT TERM VS. LONG TERM

In the defense of leaders who haven't yet adopted honesty as a strategic tool for greatness, the fundamental relationship between honesty and sustained business success can be especially volatile in the short term. For instance, David Crane, the former CEO of the energy corporation NRG, was unceremoniously booted from his role as top dog due in part to his big and often controversial push into renewable energy sources over traditional sources. "The thing I struggle with most in having gotten fired," he later reflected, "is that I thought my special contribution to the [climate] cause was showing how a fossil fuel company can become a green company; but, by getting fired and not getting there,

I've sent the opposite message: 'If you think you can transform your company and get rewarded for it—you can't.'"[7]

Honest? You bet. Effective? That depends on how you define it. Few would agree that getting fired equals success, but then again, all would laud his standing up for what he knew was right. If we're honest with ourselves, we all know that fossil fuels are going the way of the dodo bird, and that renewable energy is unequivocally the way of the future. But as with many things in life, timing is everything. Crane's case proves that honesty doesn't always light the best path forward for self-preservation . . . but as we'll see, self-preservation doesn't lead to success, either; in fact, in most cases the pursuit of self-preservation can actually crush an organization's chances to achieve greatness *in the long run*. Look around and ask yourself how long NRG will survive as a traditional energy company, and you'll likely agree that Crane was directionally correct, though perhaps a bit early. Scores of other leaders have followed Crane's technique and won big, including one former CEO of Sprint, Dan Hesse, who took the reins as CEO in 2007. Like Crane, Hesse insisted that his telecom company be environmentally friendly. As he recounted to me, he would get drilled on Sprint's quarterly conference calls by analysts asking, "How can you justify spending so much time on being green, when Delaware law says that if it's not in the shareholder's interest *this quarter*, you shouldn't be doing it?" Focused on caring for his customers over the long run instead of on short-term Wall Street metrics, Hesse took Sprint from last to first place in customer satisfaction, winning twenty J.D. Power awards in customer service. With an insane focus on what's best for customers—environmentally or otherwise—Hesse returned 205 percent to shareholders from the bottom of the financial crisis in 2009 to his last full month as CEO in July 2014, roughly 30 percent more than the S&P 500 Index and nearly 50 percent more than Sprint's telecom competitors.[8] Hesse was honest about what mattered to his customers and to his planet, and he used it to help Sprint outperform in every sense of the word. We'll learn more about Hesse's approach to Sprint later in the book.

THE MODERN PHILOSOPHY OF GREATNESS

Your inclination to fear Crane's outcome or herald Hesse's indicates whether you can embrace honesty as a strategic tool for greatness or not. Perhaps, given enough time or a different set of boardroom politics, Crane could have swayed his board and investors to embrace renewables. Perhaps Crane wasn't honest enough about those around him—that is, he wasn't honest enough about what it would truly take to change minds and transform a fossil fuel company into a leading renewable energy company. In any event, he stuck to his core values and beliefs, and through his efforts at NRG, he made a lasting impact on his industry and the world by investing in residential solar projects and championing a future where we can all contribute to a sustainable power grid. In fact, if he hadn't been metaphorically executed in such spectacular fashion, perhaps he wouldn't have acquired the platform he has today to reinforce his message and encourage lasting change.

His story reminds me of the classic dichotomy between the way the Greek philosopher Plato defined the ideal leader and the way the fifteenth-century Italian philosopher Niccolo Machiavelli defined it. To Plato, the ideal leader must be fair, virtuous, and an upholder of truth above all in order to serve as an effective example to the public. Meanwhile, Machiavelli famously argued that a wise ruler should have two faces: the benevolent ruler who publicly preaches "peace and good faith," and the ruthless politician who privately rules with an iron fist and a healthy dose of deceitful politics.[9]

Of course, Machiavelli benefitted from additional centuries of kingships and political turmoil upon which to build a strategy. But is he right, even today? Looking around at our own current politicians and CEOs, you might be tempted to side with Machiavelli. But honesty is about time and place, and the business kingdoms of tomorrow will look very different from the fiefdoms of years past. We've entered the age of the consumer, with ubiquitous information transparency. Today's level of forced transparency defines the future, particularly—though certainly not exclusively—to millennials and Generation Z, who grew up with the ability to fact-check anything by uttering, "Hey, Siri?"

When it comes to choosing honesty, we simply won't have a choice much longer. The climate in which our society exists right now is very different from what has ever come before, which is why *we need a new set of rules in our business playbook* that are fundamental to a world in which there is nowhere to hide. In the defense of corporations everywhere, it was only a mere fifty years ago that the British philosopher Bertrand Russell believed that "life is nothing but a competition to be the criminal rather than the victim."[10] Russell died in 1970, two decades before the internet took inexorable hold of our society and changed human behavior as we've known it since we started walking on two legs. I suspect that if Russell had seen the dot-com bubble or

> Honesty is about time and place, and the business kingdoms of tomorrow will look very different from the fiefdoms of years past.

witnessed the rise of chat rooms, work-from-home jobs, or Glassdoor, he might have changed his stance and instead fashioned a worldview in which leaders, managers, employees, investors, suppliers, distributors, the public, the planet, and, especially, customers can—and must—win *together* in order to create lasting, successful, *honest* businesses. The businessperson who's bully and curator of the truth, who's selective about what the customer sees, is no longer a valid model or effective modus operandi.

———

Over the course of this book, we're going to take a look at what in the world has happened to our world—why we see dishonesty everywhere, why fake news rules our airwaves and social media, and why we must not give in to the temptation to deceive in the short term if we want to achieve success in the long term. We'll examine some obvious, scandalous cases of outright dishonesty to see whether or not dishonesty can still produce positive results in our modern society. Then we'll zoom out to put those cautionary tales into context by studying what has changed in the twenty-first century that is steadily forcing us to be honest and transparent, lest we end up fighting the likes of review sites, social media testimonials (good and bad), and the public relations wrath of angry customers.

Then we'll turn our attention to some of the most influential business leaders of our time to show how they have used honesty as a strategic tool for effective sales, marketing, finance, management, communication, innovation, and leadership, so you can discover how to spot opportunities to harness the power of honesty across your entire organization, whether you're in a leadership role or still rising through the ranks. We'll see how start-up entrepreneurs, small business owners, presidents of midsize companies, and the leaders of Sprint, Quicken Loans, Berkshire Hathaway, Domino's Pizza, Bridgewater Associates, Tropicana, and others use honesty and transparency to win. Spoiler alert: they don't sketch these touchy-feely

> The businessperson who's bully and curator of the truth, who's selective about what the customer sees, is no longer a valid model or effective modus operandi.

values onto their conference room walls and smile at them before each meeting. Instead, they *wield* honesty, and all that it encompasses, as a strategic technique to *thrive*. In this way, honesty is a value that gets etched into the souls of their organizations.

Along the way, we'll consider honesty from multiple angles and with several different lenses to see if we can take that nebulous concept and usefully define it, both in terms of what it is and what it surely isn't. Through that journey you'll doubtless find honesty compelling as a business growth strategy, but it isn't always easy to implement, as John Antioco proves. That's why we'll also discuss ways to cultivate honesty within your teams, from the C Suite to the front lines, and we'll even discover how to gently introduce honesty into the culture of your organization so you don't end up like NRG's Mr. Crane. Along the way, I'll provide you with critical frameworks that you can use to enhance your leadership skills, create a culture of innovation, and achieve industry-dominating success.

The techniques in this book transcend business size, industry, and purpose. Honesty, unsurprisingly, works universally; it creates opportunities to ask better questions, get more insightful answers, and overcome the roadblocks we face as leaders who lie—sometimes to others, but most often, egregiously, to ourselves.

Whether you're starting a new business and looking for the next big wave, growing a company and needing a rocket-fuel additive, or transforming your organization into its next phase of success, the frameworks in this book will help you get honest on three main levels—the same three levels that Blockbuster failed to identify.

First, you'll learn to get honest about what's going on in your *community*—including what's changing in your industry and what's happening in our evolving world.

Second, you'll learn to get honest about how you view the *others* around you, whether those others are your team, your customers, your prospects, or something else entirely.

Third, you'll learn how to get honest with and about *yourself*, so that you can easily recognize whether you're saying no to just another cold call or turning down the next Netflix-sized opportunity.

After more than a decade of working on behalf of leaders from local car dealers to Warren Buffett, I've discovered that honesty truly is the best policy—for your principles *and* your profits. Now I want to inspire *you* to use honesty to achieve greatness.

Let's begin.

PART I

Why Honesty?
Why Now?

Look at the news today and you see it everywhere: *dishonesty*. Today's most public CEOs, politicians, and celebrities seem to bask in the glow of deceit. We might even be tempted to believe that fakers make it farther. But here's the skinny: the world has changed in a way that human society has never before seen, and it's not changing back. Transparency is the new norm, and eventually, today's charlatans are getting permanently exposed. To kick off this truth-telling tale, we must first understand why honesty isn't just the best policy today; instead, it's the *only* policy for surviving—and thriving—in twenty-first-century business.

CHAPTER 1

Fraud Is Our Fault

Have you ever thought about your relationship with honesty? I bet you have at some point, given all the idioms and expressions we have about honesty and the truth. Look for it and you'll notice that the idea shows up in our books, shows, songs, and films. Listen for it and you'll hear the words everywhere; truth permeates our language like water in a sponge . . .

As honest as the day is long.
An honest buck.
An honest mistake.
A moment of truth.
Stretch the truth.
Let the truth be known!
The truth of the matter.
Truth be told . . .
To tell you the truth . . .
Ain't that the truth!
The truth, the whole truth, and nothing but the truth.
The naked truth.
Keep me honest?
If I'm honest . . .

At least you're honest!
Nothing could be further from the truth.
Honestly!
In all honesty . . .
Honesty is the best policy.
Honest to goodness.
Honest to greatness?

And yet, here's the cold, hard truth: we're all a bunch of no-good, dirty liars. And by the end of our time together, I'm confident you'll agree that our dishonesty—as individuals, as groups, and as organizations—keeps us from success.

But, sadly, that's not the worst part. The worst part is that most of us don't even know that we're lying. What are we lying about? Everything. We lie about the state of the world and what's going on around us. We lie about the people around us. And, worst of all, we lie to *ourselves.* We have no clue that we're even sabotaging ourselves with deceitful bullshit of the highest order. As a society, we humans have been acting dishonestly for millennia. We have dishonesty ingrained in us so deeply that getting it out will take a journey of self-discovery the likes of which you may never have considered before this moment. Luckily for you, your journey toward honesty is the exact same journey that the greatest leaders of our time have undertaken to create some of the world's most prolific, industry-dominating, and game-changing organizations. Actually, that's not even true. They haven't *undertaken* them, as in the past tense; they are still, every day, *undertaking* their journeys toward honesty—and it's the lifelong commitment to the journey that makes them successful.

That journey is the exact same one we're going to undertake together—and through shocking revelations, thought-provoking questions, and surprising stories from some of the world's greatest business leaders, you're going to learn exactly how to *use* honesty. And when I say "use" honesty, I don't mean put the word up on your wall at work, stare at it lovingly, toast it daily with champagne and crumpets (whatever *those* are), and develop a warm, fuzzy feeling about your moral compass.

Instead, I mean *wield* honesty just as you'd use any other business strategy to drive organizational growth, game-changing profits, and industry-dominating results.

How challenging is it to use honesty as a business strategy? Well, the problem is that *dishonesty* still seems to work. Examples abound of fraudulent actors using BS as a powerful currency that produces results. The question is, will dishonesty continue to work in the future, and can we even rightly say that it's working *now*? To figure that out, we need to see what happens when modern-day liars use dishonesty to get ahead.

> Wield honesty just as you'd use any other business strategy to drive organizational growth, game-changing profits, and industry-dominating results.

CHEATERS NEVER WIN ... OR DO THEY?

Are you an honest person? Don't worry, you don't have to answer that. I lie like a rug sometimes when the situation calls for it, so you should know that up front if we're going to be friends. But hey, at least I'm honest about it, right? Nobody can tell the truth 100 percent of the time. I mean, if your terminally ill friend were to ask you, "Hey, do you think I might die today?" what are you going to say? "Well, chances are good that today'll be it, bro. You best enjoy those last breaths just in case! It was real good knowin' ya. Do you mind if I borrow your Xbox?"

Of course not.

We all have our own set of values—our own personal spectrum of right, wrong, honest, and dishonest. The vast majority of us live in the acceptable middle of a normal distribution of honesty—a bell curve of agreeable morality in which my dying-friend example exists among other beneficial half-truths. But some cheaters—existing in the tails of that curve—have no qualms about lying right to your face about who they are and what they do. And egregious though it is, those same peeps seem to be the ones rolling around in Scrooge McDuck–style success! WTF?

Over Thanksgiving, I was standing in my mother-in-law's kitchen when she asked how I was. I answered that I was in the throes of producing what you are now reading, which was proving to be an arduous but highly enjoyable process.

When she asked what this book is all about, I told her it's about showing how today's most dominant leaders use honesty to achieve massive success. She paused momentarily before going back to assembling the jigsaw puzzle of deliciousness in the oven, then responded, simply, "Good for you. It always seems like you have to be dishonest to get anywhere in this world."

Well ain't that just the saddest thing? Her observation was not untrue; the truth of the matter is that unscrupulous people and dishonest companies *are* surviving and thriving, even in today's increasingly transparent world. I'm sure you can conjure up a few "successful" individuals and organizations with virtually no scruples. Any politicians, CEOs, entrepreneurs, government entities, or businesses come to mind?

Just because honesty can produce industry-leading profits (as we'll see in part two), and just because dishonesty is on its way out as the world becomes more transparent, doesn't mean that dishonesty *isn't* working for the time being; in fact, it's working literally in every corner of life. But as with all elements of our discussion, I hope you'll pause and ask, Is that entirely true? Does dishonesty *always* work? As with all good questions, the answer is *it depends.* Dishonesty often works *for a time,* just as the wax-hewn wings of Icarus helped him soar close to the sun. But just as Icarus learned that the penalty for flying without the proper ingredients can be quite severe, practicing dishonesty long term can also lead to disastrous results. Let's look at a few

> Dishonesty often works for a time, just as the wax-hewn wings of Icarus helped him soar close to the sun. But just as Icarus learned that the penalty for flying without the proper ingredients can be quite severe, so, too, can practicing dishonesty long term.

juicy cautionary tales of modern-day Icaruses who disregarded honesty and ended up scorched. As you read, keep this question in mind: *Is the risk of being dishonest worth the reward?*

Health Care's Billion-Dollar Bluff

Allow me to introduce you to a once-high-flying start-up called Theranos, formerly heralded as Silicon Valley's next great "unicorn" company. Theranos was founded and led by Stanford dropout and company CEO Elizabeth Holmes, who quickly became the youngest female self-made billionaire—at least according to her sky-high valuation.

Started in 2003, Theranos grew over a short eleven years to be valued at $10 billion[1]—yes, that's $10 billion with a *b*. This success rocketed Holmes to the covers of the biggest business magazines in the world. But by mid-2016, Theranos stumbled into the crosshairs of both the United States Justice Department and Securities and Exchange Commission. Regulators initially imposed sanctions, including banning Holmes from "owning or operating a medical laboratory for at least two years."[2] Shortly thereafter, she was indicted by a grand jury for fraud.

If you know the story, you know the heart of the matter: Elizabeth Holmes lied. She had promised that Theranos's groundbreaking machines could detect health problems at an unprecedented low cost by testing only a mere drop of blood, a method that would drastically shorten the time and cut the cost of diagnosis using traditional tools. That would be quite helpful to our world—if only it worked.

In *Wired* magazine, reporter Virginia Heffernan wrote one of the most scathing accounts of Holmes's downfall: "It's clear . . . that it was she—and no one else—who managed to drive the company's value up to $9 billion [at the time] without a working product." Her modern-day bank robbery left legendary investors like the DeVos family (whose members include the former CEO of Amway and the US Secretary of Education) and the media mogul Rupert Murdoch down by about $100 million apiece, with another $700 million lost from a veritable who's who of investing mavens. Heffernan called Holmes "a cheat, a pyramid schemer, an evil scientist, for heaven's sake . . ."[3]

Most interesting is that Holmes's cadre of investors could have easily spotted the signs, just as investors could have chosen to see the signs Bernie Madoff exhibited throughout his tenure as master con man (which is why many have compared Holmes to Madoff). Given her race to keep her deception under wraps, many close to Holmes shared that she went to drastic lengths to conceal the truth, publicly disparaging the investors, employees, and board members who asked too many questions about obtaining valid proof, even firing those who doubted her.[4]

> Many close to Holmes shared that she went to drastic lengths to conceal the truth, publicly disparaging the investors, employees, and board members who asked too many questions about obtaining valid proof, even firing those who doubted her.

But eventually, the fear Holmes created put too much doubt into the minds of everyone around her, and piece by piece her narrative began to unravel. The deeper she got, the harder she pressed against her detractors, frequently gracing global stages to demonstrate how she would save lives all over the planet. "Bernie Madoff would never have sounded so earnest," Heffernan quips, "P. T. Barnum would never have played his con as morally urgent. But that's why Holmes was—for a time—the billionaire they never were. Eventually Holmes, like so many of us, got what she feared most: a whole universe of people who don't believe in her."

For Holmes, was the risk of being dishonest worth the reward? Clearly, she thought so at the time (though I suspect she might have a different opinion today, in retrospect).

Capitalizing on a Vice

Holmes is certainly not alone in her ability to bluff for profit; take, for instance, the ongoing saga of Shane Smith, the infamous cofounder of Vice Media. If you haven't heard of Vice Media, that wouldn't surprise me. Vice Media's content is created especially for a young audience interested in fast-paced, transparent, and—yes—*honest* takes on people, places, and world affairs. (Don't worry, the ironic part is coming.)

Vice was founded in 1994 when Smith and two colleagues used money from a Canadian welfare program to start a youth-oriented magazine in Montreal (think *National Lampoon* for millennials, but even more offensive). According to Reeves Wiedeman's analysis in *New York* magazine, Smith did all the selling in those early days and was easily found running around the office proclaiming loudly that everyone who joined him would get wildly rich. His cofounder called him Bullshitter Shane, and Smith mainly sold advertising by sending a few copies of the magazine to random record stores and skate shops in far-flung cities across the United States so that he could tell advertisers they had a broad, North American distribution. "Shane would talk all the time about how stupid people were for giving them money," said one of Smith's girlfriends at the time, according to Wiedeman.[5]

> It turns out that "Bullshitter Shane" had a knack for turning BS into USD.

It turns out that "Bullshitter Shane" had a knack for turning BS into USD. In 1998, Smith told a reporter that Richard Szalwinski, a wealthy tech tycoon, had invested in Vice. Szalwinski had done nothing of the sort, but—and get ready to use that face-palm emoji—he was impressed enough with Vice's boldness that he *did* invest in Vice, and moved the publication to New York City. One of Vice's cofounders would later recount, "The reason those lies were so successful was because even we believed them after a while."[6]

Later, after Smith moved to New York, a Canadian reporter came calling to do a profile. Smith doubled down on his deceit, paying a friend to pretend he was an MTV executive who was interested in a Vice show so the reporter would seed the idea into the story. And the story quickly picked up steam; as Smith ranted to his employees about a soon-to-come IPO, filling their heads with visions of glory, he perpetuated his appearance of success by pulling stunt after stunt. He once paid a neighboring architectural firm in Brooklyn to move out of their offices so that Vice's people—along with an army of friends and family—could move in and make it look like they had been there all along. The swap was designed for a group of Intel executives who were interested in Vice's marketing agency abilities, and the execs fell for it. Later, Smith famously sent Dennis Rodman to North Korea in a publicity stunt disguised as a documentary.

Former MTV chief Van Toffler would later recount that Smith boasted, "MTV's over. You suck; we're the new kids on the block."[7] And by the droves, investor after investor bought Smith's story and invested millions, then tens of millions, and then hundreds of millions of dollars at sky-high valuations.

But that's not the most shocking part. What's most shocking is that even family-friendly brands like Disney created partnerships with Vice Media, ignoring its indecent reputation. For instance, Vice reportedly asked employees to sign a "nontraditional workplace agreement" in which employees specifically agreed they would not be offended by Vice's indecent, violent, or disturbing environment. Even as investor money flowed in, Vice's culture of widespread sexual misconduct began to get some unwanted attention from the *New York Times*. And, adding insult to injury, Vice had a reputation for underpaying employees. One senior manager reportedly joked about a "22 Rule"—"Hire twenty-two-year-olds, pay them twenty-two thousand dollars, and work them twenty-two hours a day."[8]

Smith spent his growing, investor-made fortune on helicopter rides, acquiring the mansion featured in the HBO show *Entourage*, and wooing new investors by throwing all-nighters at New York City's hot spots at which chief marketing officers would be treated to a noxious cocktail of booze, drugs, strippers, and more. That's when Rupert Murdoch strode through the office with Bullshitter Shane, who would later brag, "I said to Rupert, 'I have Gen Y, I have social, I have online video. You have none of that. I have the future, you have the past.'"[9] His confidence garnered a whopping $70 million investment from Murdoch at a more than billion-dollar valuation. In addition, Murdoch's blessing gave other would-be investors a peace of mind that would prove to be worth billions more to Smith.

Yet those on the inside of Vice knew Smith's game. When an HBO executive congratulated Vice's then-chief creative officer, saying, "It was nice to see the good guys win," the Vice executive replied, "I'm not so sure that we're the good guys."[10]

Now the moment you've all been waiting for—the one where Icarus's wings eventually melt away, leaving him to plummet back to Earth. By 2017, when Smith and Vice should have been dominating the millennial market, the *Wall Street Journal* reported on Vice's $100 million revenue miss, painfully compounding the negative press swirling about Vice's sexual harassment issues and workplace conduct violations.[11] In 2018, Smith was replaced as chief executive by Nancy Dubuc, a veteran TV exec and former chief executive at A&E Networks.[12] Despite the founders' assertion that Vice is "the largest youth media company in the world," there is evidence that Vice is no longer as cool as it thinks it is: a 2017 Google report listed Vice as the second *least cool* brand out of 122 on the test, according to Gen Z respondents, with Vice falling behind such uncool icons as Yahoo!, the Sunglass Hut, and JCPenney—yes, even JCPenney.[13] With millennials, Vice didn't fare much better; it ranked ahead of Sunglass Hut, but about on par with such hipsters as Verizon and Dell, and behind the ultracool Old Navy (yes, I jest). Those results can't possibly be surprising. In the age of #MeToo, an old boys' club founded on bluster, drugs, and alcohol can't survive forever, regardless of which investors have blessed the beleaguered brand. Google Vice Media today, and you'll see stories of key partnership dissolutions, job cuts, and other hallmarks of a company in desperate need of a turnaround.

> When an HBO executive congratulated Vice's then-chief creative officer, saying, "It was nice to see the good guys win," the Vice executive replied, "I'm not so sure that we're the good guys."

"Shane would always say that young people are the number one bullshit detector," said one departing employee, "which was annoying once you realized that the thing he mastered is getting young people to buy shit."[14] As an editorial correction, let's make sure we understand that Smith didn't just get young people to buy shit; he got young people *and* mature, wealthy, intelligent executives to buy shit—more than $5 billion worth of shit, to be exact. At least, for as long as Vice's popular run lasted. (As an aside, Disney recently wrote off its entire 27 percent stake in Vice, suggesting it will get no return from its stake whatsoever.[15])

> In the age of #MeToo, an old boys' club founded on bluster, drugs, and alcohol can't survive forever, regardless of which investors have blessed the beleaguered brand.

What's most sad is the lesson young people might take from Smith and his meteoric rise. After all, unlike Theranos, Vice is still alive (at least as of the time of this writing), despite all the sexual misconduct, layoffs, earnings misses, and other eventualities of building a global company on a cornerstone of deceit. Yet many might be tempted to look at Smith's life and consider him a modern-day Robin Hood, laudable for his ability to swindle the "smart" big-business icons into releasing a dump truck of money into the backyard of the little guy's not-so-little *Entourage* mansion. To me, it's a testament to how far people will go to chase an opportunity that they know should be too good to be true. In Vice's case, Murdoch and his compatriot investors needed to solve the problem of reaching young people, and Smith purportedly had the solution, opaque as it was and continues to be.

IS THE RISK HONESTLY WORTH THE REWARD?

If supposedly skilled and intelligent investors didn't see Holmes's and Smith's deceit—or worse, chose not to see it—what truths are we supposed to take away? Do these examples encourage us to create our own masquerades? Can and should we "fake it 'til we make it"? Is that just the way it works in the world in which we live?

Ultimately, only you can decide if the rewards are truly worth the risks. It's your career. It's your life. You have to live with yourself at the end of the day and stave off the lawsuits and headlines that could attach a permanent anchor to your reputation.

As an entrepreneur, I must admit I admire their fake-it-'til-you-make-it attitudes. But there's that bell curve of morality again, reminding us that lying to a customer about being able to deliver only works if you actually deliver. In the early days of my first company, my business partner and I absolutely told customers, "Sure, we can do that," even if we hadn't before. But that's because we could, and we did. We had fail-safes and backup plans. We would've worked until the end of time to deliver on our promises before taking the chopper to the new mansion, because that would have been the right thing to do—the *honest* thing to do.

That particular entrepreneurial dilemma represents only one sliver of the massive gray area of life and business. When it comes to assessing the entire landscape of gray, my hope is that after you see in parts two and three what honesty can do for your sales, marketing, new product development, culture, and more, you see only risk in dishonesty and the promise of innovation in honesty. As we saw in these examples, deceit can open doors *at first*, but then what? Do the rewards mitigate the risks? What happens when the lies catch up with you?

Then again, you might be thinking that you're too smart to be deceived like Murdoch, right? You would have seen through Bullshitter Shane's bullshit. And you might have been smart enough to know that Netflix was actually the real deal. Maybe, but in truth, those are perilous assumptions. We humans are gullible. We embrace faith and belief as easily as the air we breathe. We love to tell ourselves stories and then wholeheartedly believe those stories without going deeper to find the kernel of truth that might run against what we already "know." But in our defense, we can't expect to save ourselves from believing our own stories *when we have no better information*. People were perfectly comfortable believing the Earth was at the center of the universe until they had new facts proving otherwise; then it was only a matter of time until they shifted their belief system.

And if you accept that line of reasoning, you must also accept that with more information about Vice Media's or Theranos's true inner workings, a lot of wealthy people could have bought a few (more) luxury yachts or rid a continent of dengue fever with the money they would have saved. Consider the sheer number of people who were affected by these dishonest organizations; consider the ripple effects and subliminal messages that these stories send to investors, employees, and watchful would-be entrepreneurs. I offer these stories up first to show the counterpoint to honesty, which right now can still work to lure powerful allies whose lack of vigilance can prop up bluster-filled charades. The good news is that transparency will save us from ourselves, and the organizations who jump on that trend first will prosper.

Beware the Herd Mentality or You Might Get Trampled

Today's fraud is our fault: we enable fake news by giving it attention; we empower stories by clicking on their hyped-up headlines and sharing them neglectfully across social media; we embolden founders to defraud us when we shower them with money and praise without doing our due diligence (and/or without holding them accountable to basic moral tenets). Choosing to be honest is key, but it's only part of the battle— because even if we consciously decide to be honest, we can (and do) subconsciously lead ourselves astray. Our human brains have an innate bent toward dishonesty—sometimes with others, but mostly with ourselves and our own biases. Having the ability to *spot* deceit takes an extra kind of personal honesty, the type of personal honesty that can make us better, more skeptical leaders who ferret out the truth instead of blindly following others. But that ain't natural. Rather, we humans instinctively want to build community and look for social proof to guide and reinforce our beliefs and decisions. Few leaders are brave enough to admit how easily they can fall into the trap of herd mentality.

I can't tell you how many "leaders" I've encountered who are obsessed with copying whatever their competitors are doing, which makes me eye-roll so hard that my eyebrows seize up. Crazily, in industries like venture capital, firms actively strive to be herd followers rather than independent-thinking leaders. Umm . . . no wonder Shane Smith did so well! Curiously, this follower-type mind-set broke Blockbuster just as it did Theranos and Vice, but in opposite ways. With Blockbuster, the powers-that-be couldn't believe that the herd they'd known for decades was changing directions; with Theranos and Vice, investors believed that the herd was running away and that they needed to cling on for dear life. In both cases, a bit more objective truth seeking would have made billions of dollars' worth of difference. Instead, herd mentality led to dishonest outcomes—en masse. In fact, if you really want to chuckle about herd mentality, allow me to tell you the story of a young British couple who waited months to dine at the hottest restaurant in Britain.

The Shed, as it was branded, was the number-one-rated restaurant on TripAdvisor for weeks at a time. Even getting The Shed to pick up the phone and take your reservation was a gift you could use as a badge of honor in your cocktail party banter and in your social media updates. Founded by Oobah Butler, The Shed quickly rose to fame on TripAdvisor, and the young British couple that finally scored a table couldn't wait to dine there.

When they arrived in the middle of an innocuous suburban neighborhood, they took a space on the street alongside very few other cars. The house in front of them seemed ordinary enough; who would ever know that this place was *the* place? The couple was finally greeted by what must have been the host and ushered to the rear of the house, where a small, unspectacular courtyard greeted them. Their table awaited, situated in between the house and a small garden shed that framed the tiny backyard. This was certainly an experience! The couple went to work, busily snapping social media photos and posting pictures of themselves in this culinary hot spot. After eons of anticipation, they finally spotted the waiters dawdling out of the kitchen with dishes held high. This was it! When the waiters got to the couple's table, they plunked the plates down with all the ceremony of serving a dog its Wednesday-night kibble. That might have struck the couple as odd, and, admittedly, they weren't delighted by the food, but what does presentation or taste matter when the date-night war had already been won, with all the social proof this couple would need to punch their cool-crowd tickets for the rest of the year?

You might be surprised and entertained—more so than that young couple, I assure you—to learn that Oobah Butler has never owned or run a restaurant. Instead, he successfully turned his everyday backyard shed into the number-one restaurant on TripAdvisor by using the platform's own procedures against it.[16] The shed was just an ordinary, run-of-the-mill garden shed behind an ordinary house in an ordinary neighborhood—the very epitome of fake news. The entrees tasted exactly like frozen TV dinners—because that's exactly what they were!

Recap: Butler, the most brilliant restaurant owner who never was, generated a waiting list for his "restaurant" and served frozen dinners on opening night, when people lined up to get a table in his backyard. Funnier still: even after dining there, no customer honored to earn a reservation wrote one negative word online about the unusual nature of the coveted dining spot.

And who was investing in Mr. Butler's work while he was performing this and other feats of sensational bullshit?

Vice Magazine, of course.

We Need to Beef Up That BS Radar If We Want to Win

Not every organization is as deceitful as Theranos, as brash as Vice, or as purposely deceptive as The Shed, but be honest: How good are *you* at spotting fraudulent people and unscrupulous organizations? We humans love to blindly follow others, not ask too many obvious questions, and generally avoid the truth if it might contradict what we already believe is true—just like when we humans so fervently resisted Galileo's radical idea that the Earth revolved around the sun.

But if we don't fight those natural tendencies, they can lead us to catastrophic ends. We must dig deeper to see truths that could rise up and hurt us and the others around us. We must face the fact that we—the people—empower fraudsters by *allowing* ourselves to be deceived.

As a leader, ask yourself: What happens every time you bury your head in the sand, just going along with what everyone else is doing rather than really assessing what's going on in the world? What happens when you lie to the colleagues in your boardroom by putting your own beliefs ahead of the objective truth? What happens when you lie to yourself about what you want in life, or fail to test your most basic assumptions? Compounded, these small, oft-hidden lies are just as dangerous as billion-dollar deceptions—not only because you might get caught but also because you lose the opportunity to find the truth and all the doors to innovation and advancement that the truth naturally opens. Dishonesty is a sneaky threat; one small step toward deception can hurt you just as much as the big, glaring lies from those deceitful examples.

> Compounded, these small, oft-hidden lies are just as dangerous as billion-dollar deceptions—not only because you might get caught but also because you lose the opportunity to find the truth and all the doors to innovation and advancement that the truth naturally opens.

Stories like Theranos, Vice, and The Shed are testaments to our biases, and demonstrate how much we're willing to look beyond the surface and believe only what we want to desperately believe is true. In the case of Theranos, investors wanted to believe they had a golden goose in the lucrative health care industry. With Vice, investors wanted to believe that they had found the key to entertaining the next generation. With Butler's shed, customers wanted to believe they had earned a coveted reservation at an exclusive venue—and, more importantly, that they had earned the social rank that came with such an honor.

They were wrong.

Lest we be too hard on them, however, we must remember that we humans are wired for deceit. If you've ever spent any time with a child, you know that children are born compulsive liars. We emerge from the womb able to say, "No . . . I didn't eat the cookie you told me not to eat." Our rocky relationship with honesty is as old as our ability to lie. That means we must actively work at transforming ourselves into honest, effective leaders. But before we can transform ourselves as individuals, we must deeply understand our complicated relationship with honesty as a society—because unless we understand the context around what we're fighting, we won't stand a chance.

———— QUESTIONS FOR HONEST REFLECTION ————

1. How might you develop a stronger "BS radar" to question what you're seeing and hearing with healthy skepticism?
2. What are some of the behind-the-scenes motivations of the organizations, politicians, and news outlets around you? How honest are they?
3. To what extent do you succumb to herd mentality? How might you be following a trend without even realizing it?

CHAPTER 2

The Complicated Story of Why We Lie

Dear Reader: I'm sorry to report that you're a no-good dirty liar. Yeah. There. I said it.

It's not you, it's me. Well, and you. And everyone, really. Together, as a collective of people hungry for success, we've turned the world into a veritable shitshow of moral uncertainty. No matter what industry you're in, what politics you follow, and which flag you fly outside your home, the whole truth and nothing but the truth is damn near impossible to find these days. Our news has been hijacked by clickbait. On TV and social media, we're inundated with opinions pretending to be facts and barraged with views that polarize the world. And in the business world, as in society at large, we see people coloring what they say so it's more "palatable" to our sensitive, politically correct eardrums.

With the facts being so difficult to discern, can we honestly be too surprised that we live in a sea of deceit? I don't know about you, but I don't trust anything I see and hear. But I do hear it . . . and the siren song of cheating has perhaps never been so loud, as we saw in the last chapter. We can hardly help but be wooed by it—the promises of yachts, jets, and the Lifestyles of the Rich and Instagram-Famous. We wonder, *Why bother playing fair if everyone else is using bluster to profit?*

Why emphasize the facts if nobody trusts them anyway? Why think about long-term reputation when I might not even be in this role for the long run?

All good questions. And to get at the answers, we must return to our roots and understand how we've ended up here, so that we can appropriately gauge where we are as a society and then accurately predict what might happen next.

A BRIEF HUMAN HISTORY OF (DIS)HONESTY

Unfortunately, humanity holds a long-standing, damaging belief about the connection between money and morality. For millennia, we humans have built societies that teach us contradictory notions about right and wrong and about how we can use money to tip those scales in our favor. I can't very well expect you to believe that we're at a tipping point of change for the future if I don't show you where we've been in the past, right? And to measure how we've traditionally linked money and morality, we need to go back in time.

When in Rome . . .

The year is 1517. The place: Rome. Your wealthy, despotic uncle has just passed away. *Good riddance,* you think. He spent his life proclaiming his pious dedication to Catholic values and community service, but you and your siblings know the truth: he sought to make himself wealthy above all else and all others, and he succeeded by acting as an unrepentant thief in his business dealings. Of course, Rome doesn't have Facebook or Yelp during the Renaissance, so every customer with the misfortune of dealing with your rich uncle has had to learn, from scratch, that there was a reason why he had more shekels than the rest of his competitors.

But fortunately for your uncle, his religion offered him a loophole for eternal redemption (cue heavenly chorus, please). St. Peter's Basilica in Rome has been in dire need of some updating, and it's looking for a few coins to help with the renovation. So, to fill the investment gap, Pope Leo X has expanded the use of "indulgences"—spiritual pardons for lifelong sins that the pope can, at his discretion, hand out to "worthy" Catholics. All that's needed to acquire one of these indulgences is a fairly sizeable chunk of cold, hard cash—which, luckily for your uncle, was no problem at all. With a casual transfer of wealth from your uncle to the Catholic Church ahead of his demise, your uncle earned his pardon and set his spirit free to go to heaven, a life full of sin notwithstanding.

How to Walk Like an Egyptian

The powers that be in Rome made it relatively easy for sinful leaders to act dishonestly for a lifetime with no one the wiser *and* get their sins pardoned as a sort of twisted *have your cake and eat it, too.* But Rome was not alone in conditioning society to the vicious circle of money and morals in which immoral behavior could be used to pursue money, which could then be used to offset immoral behavior, and 'round and 'round it goes. Rome was just one in a long line of societies that placed money over morals this way. Take, for example, the curious phenomenon that occurred within the high priests of Amun in ancient Egypt, who rose to great power from the fifteenth to the tenth centuries BCE.

Imagine, for a moment, that as you step outside your favorite local market, you become momentarily blinded by the desert-hot sun and go ass-over-teakettle down a flight of rock steps, landing you forcefully face-first into a cart of unforgivingly unripe melons (a sorrowful but quick way to go, at least). Instantly, you are transported to a firelit hallway, appropriately called the Hall of Two Truths. As you approach the end of the hall, you begin to make out a giant scale with a pulsing, red organ on one end—your own beating heart. On the other end of the scale, you can see the outline of an ostrich feather—the feather of Ma'at, the goddess of truth, balance, justice, harmony, and other elements of an honest life.

You watch anxiously as the scales tip back and forth; you hurriedly recite an ancient incantation, praying that your sins don't weigh down your heart and make it heavier than that feather of truth. If your heart doesn't pass this test, it will be devoured by the part-hippopotamus, part-crocodile god Ammit, whose snacking on your cardiac organ will permanently erase your soul from the world, thereby preventing you from reaching the afterlife.

For all intents and purposes, the story of the Hall of Two Truths was a remarkable way to encourage ancient Egyptians to embrace honest values as a way of life. In fact, it's not unlike many other cultural and religious stories designed to help us make honest decisions and act harmoniously within our societies (read: formulated with the best of intentions). Except that, as we saw in Rome, there was a loophole in ancient Egypt (read: leave it to us humans to fuck it up).

Although ancient Egypt's weighing of the heart ceremony was designed to apply to all Egyptians regardless of status, the Amun priests began allowing wealthy Egyptians to purchase special documents and funerary objects with protective spells to give them an edge. In one available trade, wealthy Egyptians could buy a ready-made papyrus to bring with them into the afterlife, so all they had to do was fill in their name and voilà, they could punch their ticket to eternal bliss. With enough moola, they could even customize those spells to absolutely ensure that their hearts wouldn't become Ammit's lunch. And if that most pious judgment of all could simply be bought, what reason would a wealthy ancient Egyptian have for living an honest life in the first place?

Dishonesty Is an Easy (But Potentially Deadly) Habit

To put it simply, we've given ourselves an out when it comes to morals and money. Duplicity has been ingrained in our societies through our traditions and habits. Time and time again, we followed the path of dishonest gains *because we could*, because the consequences could be skirted. And sometimes, instead of disapproving of our deceit, society allowed and even incentivized our dishonest natures—especially if a few influential souls stood to make a profit.

To make matters worse, it isn't easy for us to change course. To resist deceit, we fight not only society's allowances but also the way our brains fundamentally work. A 2016 study in the journal *Nature Neuroscience* showed that being dishonest actually alters our brain chemistry, making it increasingly easier to lie the next time and the next. That sinking feeling we get from being dishonest comes from the part of the brain called the amygdala, and repeatedly telling lies—even to ourselves—eventually suppresses the amygdala's negative signals that remind us we're being dishonest. Unsurprisingly, a cognitive neuroscientist that led the research concluded, "If you give people multiple opportunities to lie for their own benefit . . . they start with little white lies [which] get bigger and bigger over time."[1] It's as if we've made a developmental line into a circle: We start out lying for our own benefit (to avoid the pain that comes with admitting we ate the cookie). Then we're taught explicitly that lying is wrong. And then, instead of stopping there, we turn into adults, learn that society has provided us loopholes to suppress our learned morality, ignore the warnings we ingrained into our amygdalae, and turn back into self-preservationists, truth be damned.

> Time and time again, we followed the path of dishonest gains. And sometimes, instead of disapproving of our deceit, society allowed and even incentivized our dishonest natures—especially if a few influential souls stood to make a profit.

As it is, when we face any habit-forming activity, it is up to us to admit we have a problem and admit that we need to be more conscious about how we live our lives. Do we wield lies or the truth? Do we know we're lying, and do we honestly understand why? If we get away with deceit, we feed more and more power to it, as the neuroscience study, Elizabeth Holmes, and Shane Smith all show. Now add social media. Add fake news. Add a few notable examples of liars in top positions in business and politics. And it's enough to almost convince ourselves that it's easier than ever to go with the dishonest flow and capitalize on our societal and personal loopholes in morality.

But that's where the tipping point comes in. We're not descending into more deceitful darkness; instead, we're approaching a cliff. Rome and Egypt of yesteryear didn't have smartphones. They didn't have a scientific community as we know it today. Their information didn't flow rapidly around the world in a heartbeat. Sure, lying is easy when we can get away with it. We deceive ourselves and others more easily when it's easy to do so and there are no repercussions. But the easy times are rapidly ending. Remember: people exchange money for value. That's the basis of commerce and capitalism. When we consumers know more, we assign value based on better information. And when that happens, the entire system shifts—in favor of honesty.

A WINDOW INTO TOMORROW'S TRUTH

For the first time in human history, something is different about the here and now when it comes to the core value of honesty. Something fundamental has changed, which has—for the first time ever—put the feather of truth in perfect balance with the pursuit of achievement *and* profits.

In earlier times truth and profits might have functioned as opposing forces, but today honesty and profitability are both intertwined. Better yet, you can even use each one to *cause* the other to occur. Did a velvet-robed wizard shift thousands of years of human behavior with a magical wand? Nope—like many good things in life, all it took was a few computer geeks and a dream.

See, something remarkable occurred just a few decades ago, something you might have heard of through your local news outlet or your mobile telephone. It's called the *internet*. The internet made *transparency* the buzzword of our time, because for the first time ever, anyone with an internet connection can look into the windows of companies in a way that was never possible before.

Whereas before a company could say one thing and do another, that is no longer true. Whereas before a company could praise their employees but actually treat them terribly, that is no longer true (or at least they can't get away with it without being called out on it). Whereas before a company could pollute the environment, or mishandle its finances, or employ unfair labor practices, that is—increasingly and for the most part—nearly impossible to pull off without getting brutally exposed.

And whereas before a few wealthy celebs might have continued matriculating their offspring into elite universities with the leathery creak of a bountiful checkbook and a few tall tales about their children's athleticism, that is, apparently, no longer an effective method. Eleven schools and fifty people were implicated when the college admissions scandal broke in the spring of 2019. It turns out that wealthy parents had a long-standing tradition of getting their kids into the college of their choice through bribery instead of merit (raise your hand if you were shocked . . . yeah . . . didn't think so). I don't know about you, but I wasn't surprised to hear yet another account of using deceit for personal gain. But that scandal served my point beautifully: those who tried to cheat the system were caught and publicly exposed, proving how difficult it's becoming to cheat and get away with it with today's easy access to information.

My argument for why to resist cheating's lure is simple: what got you here won't get you there (as author Marshall Goldsmith said long ago). Dishonesty might be working for some people, some of the time, but its efficacy will not last in today's increasingly transparent environment. In this environment, we're all growing tired of bullshit. Aren't you? Our awareness of fake news grows stronger by the day. We leave our phones open to fact-check the talking heads on TV. Scandal after scandal hardens us into professional skeptics, wary of almost everything we see and hear.

That's today; what about tomorrow? As a thought experiment, let's play these trends forward and ask ourselves some important questions. For instance, do we believe that technology will solve our fact-checking needs? Do we think that someday Robey—the name I've chosen for your personal AI robot (you're welcome)—will be able to gauge an organization's or leader's reputation with an automatic online search? Can you envision saying, "Hey, Siri, is this CEO full of shit?" Can you imagine Alexa automatically fact-checking TV pundits and correcting every assertion as it leaves their lips? Do we foresee that, given the incredible number of first-person photos and videos being posted to social media every second, we will soon live in a world where nobody has to guess what happened because everything will be recorded by someone, somewhere?

We don't need to have wild imaginations to conjure a world like this; we're already living in the early days of such a future. And in that future, leaders and organizations will be measured by exactly what they say and what they do—no more and no less. In such a world, who will win? That's right—the leaders who create incredibly honest organizations with nothing to hide. When I ask Robey to find me the most reputable company that sells a product or service I'm looking for, it won't have far to go. That might just be the easiest question we ask our current robotic friends, Siri and Alexa. Someday soon, the window for using lies to get ahead will permanently close. That day is approaching more quickly than some unscrupulous leaders would care to admit.

> Someday soon, the window for using lies to get ahead will permanently close. That day is approaching more quickly than some unscrupulous leaders would care to admit.

As we, the consumer public, have been given the right to transparently examine people and organizations, we've borne witness to a world thrown into chaos as many organizations are struggling to keep up, to change, to transform, to adapt, to adopt new ways of being and new belief systems and new core values (which *must* now include honesty).

For the business world in particular, information transparency brought on the infamous *age of the consumer*, a dreaded (by some) state of commerce in which boardrooms have been stripped of their superpowers while their customers have picked up the controls like a group of giddy kids in an after-hours Toys "R" Us. It's no wonder why many organizations have failed to keep pace; a medieval monarch informed that the farmers had taken charge would have been desperately unable to cope. He might have considered exiling himself or worse as an alternative to such a terrible coup. And yet, if that king had been honest with himself, he might have willingly adapted to his new role and even prospered because of it.

In fact, that's exactly what we'll learn how to do with this whole honesty thing, because, to be quite clear, this is a book about making *money*. And that's what makes our society different from those that came before: we are finally at a place in time where it *pays* to fight our millennia-old, innate human tendency toward using dishonesty to get ahead. Honesty is soon becoming the *only* policy that can guarantee your ability to *survive* as we accelerate into information transparency. It's honesty . . . or it's gambling with your life, your career, or your child's dreams of going to their first-choice college.

Cheaters need not apply.

THE CAPITALIST CONUNDRUM

The dangers of dishonesty abound in our personal and professional lives, from buying your kids into a better school to inflating the number of new accounts your company opened this quarter. We must fight the habit of dishonesty before it catches us with our proverbial pants down in our newly transparent world. Furthermore, if we want to succeed in business, we need to check our *beliefs* about business—because despite commerce being created by deceptive human beings (because that's what we all are), the business world was never designed to exist on a foundation of deceit.

To help us remember what business and capitalism were honestly meant to be, let's pop over to eighteenth-century Scotland, where we'll toast a glass of Scotch to the young philosopher who first opined on the subject of capitalism. His name, which some econ majors may remember from class (unless they got too involved in the whiskey), was Adam Smith.

The Humble Origins of Capitalism

Today's systemic corporate greed is only partially Adam Smith's fault. Sure, Smith invented capitalism as we know it, and economics majors worldwide study his works. But few realize that Smith was a *moral* philosopher first, having written *The Theory of Moral Sentiments* before he ever thought about laying the foundations of classical free-market economic theory (which is a fancy way of saying, "how people can sell stuff to each other so they can make mo' money").

Most importantly, Smith's original concept of capitalism emphasized *creating value for the benefit of everyone involved*. As an antitheses to unwieldy corporations that pollute our environment and employ slave labor, some of today's memorable start-ups have returned to Smith's balance of delivering profits *and* benefitting all involved. TOMS Shoes, Patagonia, Ben & Jerry's, and other ecologically- and charity-minded companies show us that businesses that crusade for the social good can prevail. Unfortunately, for every one of those examples, we can point to countless others that ruin the water supply, screw their suppliers, or subject their customers to an hours-long phone tree.

> As long as business schools teach Maximizing Income and not Maximizing Value for Everyone Involved, we'll continue to misunderstand what paradoxically produces outsized business profits.

Since every company—even the ones in the Fortune 500—started as an entrepreneurial venture, it's worth asking how (and why) many of those organizations veered from what I hope started as an agreeable, perhaps even world-improving, vision. In many cases, somewhere along the line, a once-honest insight about how to make the world better through business turned into a singular pursuit to make the enterprise wealthier. It doesn't take an entrepreneur, an MBA, or even a Scottish philosopher-economist to understand that creating mutual benefit is actually a good idea, but as long as business schools teach Maximizing Income and not Maximizing Value for Everyone Involved, we'll continue to misunderstand what paradoxically produces outsized business profits.

Can Capitalism Survive As We Know It?

We've certainly come a long way from Smith's philosophical vision of capitalism. Today, an MBA candidate practically drowns in drool-worthy

Instagram photos of yachts, exotic cars, and private jets. Our society emphasizes, as pop singer/philosopher Rihanna points out, "the money, the fame, the cars, the clothes." Meanwhile, few pop-culture icons sing songs about giving free shoes to impoverished children. I suppose it'd be tough to rhyme.

That said, it wasn't so long ago that we were occupying Wall Street and rethinking Gordon Gekko's assertion that "greed is good." Post-2008, we heard some of the best and worst arguments for and against capitalism. We recognized a shrinking middle class. We witnessed otherwise dulcet Americans railing against the 1 percent, and we experienced a whole host of finger pointing aimed mainly at Wall Street and the federal government. But, silver lining: from the ashes of that financial catastrophe there arose an organization whose sole purpose is to remind us about Adam Smith's original intention for capitalism. The organization—which has turned into an international movement—is called *Conscious Capitalism*, and it's helping to evolve business right back to where it started.

Conscious Capitalism, led by millennial CEO Alexander McCobin, believes that capitalism is about maximizing profit for all constituents involved—from customers to vendors, employees to managers, and everyone in between. It's a modus operandi that inserts the human equation back into the income statements of our enterprises. The organization teaches businesses how to maximize the value of every affected party instead of only stuffing the pockets of executives and shareholders. Its credo describes a belief system that seems old-fashioned compared to today's state of commerce, in which the lines between Kardashian and corporation are blurry at best and companies inexplicably survive on shady advertising and sexual harassment alike.

"We believe," the credo begins, "that business is good because it creates value, it is ethical because it is based on voluntary exchange, it is noble because it can elevate our existence, and it is heroic because it lifts people out of poverty and creates prosperity. Free enterprise capitalism is the most powerful system for social cooperation and human progress ever conceived. It is one of the most compelling ideas we humans have ever had."

In a world where Theranos and Vice can swindle smart investors out of hundreds of millions of dollars, I wouldn't blame you for asking why we should be so conscious about the way we do business. Well, in an increasingly transparent world, there's more incentive than ever. Customers are voting—not with ballots but with dollars. They are choosing, among an incredible number of options, to do business with you or with your competitors. Today, buyers' rationale for opting to do business with your company extends far beyond the value of your product or service.

> A whopping 75 percent of millennials are willing to change their buying habits to reduce their environmental impact, and 90 percent are willing to pay more for sustainable brands.

Travelers start with Kayak reviews before they even consider booking. Employees check Glassdoor before even applying. And millennials? In Nielsen's 2018 review of sustainability trends, it found that a whopping 75 percent of millennials are willing to change their buying habits to reduce their environmental impact, and 90 percent are willing to pay more for sustainable brands.[2]

In part, this transition—the one already happening right underneath our feet—is what has enabled Conscious Capitalism to spring forth as a growing, global institution with communities in more than seventy cities worldwide and thousands of event participants each year. The movement features board members like John Mackey, the cofounder of Whole Foods, and supporters like Howard Schultz, the former CEO of Starbucks.[3] Thousands of Conscious Capitalism followers across a wide variety of industries have realized that it makes a lot of sense to be a little more honest about the mission, vision, values, culture, and code of conduct at their organizations, which range from small businesses to massive enterprises. With a little help from a pie-in-the-sky credo and an earnest belief in the good that business can do, these leaders have deliberately chosen to make their companies into community support systems rather than production facilities that simply take inputs and produce profits.

MEASURING UP TO CONSCIOUS COMMERCE

Lying is not new; throughout the ages, we've consistently struggled with the balance between advancement at all costs and virtuous behavior. Now, in our newly transparent world, the pendulum is swinging back to what used to reside at the heart of free-market enterprise when the idea originated. Organizations like Conscious Capitalism are paving the way for how to do honest-to-greatness business in the twenty-first century.

Depending on your own value system, you might judge Conscious Capitalism's ideals as obvious or scary. Either way, the point is that society is moving toward honesty, and the signs are all around us. Even if your organization has begun thinking consciously about supporting every constituent you interact with, how will you know it's enough? That's going to take some honesty—with your employees, with your customers, with your prospects, and with the way the world is evolving.

> Employees, customers, and others trust and even love companies that have an inspiring purpose.

To check if your organization is embracing a conscious way of doing business, consider the four pillars of Conscious Capitalism to see where you stack up.

1. **Higher Purpose:** While making money is essential for the vitality and sustainability of a business, it is not the only or even the most important reason a business exists. Conscious businesses focus on their purpose beyond profit. By focusing on its deeper purpose, a conscious business inspires, engages, and energizes its stakeholders. Employees, customers, and others trust and even love companies that have an inspiring purpose.

2. **Stakeholder Orientation:** Unlike some businesses that believe they only exist to maximize return on investment for their shareholders, conscious businesses focus on their whole business ecosystem, creating and optimizing value for all their stakeholders,

understanding that strong and engaged stakeholders lead to a healthy, sustainable, resilient business. They recognize that without employees, customers, suppliers, funders, supportive communities, and a life-sustaining ecosystem, there is no business. Conscious business is a win-win-win proposition, which includes a healthy return to shareholders.

3. **Conscious Leadership:** Conscious leaders focus on "we" rather than "me." They inspire, foster transformation, and bring out the best in those around them. They understand that their role is to serve the purpose of the organization, support the people within the organization, and create value for all the organization's stakeholders. They recognize the integral role of culture and purposefully cultivate a conscious culture of trust and care.

4. **Conscious Culture:** A conscious culture fosters love, care, and inclusiveness and builds trust among the company's team members and all its other stakeholders. Conscious culture is an energizing and unifying force that truly brings a conscious business to life.

How would your organization rank according to these four pillars? Even if your report card needs some work, the key is to develop an organizational habit—the habit of being conscious about your purpose, stakeholders, leadership, and culture. If you're a leader in your organization, you can create change by introducing these ideas and helping shift your organization's beliefs about business. If you're not a leader in your organization, you can still create enormous change in your organization—and with the help of the CEOs in this book, you're going to learn how.

The first step, though, is becoming *conscious* that an alternative, even old-fashioned, view of business is quickly gaining traction around the world. In fact, Conscious Capitalism's credo reminds me of Rotary International's Four-Way Test[4]:

1. Is it the TRUTH?
2. Is it FAIR to all concerned?
3. Will it build GOODWILL and BETTER FRIENDSHIPS?
4. Will it be BENEFICIAL to all concerned?

Apparently, way back in 1905 when Rotary was founded in Chicago, the first group of professionals realized that honesty, fairness, and mutual benefit form the foundation of prosperity. They also understood that honesty comes *first*—and today, 1.2 million members in more than 35,000 clubs worldwide rely on truth to guide their actions. Today, getting honest about the shifts in our societal beliefs requires the same level of thoughtfulness, mindfulness, and awareness to accept that change is here and real. Whether we think we're going back to old-fashioned values or forward into an evolved take on honesty, the truth is that every challenge your business faces, in every department, is an opportunity in disguise, waiting for you to figure out the win-win-win solution.

Unfortunately, not every business thinks this way, as many newsworthy, dishonest organizations show: take Wells Fargo, which falsified customer accounts, or VW, which lied about their diesel emissions. Conscious Capitalism's CEO, Alexander McCobin, reminded me that "what we need to undo and try to help people understand is that business is about something much bigger than (short-term) profits—it's about a higher purpose, creating value for everyone. In some ways it's about reminding ourselves that business involves big, philosophical, moral questions about what is valuable and what is good." If we listen to what our society is whispering, we'll hear what McCobin hears: his organization reflects where we are in human evolution, the state of our world today, and the innate potential of business to make a positive impact on the world.

> Every challenge your business faces, in every department, is an opportunity in disguise, waiting for you to figure out the win-win-win solution.

Choosing sustainability, supporting people, and being honest—these are core concepts. It ain't rocket science, people. Which is why it's so odd that we have to talk about it in the first place, and why it's sort of sad that an organization like Conscious Capitalism needs to exist at all. "A lot of this actually is pretty simple," McCobin told me in conclusion. Fortunately, capitalism is returning to the way it was always meant to be—as McCobin says, "valuable" and "good."

That is, good for *everyone*—and *especially* good for the bottom line. And that's exactly how we know we're not in ancient Egypt or Renaissance Rome anymore. Instead, we're here—at a crossroads where the right thing to do is quickly becoming the most profitable thing to do. We've never had near-perfect information like we do today; we humans have never experienced an environment that makes it profitable to be honest and ineffective to lie. And if you believe, like I do, that we're only at the beginning of this trend, then congratulations—you're in the perfect place to capitalize on it.

————— QUESTIONS FOR HONEST REFLECTION —————

1. Which people and organizations have influenced you to be more or less honest? What impacts have they had on your belief system?
2. When might you justify telling lies? Under what circumstances is lying a good idea vs. simply telling the truth?
3. Does the organization you work for believe in supporting all stakeholders, or just a few? How might your organization become more "conscious" about the way it operates?

CHAPTER 3

Giving Power to the People Will Make You Rich

As the head of Conscious Capitalism, Alexander McCobin doesn't just encourage businesses to be honest; he fights human instinct. Dishonesty, he points out, is a "human endeavor" that gets in the way of our business (and personal) success. If you're not quite buying that honesty is the first step in business innovation, don't worry, we'll get there. First, invite yourself to consider an extension of honesty that's getting more scarce every day: *trust*. If you can't trust the people you work with, the vendors you buy from, the executives who surround you, or your managers or employees, then how can your organization move forward at all? If dishonesty creates distrust, then honesty is our only way out of a world filled with fake news, fake accounts, fake emissions reports, fake social media profiles, fake advertising claims, and other falsehoods that we live with every day.

Some blame famed economist Milton Friedman. In his book, *Capitalism and Freedom*, published in 1962, he wrote, "There is one and only one social responsibility of business: to use its resources and engage in activities designed to increase its profits." Profit-hungry executives were all too happy to receive that message over the latter half of the twentieth century. And sure, some benefitted from the innovations that came from the pursuit of cash. But others, like our environment or Enron's investors, suffered because of it.

In truth, the pursuit of profits is not where Friedman's dictum stopped; in fact, his caveat continues. It was a grave one, and one that now defines the elephant in the (board)room. After "there is one and only one social responsibility of business: to use its resources and engage in activities designed to increase its profits," Friedman wrote, "*so long as it stays in the rules of the game . . . without deception or fraud.*" (Emphasis mine.)

> "There is one and only one social responsibility of business: to use its resources and engage in activities designed to increase its profits so long as it stays in the rules of the game ... without deception or fraud."
> —Milton Friedman

Today, the currency of business isn't dollars or bitcoin; it's trust. With trust, a business can inspire a movement and destroy its competitors. The more honesty, the more trust. The more trust, the more profits. It's a strategy as simple as it was on the day we were taught that honesty is the best policy. Only now, we have more data to back up the claim.

LEARNING WHAT PEOPLE WANT GIVES YOUR BUSINESS POWER

In a world where it's easier to see what's honestly happening and harder to get away with lyin' like a rug, the logical next step for any business is to get its own values into alignment with the values of its customers. The big question is, how can we get better data about what our customers are thinking and feeling so we can catch a profitable wave and ride it, lest we get swept under it and drown?

To get at those critical signals in the noise, allow me to ask you a different question (and no, this isn't the start of a joke): What do a hedge fund manager, media mogul, serial entrepreneur, and New Age alternative medicine guru have in common?

Answer: They all think that the state of business today is in deep, deep doo-doo.

In 2013, a motley but powerful group of leaders came together to form JUST Capital. That group—including hedge fund manager Paul Tudor Jones II, media mogul Arianna Huffington, serial entrepreneur Rinaldo Brutoco, and alternative medicine advocate Deepak Chopra—decided that enough was enough with the greed, corporate abuse, and institutional dishonesty in today's business climate. Formed as a 501(c)(3) registered charity, JUST Capital "helps people, companies, and markets do the right thing by tracking the business behaviors Americans care about most." Like Conscious Capitalism, the folks at JUST believe that business should be a positive force for change, and that organizations today have a responsibility to win back the public's trust, which has been lost in our scandalous times. JUST's thesis goes on to say that the nonprofit sector alone can't solve the world's most pressing issues—and that the private sector, with its market cap worth tens of trillions of dollars, is needed if we're going to solve the big, systemic problems of our time.

> The folks at JUST believe that business should be a positive force for change, and that organizations today have a responsibility to win back the public's trust, which has been lost in our scandalous times.

JUST Capital decided early on that it would be honest with itself, which meant that the executive leaders at JUST had to admit they couldn't speak for the values and expectations of the entire American public. Instead, they agreed that the only people who could decide what a "just" company looks like is the American people themselves—not the executives but the *customers.*

JUST's ranking—called the JUST 100—lists the top 100 most "just" companies out of 922 of America's largest publicly traded firms (the Russell 1000 minus REITs and pending mergers, for the 2019 list).[1] JUST categorizes and awards firms according to the public's idea of how a just, fair, and honest company should be. They capture the public's preferences using nationwide polls of real Americans—in other words, they simply call up ordinary people across the country and ask what's important (I know . . . asking customers what they think. Crazy, right?). Those surveys have revealed five main "issues" that influence buyer behavior, weighted according to how important each issue is in the eyes of the American public. The five issues, in order of importance at the time of writing, are:

1. **Workers:** How a company invests in its employees.
2. **Customers:** How a company treats its customers.
3. **Communities:** How a company supports its communities.
4. **Environment:** How a company reduces its environmental impact.
5. **Shareholders:** How a company delivers value to its shareholders.

One critical takeaway emerges from this mix that directly conflicts with today's typical business practices: *the American people want businesses to care about people, and even our planet, over profits.* That might not surprise you, yet listen in to the next quarterly earnings call from your favorite publicly traded company. C'mon, you know you love to do that on a sunny Sunday morning in your cartoon pj's. As you're listening, notice how many times the company says "people" vs. how many times it says "profits."

Customers Care about People over Profits . . . Period

To better understand this strange dichotomy, I sat down with the CEO of JUST Capital and longtime leader in the impact investing space, Martin Whittaker. Whittaker, who has testified to the US Senate on environmental markets and has dedicated his life to creating a more just business climate, joined JUST Capital knowing full well that its Sisyphean challenge would face enormous headwinds, as one would expect going up against a status quo driven by some of the most powerful companies in the world.

So why take it on? And what makes Whittaker think that judging businesses on their justness might provide a better world for us all? Ultimately, he recognized that we "can't solve systemic social, economic, or even environmental health challenges without the private sector. Our government doesn't have the money, and our philanthropic organizations aren't big enough to be able to promote sustainable solutions."

In other words, and perhaps paradoxically, we need those big corporate behemoths—their time, money, manpower, and even political power—to help change the way workers are mistreated, customers are cheated, harmful products are created, or environments are polluted. Of course, that might be problematic for companies who ignore or even *create* those problems in the first place (if you're having trouble thinking of a few, pick up today's news for some fresh examples). Up until the twenty-first century, companies have willingly bent the rules in pursuit of profits because they could, just like the Egyptians and Romans could. But times are changing, and with no thanks to governmental doctrines or new laws. Think about it: throughout the last century, regulations have come and gone, with rules and fines and laws. Did fines stop the financial crisis? Did laws stop VW from falsifying their emissions testing? Did the foundation of meritocracy stop elite universities from taking bribes? Of course not . . . because as long as the motives exist to make money, and we can trick our amygdalae into building up a tolerance for deceit, we inexorably end up in the business environment we experienced over the twentieth century. But here, in *this* century, information transparency is giving us a different set of incentives.

> The American people want businesses to care about people over profits, yet listen in to the next quarterly earnings call from your favorite publicly traded company. How many times does the company say "people" vs. how many times it says "profits"?

As Whittaker notes, the line between "business success" and "profits" appears murkier as of late, and our understanding of exactly what drives business performance and high profitability is rapidly evolving. We do know that ending up in the headlines is decidedly *not* good for profits. Luckily, the components that make for outsized profits are getting clearer as we can measure more data, which is exactly what JUST Capital and its rankings are seeking to accomplish.

"Any good accountant will admit that whether a company is making a profit or loss is an *art*, not a science," Whittaker pointed out, "so imagine the complex drivers of value that include things like people and community relations and product development, and it's not surprising that those drivers haven't been exactly quantified and systematized and turned into tools that can help connect those things to financial performance in business." If we want to make more money in business, we have to be honest: the formula we've used to assess profit is at best only partially correct. It's now time to expand our understanding of how buyers buy, which *does* translate directly into revenues and profits.

Consumers Want a More Just Business (and Will Reward You for It)

The most skeptical among us—a group that, by the way, includes yours truly—might be wondering how we can abandon focusing on the income statement in favor of such touchy-feelies as nurturing our communities and taking better care of employees. I don't know about you, but that sounds *exhausting*. But consider this: if you look back to the Industrial Revolution and consider how companies treated their workers then compared with how companies treat workers today, you'll see that things have improved. In times past, employees literally put their lives at risk to fatten the coffers of owners and executives. Today, unions have enabled better working conditions, workplace safety is a top priority, and perks like gyms, unlimited vacation, and flexible hours run rampant. Don't forget the power of the almighty ping-pong table, either. And if employees' choices have steadily improved, what makes us think that customers' options haven't improved and broadened as well?

Formerly, the difference between those two constituencies was only in the degree of transparency—employees could know for sure how they were treated, while customers didn't have that inside information about product quality, company policies, worker treatment, environmental impact, and so on. Fast-forward to today, when companies are getting exposed in the best and worst of ways, and you can quickly see a future where some companies might be at DEF-CON 1 when it comes to their internal policies and practices. When JUST Capital conducted its nationwide poll to measure how much consumers even cared about justness, 96 percent said they believe it's important to measure just behavior; more than 80 percent indicated they would seek out and use information on justness in purchasing; 63 percent continue to believe in business, which is sort of a sad figure; but 56 percent believe that corporations have become *less* just over the last decade.[2]

Ouch.

The numbers don't lie, and fortunately our crystal ball doesn't have to look far to see that meaningful money is flowing into more just businesses as consumers get more information and make better choices. As Whittaker noted, "When I started out doing impact investing twenty years ago, you had to telephone the investor relations person to say, 'I'm interested in your company's environmental profile or how you treat your workers well,' and they would respond, 'What? Who do you represent?' Finally, if you were lucky, you would receive a little glossy corporate social responsibility [CSR] report, which was more of an exercise in creative writing and photography than in mathematical analysis."

Of course, today is completely different, with companies creating entire CSR departments with the sole focus of enhancing responsible

> In times past, employees literally put their lives at risk to fatten the coffers of owners and executives. Today, unions have enabled better working conditions, workplace safety is a top priority, and perks like gyms, unlimited vacation, and flexible hours run rampant.

practices, including but certainly not limited to the value drivers that JUST Capital has found to be important to the American people. But is that enough? Is a relatively small team of CSR-focused employees enough to prevent VW lying about its emissions tests, or Wells Fargo creating fake accounts to boost sales? How can we regulate against those deceptive practices to create a more honest business climate so organizations start doing the right thing?

According to Whittaker, that's exactly the wrong question to ask.

THE REAL, UNAVOIDABLE DRIVER OF ORGANIZATIONAL CHANGE

"When you look at what makes businesses tick," Whittaker told me, "I don't believe that changing the rules is necessarily the best way to go—force disclosure, change the definition of what a corporation can and can't do, and so on. That kind of change is great and important, but at the core, you have to provide the market incentives and rewards for more just behavior."

> Bringing fairness and equality into a boardroom that only speaks "profit" is like bringing a knife to a gunfight. We must fight corporate behavior with corporate behavior.

If we must fight fire with fire, then it follows that we must fight corporate behavior with corporate behavior. Put another way, bringing fairness and equality into a boardroom that only speaks "profit" is like bringing a knife to a gunfight. But Whittaker and his team stumbled on something even more powerful than fairness and equality. They found a weapon so powerful, even the most staunch CEOs in the most capitalist C Suites can't resist it.

What is this source of insurmountable power, you ask? Easy: customers voting with their wallets, otherwise known as "sales."

That's why it's so critical that the JUST 100 doesn't rank businesses on the basis of what a few executives think; instead, it ranks them according to what customers find most important in their buying decisions.

Regulation, I would agree with Whittaker, hasn't done a whole lot to change corporate attitudes. How well regulated is the pharmaceutical industry? Very. How many scandals have we endured in that industry? Many. Instead of regulation, the consumer public's decision to support a business (or not) by purchasing products and services is the tiny underwater earthquake that can begin the tidal wave of change.

Irony of ironies: in the beginning, Whittaker and his team received negative feedback about polling the public. "The public doesn't know about these things—sustainability or climate change or the connections between gender-pay equity and performance, and the trade-offs between jobs in America and low-cost goods," Whittaker quoted from some early naysayers, shaking his head. But it turns out that we lowly consumers actually do know about those things. Yep—we're smarter than we look (*fist bump*).

Ultimately, JUST's research turns up a set of basic values that any business leader would recognize as vital to a well-run organization. The results legitimize an intrinsic, human point of view we all possess—the very same point of view that we consumers use when we make decisions to *buy*. It turns out that when you ask Americans about their values, you develop some really interesting insights. Every year, JUST's research team conducts new focus groups that yield surprisingly consistent results concerning what the interviewees care about: treating people well, supporting the community, and generally being honest and trustworthy. Sadly, both our government and corporate America have shown a long history of ignoring what we ordinary folks think because, well, they *could*. It's made many of us feel relatively hopeless about the opportunity to create large-scale change, even if that change is simply a reversion to the

> Both our government and corporate America have shown a long history of ignoring what we ordinary folks think because, well, they *could*, and it's made many of us feel relatively hopeless about the opportunity to create large-scale change.

values we all agree are the bedrock of our individual, organizational, and societal identity.

Unfortunately, we're living in a tremendously dichotomous time, where some leaders are being rewarded for being just (like the leaders featured in this book), while others are being rewarded for being unjust (did the CEOs of VW and Wells Fargo give back their mansions or yachts?). But what's at stake here isn't just profits, as I hope you'll agree. What JUST's researchers have found is that people want to feel they can trust their institutions and their neighbors alike, and that they can live in a country we're all proud of. It'll be up to us as individuals to define *who* we are, and to decide whether our shift toward honest values is simply a generational fad (darn you, millennials!) or something more. By the way, we're deciding that fate every day, simply by voting with our wallets.

> People want to feel they can trust their institutions and their neighbors alike, and that they can live in a country we're all proud of.

If you're a leader interested only in short-term profits, I have no strategy to offer. I can only appeal to your identity, core values, and willingness to make the world a better place. But if you want to thrive long-term, then wow do I have the strategy for you.

Let's be brutally honest for a moment about where we are as a society. If we think about society as a whole—our politics, social norms, even casual conversations—we've been on a journey over the last fifty years in this country to stop treating people as manufacturing inputs and start treating them like humans. Many elements of social life that were simply part of the way the world worked have forever changed, and the way we do business is changing, too. As a nation and throughout the world, we've been on a trajectory toward treating people better—whether interpersonally, between neighbors, or organizationally, as employers and employees and vendors and customers. Play it forward, and anyone with even a small amount of foresight can see that the businesses that ultimately win will be those that lead with honesty and transparency.

THE SHOCKING BUSINESS CASE FOR BEING A JUST ORGANIZATION

Each year, JUST Capital illuminates what the consumer public wants and how today's largest companies stack up to those expectations. JUST is tracking company performance on data points that have never been tracked before, so we can all see what happens when people gain access to more information than they've ever had about their beloved brands. Chances are, most of those brands will begin to behave differently, more justly. Companies, after all, are made up of humans, and, as Whittaker offered, "People behave differently in the dark than they do in the light."

As more companies have reported data, JUST has been able to collate that data into a phenomenally compelling case for justness; companies who make the JUST 100 list also, on average:

- pay their median US employees 33 percent more than other companies
- employ an average 38 percent more workers in the US than other companies
- have paid no consumer product safety fines over the last three years
- have zero FDA fines
- donate 3.8 times more to charity per dollar of revenue
- emit 72 percent less greenhouse gases per dollar of revenue
- pay 99 percent fewer environmental fines per dollar of revenue
- pay 96 percent fewer sales term fines per dollar of revenue
- face 74 percent fewer employment discrimination cases per dollar of revenue
- face 73 percent fewer labeling controversies per dollar of revenue
- use 80 percent less fossil fuel per dollar of revenue

And the metric you've been waiting for: it doesn't cost these companies even a dime to live by generally honest business practices. In fact, JUST 100 companies deliver an average 8 percent *higher* return on equity than their peer companies,[3] which makes acting justly, according to JUST Capital, "*just* plain smart."

Now we know. We consumers *know* that making the choice to buy from a just company makes it possible for its employees to earn better wages, for the environment to sustain less damage, and for us to be better protected, knowing that what we buy has better quality. And if that level of transparency excites you, we're only at the beginning.

"In the next twenty years," Whittaker mused, "I imagine you'll be able to know what women and men get paid in the same job in the same company. All that data is going to be out there. You'll know exactly whether or not a company is polluting locally or not in the zip code where you live. Think about corporate disclosure reporting going back to the Depression, and you'll see that companies have been resistant to giving out information. Fifty years ago, companies didn't even give up where they were getting their revenues from because of 'competition,' which today is totally different. It's inevitable to me that anyone's going to be able to get the kind of information that we struggle to get today, and once you embrace the fact that that's going to happen, it requires an honesty about what actually drives performance."

Whittaker and JUST Capital's founding team have bet big that the business world is ready to expose the honest drivers of profitability, and they firmly believe that all that's missing is access to more data. Already, big multinational companies are thinking more critically about how to more deeply measure *all* the components of business success, and the more serious businesspeople there are who are willing to be honest and transparent, the more this snowball will accumulate.

This being a book about honesty, there are, admittedly, some holes worth addressing. For instance, fossil-fuel-producing oil and gas companies grace the JUST 100 list, as does Facebook, despite recent scandals. To that, JUST Capital's staff members explained that, ultimately, the American public is the judge, jury, and executioner when it comes to which companies deserve to be on the list and which don't. That's why, each year, JUST redoes its nationwide polls to gauge which issues are important and how those issues change in importance over time. Thus, the public might be willing to forgive Facebook because data privacy may not be a strong enough criteria, while fracking for natural gas might be much more egregious. In fact, as one researcher put it, the rankings "do allow for companies to make mistakes, or, for instance, to be ongoing polluters, and still be just in other ways."

Nuances indeed exist; for instance, when you fill up your car with gas, it might be difficult to pinpoint whether the gas company, your automobile manufacturer, or *you* are the one to hold responsible for polluting the environment. JUST also found that for some companies, treating employees well or giving to charities couldn't offset the core of the business. For example, tobacco producers couldn't overcome creating a product that inherently damages people's health, so JUST Capital made the decision to permanently pull cigarette maker Philip Morris International from the list in 2017, as the public demanded.

Furthermore, there exists a conspicuously large number of technology companies on the JUST 100, which made me wonder whether justness was a function of profitability (instead of the other way around), or perhaps simply a birthmark of newer, millennial-driven cultures. To that, the JUST researchers noted that tech companies do inherently tick a lot of boxes by being in a high-wage industry with products that people love, close relationships with end consumers, and so on. But even more importantly, tech companies are often younger, nimbler organizations that can move more quickly on the issues that people care about, and they're less likely to be stuck in practices they developed decades ago that today aren't socially relevant or appropriate.

> Now that companies can see us consumers coming for their data, they will doubtless move to clean up their acts.

Even more frustrating, the rankings are still constrained by publicly available and crowdsourced information. Of note, there are issues bubbling up in the tech community around sexual harassment, gender pay gaps, how those companies treat contractors who are outside the purview of the employer-employee relationship, and so on. Those are factors that, over time and with ever-more data, the JUST team can integrate into their rankings to create a more complete picture of organizational honesty. Hopefully, with help from Wall Street analysts who are keen to collect more information to produce more accurate guidance, companies will have an incentive to create and share more data over time. And now that companies can see us consumers coming for their data, they will doubtless move to clean up their acts.

IF YOU WANT TO COMPETE, THE TIME FOR HONESTY IS *NOW*

The race is on to be the most honest, most transparent, most conscientious company, and we won't have to wait too long for organizations worldwide to fall in line. "It's not that all business is adapting to a changing culture," one JUST researcher noted, "but that businesses exist on a continuum of competitiveness, so the ones that are leading anticipate what's coming and adjust as a result." The entire distribution curve for organizational honesty is shifting, and the opportunity standing before you gives you the chance to occupy the leading edge of that curve. By definition, being a leader means exploring new ground and charting new territory, which is what the JUST researchers, CEO Martin Whittaker, and JUST Capital's powerful founders hope to inspire.

> Honesty isn't a cost; it's an investment that will drive better products, experiences, sales, marketing, finance, culture, and more.

No matter where you are—on the left or on the right, on the front lines of an oil and gas company or the C Suite of a tech firm—you can see from JUST's mission that you have a compelling excuse to be honest about what needs to change. Trust is at an all-time low, and we don't need data to look around and notice how skeptical we've all become. Capitalism is increasingly being called into question as a sustainable system. And if that's true, it's time to bring America's values and America's firms into alignment so that businesses can sustainably benefit everyone as we move into our transparent future. If you're thinking, *We can't afford to do good*, you need to know that there's a business case here. Honesty isn't a cost; it's an investment that will drive better products, experiences, sales, marketing, finance, culture, and more. If you don't believe me—and I don't blame you—I'll soon prove it.

For JUST, the *how* is probably best left to market forces—peer pressure, the desire to attract and retain the best talent, the pursuit of industry awards, the perils of public perception, the ubiquity of social media, and, of course, the pursuit of profit. A company that does as it says, keeps promises, and acts honestly will, ultimately, win that race—along with a nearly insurmountable competitive advantage, as we'll soon see with the cases in this book. Mark my words: the firm that embraces honesty will always win in a world where consumers have near-perfect information. Sadly, many leaders I encounter would rather plunge a chopstick into their eyeballs than admit they must finally stop pulling the wool over the eyes of customers and employees.

Yet the age-old principles of microeconomics hold fast here: consumers buy things when they believe the products they're purchasing hold more value than the money they're paying. When consumers have bad information, they make bad choices—choices that they wouldn't make if they had better information about the value of what they're buying. We're already making better, more informed decisions as more information becomes available, and the organizations that hold out will lose out to their more transparent competitors.

> Consumers buy things when they believe the products they're purchasing hold more value than the money they're paying. When consumers have bad information, they make bad choices—choices that they wouldn't make if they had better information about the value of what they're buying.

Finally, it's worth noting that JUST's rankings contain the largest companies in the United States—not Patagonia or Zappos, which have more obvious connections to just values. However, JUST's founders recognize that creating systemic change—the movement toward a more just business climate—takes some of the largest resources in the world to achieve. According to Just Capital, a tiny shift in spending by the largest publicly traded firms could create more than a trillion-dollar flow into greater employee benefits, better product development, better customer experiences, and more, so it makes sense to try to move the biggest ships in order to produce the greatest impact.

Meanwhile, some bold individuals, public companies, and private organizations—some of which are in this book—are bravely holding short-term initiatives at bay while considering the long-term sustainability and profitability of their firms. Those brave leaders have realized that success exists in the mind-set shift from "we need to cut costs" to "we need to invest in being just so we're here for the long term." If you're not a brave leader—and bravo for your honest self-assessment—consider JUST's findings that 56 percent of people think CEOs should take a stand on social issues related to the business. If that's impressive, consider that even more—63 percent—think that CEOs have a responsibility to take a stand on important social issues *whether they concern the business or not.*[4] Unsurprisingly, young people seek out justness more than any other generation: a Glassdoor survey from 2017 found that 75 percent of eighteen- to thirty-four-year-olds expect their company to "take a stand on important issues affecting the country and their constitutional rights, including immigration, equal rights, and climate change," and that young people are increasingly forgoing higher compensation in favor of companies that "align with their beliefs."[5]

And "just" in case you wanted an even bigger financial incentive, consider that on June 13, 2018, Goldman Sachs launched the JUST U.S. Large Cap Equity ETF (Ticker: JUST)—the first ever exchange-traded fund (ETF) designed to match the American public's priorities to a publicly traded investment. With both the firepower of its supporters and the zeitgeist of our time, the JUST ETF was the single most successful Environmental, Social, and Governance (ESG) ETF launch to date, and in the top ten equity ETF launches in history—proving that investors are truly interested in putting their money into companies that do good.

The movement toward information transparency and consumer choice is already here, like it or not. It's honestly up to you whether you'll capitalize on this movement or choose to hang on for as long as possible to the status quo until you're forced to spend egregious amounts of time and money playing catch-up to your bolder peers. Ultimately, if your organization can inch its way a little closer to what America cares about—leaders and organizations being just, fair, and honest—you'll be ready for the meaningful change lurking just around the corner . . . the corner of Wall Street and Main Street.

QUESTIONS FOR HONEST REFLECTION

1. To what extent does your organization behave the way everyday Americans want it to?
2. How much do you know about the brands you buy, and what could you do to learn more about their business practices?
3. Would you describe your organization as innovative or sticking to the status quo?

CHAPTER 4

The Hourglass of Honesty

If you're just and honest, you'll earn the trust of your people—inside and outside the organization's walls. With more data, consumers will make more informed choices, choosing to do business with just and honest organizations. This stuff is literally so obvious it's probably hurting your prefrontal cortex to think about, not to mention it's your clue that the author of this book is no Einstein. And yet, from every corner of our world bullshit spews forth like a Roman fountain. It gushes from the lips of execs, from the minds of founders, from conference rooms full of employees, and from the talking heads screaming at us from our flat-screens.

Let's not delude ourselves: our norm isn't normal, and we have a responsibility to at least recognize the sheer amount of lies that invade our lives. Then, and only then, can we decide to do something about it, and even ask that nasty little question, *how?* A complex query, indeed, since there are so many ways leaders and their organizations can choose to define and then embrace an "honest" way of being. And as we saw in chapter three, even consumers have different definitions of being honest—from being fair to workers, to caring for the environment, to creating better communities, and more.

When you consider your sales, marketing, operations, new product development, communications, management style, and every other aspect of your business, it can be overwhelming to consider all the ways in which you could use honesty as a strategic tool for innovation and growth. Heck, we haven't even come close to creating an exact definition of honesty yet. That's why we need a *framework* for honesty—a simple way to decide what's important, which questions to ask, and how to approach the complex problems we leaders face on a daily basis in our organizations. Furthermore, the framework must apply to every industry—from for-profit businesses to nonprofit organizations, and from start-ups to enterprise companies. If honesty is universally effective, we must have a method for applying it universally.

> If honesty is universally effective, we must have a method for applying it universally.

A bit of warning here: nothing you read in this book should shake the foundations of your beliefs. You already know this stuff. All I did was put a shiny wrapper on something you know, in your heart, to be self-evident. But that's where the power comes from: your already knowing what's right. The stories in this book will arm you with the valuable ammunition you need to fight with strength and courage, and to *win*. With that in mind, allow me to give you a little backstory of how a lowly life-form like me came to attempt codifying such an obvious truth.

DISCOVERING THE ROOT CAUSE OF HONESTY (AND INNOVATION)

I wasn't always a crusader for honesty. I started out like any other well-meaning twenty-two-year-old entrepreneur who wanted to build a thriving business and get rich doing it. With the help of a talented team, my business partner and I morphed our fledgling video production company into a content production company and then into a full-service marketing agency that worked on behalf of leaders from local car dealers to Warren Buffett himself. Over the years, we helped organizations in more than thirty industries at the local and national level clarify their messages, create better marketing, and grow. We even emerged from the perennial struggle bus to eventually grace the Inc. 5000 list of fastest-growing companies in America for two years in a row.

In the early days, we figured out a small distinction that seemed to set us apart: while most other marketing firms were concerned about making beautiful things or running focus groups with potential new customers, we were concerned about diving deeply into the psychology of our clients' *current* best customers. We knew that if we could understand what lay in the hearts of a client's most ideal customers—the ones who spent the most money, came back the most frequently, and shared their experiences with more new customers—we could create messaging that would perfectly connect the brand's unique selling proposition with more ideal customers.

That simple premise usually gave us all the firepower we needed to create compelling marketing campaigns. Instead of focusing on what executives *thought* about their brands and potentially succumbing to their biases, we simply went to their best customers and asked them what they thought; that way we ended up with a true set of insights. Over the course of a decade in business, we used this simple, honest technique to create incredible results, in some cases giving clients up to a 500 percent return on their investment with us.

> Over the course of a decade in business, we used this simple, honest technique to create incredible results for clients, in some cases giving them up to a 500 percent return on their investment with us.

I recall being in one of our first pitches with that approach, at a local college. For a year we had been collecting video testimonials from their students in our role as video production vendor. Eventually our work landed us an opportunity to pitch as the agency of record. At the pitch, we showed a video montage of what the students were saying about the college. From those insights we derived a new tag line, which we proposed as the centerpiece of the school's campaign.

At the end of the presentation, the president of the college paused momentarily while we wrung our hands in anticipation of our fate. She looked in disbelief at the tag line printed in front of her and gazed up at us. She said, "I've been looking for something like this for years. How did you come up with this?" Of course, I was tempted to say, "'Cuz we're the' biggest bunch of geniuses you've ever met!" But that would have been a lie. The truth is, all we did was get honest about whose opinion mattered most, and we simply listened to what those opinions were telling us. And with the message we crafted—the one their own best customers gave us—we were able to grow their open house attendance for prospective students by more than sevenfold.

> My colleagues and I would sit in meeting after meeting, shell-shocked at how many executives preferred to keep their heads firmly planted in the sand if it meant that nothing had to change.

Unfortunately, creating impressive results for clients wasn't always that simple. But before we get to that, I'll be honest with you: I never set out to write about, speak about, or frankly even think about honesty. Getting honest insights from current customers didn't seem all that honest to me when we started out . . . it simply made logical sense, given the work we were doing. Not every client saw it that way, though. In fact, what shocked me most about my career in marketing was witnessing the clients who disagreed with what we found. It was most curious sitting in a boardroom with key executives and having them tell us every reason why their best customers' feedback was wrong, and why it made much more sense to just maintain the status quo, or copy whatever the competition was doing, or simply create something that the executives could agree on, even if it completely missed the mark with their own customers. My colleagues and I would sit in meeting after meeting, shell-shocked at how many executives preferred to keep their heads firmly planted in the sand if it meant that nothing had to change.

Did twentysomething Peter brandish honesty in their faces and insist they tear down their presumptions? Did I jump up on the conference room table and give bombastic speeches to persuade them to remove their heads from their asses? Of course not! I had employees with families to feed. I smiled and nodded like a benevolent nun and did whatever they wanted us to do to keep those checks coming. (Don't worry, you can lambaste me over my moral ineptitudes in chapter fourteen.) And then I would watch, my nonplussed face wedged between my hands, as those campaigns would inevitably crash and burn.

After seeing the same horrific behavior in organizations large and small and in every industry under the sun, I started to ask myself, *Why did some of our clients use our growth strategies to innovate and dominate their industries, getting a massive return on their investments, while others never even got out of the starting gate . . . embroiled in politics and wedged firmly into the status quo?* It took my own personal crisis to see this enigma for what it was—a fundamental lack of honesty.

That's why, when I first learned of Netflix's failed sale to Blockbuster, I immediately recognized the root cause—not daftness but *dishonesty*. Blockbuster's well-meaning, well-educated, and experienced executives simply failed to get honest—about what had changed in the industry, the preferences of their customers, and the dangerous strategy the activist investor was thrusting upon them.

THE FRAMEWORK THAT CHANGED
MY BUSINESS—AND MY LIFE

Honesty can take on many different meanings in life and business. It can mean true, candid, direct, transparent, authentic, and more. But in my definition of honest in business, there are three very specific levels of honesty that any organization can use to innovate and dominate. All three levels fit into a framework I've come to call the Hourglass of Honesty, because the process works just like sand would move through an hourglass. It works in any organization, large or small, and in any industry. It works for start-up entrepreneurs, managers of small teams, and executives of billion-dollar companies. Right now, we're just going to look at the top part of the Hourglass, the part that asks you to take an honest journey inward through three levels—community, others, and self.

The Honest Journey Inward

Community

The first level of honesty is getting honest about the *community*. To attain this level, it's essential to understand what's happening in the world around you and what's changing in your industry. It's putting yourself in the context of your present surroundings and circumstances, and observing the zeitgeist of our society. Consider, for instance, what the #MeToo movement has brought to our global conversation; how that singular shift in our consciousness has created a cascade of reactions, stoking the fires of related issues like gender-pay inequality. Reflect on how the 2007–2008 financial crisis drastically changed the trust level between consumers and businesses. Witness the swift rise of nonbinary gender fluidity—an idea that seemed nearly impossible just a few short years ago.

Times, they are a-changin', and society seems to be shifting its belief systems at an ever-increasing clip. It's critical for leaders to continually be honest about these changes, because they provide the basis for how we operate as a cohesive society with agreed-upon social norms. Many executives fail to properly assess this level of honesty, just as Blockbuster ultimately did. Its executive team failed to change with society's evolving entertainment habits, and they paid a hefty price for letting an activist investor steer them back to the status quo.

The world at large is brimming with innovation and change. To succeed at the first level of honesty, you must embrace that. You must be adaptable. You cannot be like the many leaders who blindly choose the status quo and hide behind "the way we've always done it."

Getting honest about the community means thinking critically about the world around you, developing a keen awareness of how society's belief systems and habits are changing, and learning to consistently examine the evolving beliefs of our time. The information you need exists all around you; it bombards you every day in the form of news media and advertising, in conversations by the office Keurig, and at your dinner table at home. Today's best opportunities will float toward you as long as you're actively listening for them.

> Getting honest about the community means thinking critically about the world around you, developing a keen awareness of how society's belief systems and habits are changing, and learning to consistently examine the evolving beliefs of our time.

Others

The second level of honesty is being honest with and about the *others* in your life. The "others" are the people who make up your personal and professional worlds. They are your family, friends, colleagues, bosses, clients, neighbors, and, well, others. Most people are dishonest with and about those around them at some level. For instance, think of your friend who won't break up with her boyfriend, even though it's objectively obvious that her boyfriend is no good for her. Think about the times you've avoided a much-needed, candid conversation with another person because you think it might jeopardize the relationship. Consider a time when you've excused the bad behavior of a loved one under the excuse that you're "protecting" them.

Examples of this phenomenon abound in our professional lives. Think of your work colleague who has been verbally abused by his boss so many times but won't confront his boss about it. Think about the times you've sat in a meeting where it was clear what needed to happen but the interpersonal politics were so thick and corruptive that nothing could possibly get done. In all these examples, the subject is unwilling or unable to be honest *with* and/or *about* the others around them.

To capitalize on the second level of honesty, we must break free of the bullshit and be honest about our others. With so many outside threats and with so much change in the world, who can afford to be dishonest, particularly at the executive level? The "others" include *all* the others: customers, suppliers, vendors, direct reports, bosses, board members, chief executives, frontline employees, advisers, prospects, and more. It will always be up to you to decide which group of others you must be honest about, though I suspect you'll find that decision obvious, and you'll see how to choose your others with some of the stories in this book. The trick is to get honest about *all* your others as a continual habit of leadership—and even get honest about your family or social group, when required.

> If you believe that business is driven wholly by the people within it, then you'll agree that getting brutally honest with and about the people in your workplace is critical to making the right assessments, building the right teams, and achieving your goals.

If you believe that business is driven wholly by the people within it, then you'll agree that getting brutally honest with and about the people in your workplace is critical to making the right assessments, building the right teams, and achieving your goals. If the others around you are so critical to your success, then the question for you, as a leader, is how much time you should spend blindly *accepting* the people around you vs. honestly *assessing* them. It's the difference between accepting those around you at face value and digging deeper to get at the truth of what people around you know, believe, fear, and perceive, as well as what they can achieve.

Getting honest about your others is usually much more difficult than getting honest about your community. It takes forgetting about being "nice" and instead being thoughtfully, and yes, brutally, candid.

It's no secret that the highest-performing organizations get the right people in the right positions, and you can't hope to align your people that way without being honest with and about them in the first place.

Self

Getting honest about the community takes intense listening skills and awareness. Getting honest about others takes the resolute pursuit of objectivity and the bravery to be honest and direct with those around you—not even letting "love" and "kindness" come before truth. But in the third and final level of honesty, getting honest with the *self* requires something entirely different, an element that escapes the vast majority of leaders across every size organization, every industry, every culture, and even every country. Getting honest with the self requires *self-awareness*, that elusive character trait that all want, most insist they have, and yet very few truly possess. Getting honest with and about the self requires a lifelong pursuit of exploration into the very depths of your identity, where you find countless fears, hopes, dreams, and beliefs that serve you or defeat you by the millisecond.

Of course, you can't be honest about what you can't see, so step one is *actively* and *continually* seeking to identify your true self. As Dolly Parton said, "Find out who you are and do it on purpose." Then, once you learn to see, you must learn to parse absolute fact from subjective opinion, which is difficult enough with those around you but incredibly challenging within your own mind. And yet, we know that getting honest with and about ourselves is critical to success and happiness, as we hold in high esteem the most enlightened, self-aware folks around us: Gandhi, Oprah, Einstein, Maya Angelou, Lincoln, Shakespeare, Nelson Mandela, and all the wise folks whose quotes float around the internet as leadership gospel.

Nearly every religious doctrine teaches a measure of self-assessment, from the Christian approach of seeing and repenting sin, to the self-auditing process of Scientology, to Buddhist teachings on consistently examining one's own consciousness. All these encourage us to hold a mirror to ourselves—or, in some cases, to ask the divine to show us our true selves, as the Jewish leader King David did when he cried out, "Search me, O God, and know my heart; try me, and know my anxieties; and see if there is any wicked way in me" (Psalm 139). We have a responsibility, both as organizations and as individuals, to get honest about ourselves. This final step unlocks tremendous opportunities for you, as a leader, to achieve massive success in business.

> "Find out who you are and do it on purpose."
> —Dolly Parton

I'm blessed to coach other entrepreneurs, helping them build their own mini-empires. Time after time, founders have come to me insisting that all they need is a better strategy for sales or a better tactic for marketing, when in fact they actually need to push past uncertainty, or admit that they need to pivot their business model, or otherwise get deeply honest with themselves about their self-limiting beliefs, biases, or fears. As Mark Manson, *New York Times* best-selling author of *The Subtle Art of Not Giving A F*ck*, wrote, "We lie to ourselves as a way to protect ourselves from getting hurt [but] it disconnects us from reality." Once we learn how to stop lying to ourselves, "it empowers us to live more freely in the world and be more honest with those around us."[1] And that's where the magic begins.

HONESTY EVEN WORKS IN YOUR PERSONAL LIFE (HERE'S HOW I KNOW)

Remember that "personal crisis" I mentioned a little while ago? Well, I happen to be somewhat of an expert on getting deeply honest about self-limiting beliefs, since I've failed so miserably at it in the past. When I was seventeen, I was sure that I was on the precipice of accomplishing two childhood goals: going to the Olympics as a figure skater and attending Harvard University as my grandfather, uncle, and cousin all had. But spoiler alert: by eighteen, I had come to grips that the Olympic dream needed to die, I had been rejected by Harvard, and I found my emotional well-being spiraling out of control. I was devastated.

It's amazing how long rejection stays in the mind. Thinking I was over those two massive failures, I spent the next twelve years moving toward "success," or how I was defining it at the time. When I turned the big three-oh, I cruised past my actual birthday. *This isn't so bad,* I thought. Then, suddenly, my age hit me like a Hawaiian wave over an unsuspecting surfer. It was a full-on quarter-life crisis. (Yes, for you math buffs, I plan to live to the ripe old age of 120.)

I don't know what it was about that age. If you're over that hump, then you know what I mean. How did you ever get through it!? (As an aside, at one keynote I delivered, an energetic woman in the front row called out that she had turned thirty *twice*. Having barely survived it the first time, I still remain in awe of her feat.) When I looked around at where I was and who I was, I disliked what I saw. I beat myself up. I wavered back and forth between wanting to double down on my dreams and work harder than ever, and feeling totally beaten down and unable to move forward at all. Perhaps you can relate.

My biggest problem: I wasn't even sure what my dreams were any-more. I had been so *sure* of those two goals that when they didn't come to fruition, I got stuck in a state of subconscious shock. Somewhere shortly after those two failures, I had stopped dreaming—or, more appropriately, I had started subconsciously accepting a second-best scenario. Perhaps I was imagining that I wasn't good enough or smart enough for greatness. Perhaps that was just the simple fact of my life.

Unfortunately, it took me until a little past thirty to wake the hell up and realize that in some ways, I had been drifting along for a decade instead of marching in the right direction. Or what I thought was the right direction. You see, it's quite impossible to tell which direction is right or wrong if you have no idea where you're going. And to be honest, I had no idea where I was going. As Yogi Berra said, "If you don't know where you are going, you'll end up someplace else." *Where am I?* I began to think. *How did I get here? How far am I from where I'm supposed to be?*

Mind you, by thirty, I had what I'm sure seemed like a successful life. My business partner and I were building a multimillion-dollar business with a team of wonderful people. I had just gotten married to my amazing wife. Everyone around me was healthy. For all intents and purposes, I should have just shut the fuck up and appreciated what I had.

But each one of us measures success in different ways. To me, my achievements weren't achievements—they were minimum expectations.

> I had been drifting along for a decade instead of marching in the right direction. Or what I thought was the right direction. You see, it's quite impossible to tell which direction is right or wrong if you have no idea where you're going.

My accomplishments weren't triumphs to be celebrated; they were evidence of how I had failed to achieve anything worthy at all.

Unfortunately, I had become a preacher of *organizational* honesty who had failed to realize that I had been dishonest with myself—with my hopes, dreams, and fears. I had developed a knack for helping other leaders and organizations get honest, but I had a massive blind spot weighing me down: I had failed to get honest with myself in my own personal life.

#irony, #fail.

It was certainly a soul-searching time. Entering my fourth decade of life put me on the verge of my greatest fear: mediocrity. Something about being in my thirties kicked me into gear, and I finally became brave enough to get deeply honest about my own identity gap in order to reinvent some things in my life. I finally admitted that I wasn't being honest *about* myself: my true thoughts, feelings, dreams, goals, and potential. And I wasn't being honest *with* myself: I had been harboring self-limiting beliefs, holding back, using negative self-talk, and hiding in the safe zone instead of moving boldly forward toward what I truly wanted in life. In essence, I had unwittingly covered myself in stinky, muddy, bull-poo and then sat there dumbstruck in my self-inflicted mess.

That's when I realized that there was so much more to honesty than I had thought; there was much more power in honesty than I had ever realized. My entire life changed when I finally unlocked the third level of honesty in my own life, when I was finally able to look at the mirror and be brutally honest with myself.

When we start telling ourselves the truth, we can start reacting to that truth, simple as that. When I started being honest with myself—who I really was, what I really wanted—I started making changes. Lots of changes. I started writing, posting, and networking like crazy. I started applying to magazine columns. I sat down to write this book. I was awarded the 2016 Millennial Move Maker in my home state. I began to get articles picked up in *Inc.*, *Forbes*, the *Huffington Post*, *Crain's*, *PR Daily*, and more. I was invited to join the Entrepreneurs' Organization in New York, as well as the Young Entrepreneur Council. I applied to and got accepted into Columbia Business School. I was invited to do a TEDx Talk. I began doing keynote presentations to spread the gospel of honesty to anyone who would listen, and I started to get invited to some amazing conferences filled with others who saw honesty's potential.

In fact, I accomplished more in the few years after my thirtieth birthday than I had in the *twelve years prior*. Doors began to unlock and open. Life became clearer. The tide of my life began to turn, and I saw the tsunami of success—as I newly and honestly defined it—start to build momentum. I was hustling, and it was an honest-to-greatness hustle for what I actually wanted in this life.

HOW THE JOURNEY *THROUGH* LEADS TO CHANGE

Sure, we had used honesty to grow clients' businesses, but still, I was floored to see how quickly honesty produced results outside the business world. Seeing the by-products of honesty in my own life reinforced to me why honesty works in the first place. It works because honesty isn't just a journey *inward*; it's a journey *through*.

This is where the concept of the Hourglass was born. This is how I learned how honesty really works, in life and in business: when you get honest about what's going on in the community, and when you get honest with and about the people around you, and when you get honest with and about yourself, with your own biases and self-limiting beliefs as a leader . . . in that instant, you've changed.

Honest You is a completely different person, with different hopes, dreams, beliefs, and fears. Honest You is willing to change the others around you, to enable the innovators and ignore the status-quo detractors. And that's how you can bend the community toward you and create industry-dominating results.

This—this *Hourglass of Honesty*—is the key that unlocks the door to innovation, in business *and* in life.

Cynical me would never have believed it if I hadn't experienced it myself. Trust me, people who knew me in high school (as the class asshole) will never believe that I—of all people—am proverbially descending from Mt. Sinai with tablets inscribed with HONESTY. But there it is: Once I was honest about the world around me, honest with and about the others in my life, and brutally honest with myself, there was an instantaneous change in my mind-set. I was no longer "dishonest Peter." Instead, I was "honest Peter"—essentially an entirely different person, with an entirely different set of goals, dreams, fears, aspirations, abilities, and potential.

The true me.

The Hourglass of Honesty

As an entirely different person, I began to think differently about the others around me. I began to spend much more time curating beneficial relationships that could help me achieve my *true* goals—the ones I had been suppressing for years. And once I changed my inner circle, those new "others" helped me influence the community around me with new ideas, connections, and opportunities. They enabled me to bend the community toward me and make remarkable things happen within a very short period of time—one of those things being this very book.

All those outcomes were made possible by the key that starts the engine of change: *honesty*. And it works exactly the same way for business leaders. Once you get honest about what's going on in society at large and in your industry, and then get honest about the customers and colleagues around you, and then get honest about your own biases and beliefs, you naturally change. You're able to see different insights, assess new possibilities, and approach old problems in an entirely new way. In that instant you become an *honest* leader, one who is willing and able to strategically alter the others around you and produce incredible outcomes in your community.

If you watch for it, you can see the Hourglass all around us, hiding in plain sight. It lives in every leader you've witnessed who is unabashedly authentic to who they are—from Oprah Winfrey and Tony Robbins to Ellen DeGeneres and Steve Jobs. These and many others somehow seem predestined for greatness, like they were always going to become stars in their own right. Now I realize that's exactly the case. Because they were

> Once you get honest about what's going on in society at large and in your industry, and then get honest about the customers and colleagues around you, and then get honest about your own biases and beliefs, you naturally change. You're able to see different insights, assess new possibilities, and approach old problems in an entirely new way.

so honestly, authentically themselves, they were able to influence others and the community around them.

In fact, Steve Jobs understood this method perhaps better than anyone else. He famously wrote:

> When you grow up, you tend to get told the world is the way it is and your life is just to live your life inside the world. Try not to bash into the walls too much . . . that's a very limited life. Life can be much broader once you discover one simple fact: Everything around you that you call life was made up by people that were no smarter than you. And you can change it, you can influence it, you can build your own things that other people can use. Once you learn that, you'll never be the same again.[2]

Jobs knew that the world could be bent, influenced. He knew that people could be swayed, united, mobilized. He knew that it was not only possible but *easy* and *formulaic* if only we could remove that self-limiting cover we love to pull over our heads by fitting in with the crowd and hiding our true selves. And what's the root of that power? Pursuing one's honest self. As he advised a group of graduating Stanford students at commencement, "I'm convinced that the only thing that kept me going was that I loved what I did . . . As with all matters of the heart, you'll know when you find it."[3]

"When you grow up, you tend to get told the world is the way it is and your life is just to live your life inside the world. Try not to bash into the walls too much ... that's a very limited life."—Steve Jobs

I couldn't agree more. You'll know when you find your honest identity; if you pursue it, at least you can say you tried to just do you instead of failing at a life you might not have even wanted in the first place.

As I promised, there's no rocket science here. The idea is stupid-simple, and something we've heard countless times: be yourself, and you can influence the world. That's what Steve Jobs knew, and it's exactly what allowed me to help my clients achieve their growth goals. Though, as I've admitted,

I never truly understood the nuances of why it worked until I was able to be honest with myself and see the results in my own life. Now honesty is a lens I carry with me everywhere, like a diagnostic tool to help me understand why people behave as they do, what they believe vs. what is objectively true, and how to help people and organizations make positive change. Once you see the Hourglass, you can't unsee it. You'll recognize it in success stories large and small, here at home and around the world. You'll see it break down in business faux pas and PR disasters on the news, and the reason will be oh-so-clear to you.

> Honesty is a lens I carry with me everywhere, like a diagnostic tool to help me understand why people behave as they do, what they believe vs. what is objectively true, and how to help people and organizations make positive change.

The argument I'm selling you is that there's an old way of doing things and a new way of doing things. The old way depended on information asymmetry—a fancy way of saying that buyers didn't know any better and companies took advantage of them in order to profit. Now that we buyers know better, we're going to choose to do business with honest organizations that make a profit while taking care of all constituents in a sustainable way. If you agree that near-perfect information is rapidly approaching, and if you agree that consumers will make different decisions with near-perfect information, then you sit at an unprecedented time in human history when doing the right thing will unlock massive success for you as a leader—in your business and in your life. But none of that can happen if you aren't honest enough to *see* that oncoming wave, *assess* the people you've assembled around you to catch it, and *open* your mind to ensure that you can ride its ebbs and flows with agile confidence.

This being a book about using honesty to achieve greatness, you have a choice. You can embrace the status quo and keep on keepin' on, or you can get ahead of this tidal wave of honesty and ride it, as many of the leaders in this book are doing. But make no mistake; the time to embrace honesty is right now, because being honest, by definition, isn't a reactionary strategy. Early movers will forever be able to claim that they did the right thing *before* it was forced upon them. If you wait too long, you might find yourself battling a competitor that has embraced honesty on all three levels. Is that a game of catch-up you can afford to play?

Now that you have a working framework for honesty, let's see it in action. Because as I've noted before, this isn't a book about business ethics; it's a book about making veritable shit tons of money. And once you see honesty rake in billions of dollars, that's when it gets truly exciting.

———— QUESTIONS FOR HONEST REFLECTION ————

1. To what extent do your colleagues pursue the truth, rather than ignore it? How comfortable are you with pursuing the facts, no matter how painful they might be?

2. What can you learn from getting honest about what's going on in your community, with the others around you, and with yourself?

3. How honest are you about who you really are, what you really want, and what it's really going to take to achieve your biggest goals in life?

PART II

What It Means to Be an Honest Organization

Want to see if honesty *really* delivers business results? In the chapters that follow, we'll discover what honesty looks like across sales, marketing, finance, management, communication, innovation, and leadership. We'll also learn about key frameworks you can use to drive industry-leading growth and profitability, all by using the intrinsic power of honesty.

CHAPTER 5

Sales: The Honest-to-Goodness Technique for Explosive Sales

As Taught by the World's Most Honest Girl Scout

Think of the last time you described your suite of products or services to a prospect. How honest was your assessment? What truth did your prospects hear from you?

Funnily enough, people hate to be lied to. I know, it's a wild concept. And yet, we're bombarded with advertising messages all day long that promise the world—and we eat that shit up with a fork and knife. *If you just buy this car, you'll instantly be more sophisticated! If you only buy this face cream, you'll instantly be more beautiful!* Curiously, we all know these promises are false, yet we succumb to them. We succumb because we hold out hope . . . that maybe, just maybe, *this* product will actually fulfill our dreams of making us feel better. Because make no mistake; unless we're talking about a necessary purchase, like tires, *feeling better* is what buying is all about. Smart sales folks and marketers know this, and they use it to overextend the promise of their products and services.

Like sheep, many of us follow, myself included. But less so these days, given our rising societal skepticism. Brands are getting put into their own mini-movie version of *Backdraft*, where consumers play the firefighters and the brands play the fire that's roaring along just fine until it gets put out by a deluge and the CEO is forced into "early retirement." Just as I was editing this chapter, I got an email from JUST Capital's Martin Whittaker that highlighted a few instances of communications hypocrisy: Adam Neumann of WeWork claimed his company would "elevate the world's consciousness" before he was forced out after chicanery was exposed in their botched IPO; and Volkswagen chief executive officer Herbert Diess, chairman Hans Dieter Pötsch, and former CEO Martin Winterkorn were charged with stock market manipulation despite emphasizing during Climate Week that VW is accountable to "future generations to find the right answers."[1]

I guess the SEC didn't agree with the answers VW found.

Social media backlash against wayward marketing comes swiftly for the unscrupulous and even the unaware. Remember when Pepsi put out a commercial in which Kendall Jenner magically resolved a conflict between protesters and cops by handing a Pepsi to one of the police officers? I mean, Pepsi's tasty, but that might be a stretch for its capabilities. And what about Unilever's Dove brand ad, in which a black woman takes off her shirt to reveal a white woman? Ouch. We can only imagine what they were attempting to say about their soap's capabilities. (If you figure it out, please let me know.) And it's a shame, because Dove, with its "Real Beauty" campaign, has done some other things that are truly amazing, like remind us that real beauty is a state of mind rather than a reflection in a mirror.

In general, many marketing campaigns overstep. Pepsi can't stop riots any more than soap can turn people different colors. And on some level we sort of accept it as the entertaining hyperbole it is. I mean, who's giving up Pepsi because it's overreaching with its brand promise? Behemoths like Pepsi and Dove have size and momentum on their side, which provide some form of insulation against exaggerations and missteps. But open your Twitter app for a hot second and you'll see why even big-company insulation isn't always enough protection against social media: our online communities not only expose even the slightest untruths but they also actively hunt for deception to use in the latest round of clickbait blogs and viral memes. New brands without mega-budgets to recover from such exposure can sink their entire operations by attempting to mislead an already skeptical population. We all know this, yet I've repeatedly encountered the belief that organizations must lie to their own customers to keep them happy and keep them buying. What I'd like to suggest is that those organizations shoot themselves in the foot by not realizing that today the opposite is true: *being honest with your customers will positively blow up your pipeline in a way that no other strategy can*. Want some proof? How about nearly thirty thousand boxes of cookies to please the palate of your sales projections?

HOW BEING HONEST ABOUT YOUR ENDGAME CAN BLOW UP YOUR SALES (IN A GOOD WAY)

"I have a letter that simply must be shared with you right away," said Mike Rowe, famed television host of *Dirty Jobs*, on a video blog post he recorded on January 26, 2017. "If there's a Girl Scout in your life," Mike continued, "you've already been hit up for cookies—but not like this."[2] Those were the words that kicked off a media firestorm for an unsuspecting eleven-year-old girl named Charlotte McCourt—a storm that would involve Mike Rowe, a venture capitalist, and *CBS Sunday Morning*.

Of course, this being a book about honesty, all sides of the truth must be told—including the honest motivations of this particular Scout and the overall context of her story. So, before we examine this in full detail, know up front that one of Charlotte's guiding factors was that mother of all business pursuits: *sales*. Don't for a second think that this is anything but a capitalistic technique that created shocking sales success.

Now, some context: the winter of 2016–2017 was one of the most divisive in the history of the United States. With the presidential election decided and the inauguration just having come to a close, honesty was perhaps far from the minds of many. In fact, subverting the truth in favor of "fake news" seemed to rule the day, or at least to have become part of the fabric of a nation that was tearing apart at the proverbial seams. Meanwhile, a little girl from New Jersey was perhaps unaware—or perhaps very aware—of the world in which she was growing up.

But all the same, she was intent on her own, very important, goal: sell at least three hundred boxes of Girl Scout cookies. And although she wanted to raise money for the Girl Scouts, and of course she wanted her cookie customers to buy and enjoy the baked goods, she most of all wanted her customers to buy and ship those cookies to troops overseas to give members of the armed forces a little respite from their duties. As Charlotte's father, Sean McCourt, explained to me, "When you're overseas and you get this sleeve of cookies, it's an incredible piece of home." So Charlotte had a checkbox on her Girl Scouts order form that could be marked for this purpose.

But the question remained: How would Charlotte manage to sell a few hundred boxes of cookies and get some shipped to a far-flung locale halfway around the world? Well, Charlotte had the same idea that many of us have when it comes to starting and growing a business: follow the money! Luckily, McCourt told his daughter that he had a wealthy friend who might be interested in buying lots of Girl Scout cookies. So, with that hot lead in hand, Charlotte wrote a letter to her father's wealthy friend, a venture capitalist by the name of Jason Mendelson.

Here is the email Jason received on January 23, 2017, exactly in its original text (typos and all):[3]

Dear Mr. Mendelson,

I am Sean Patrick McCourt's daughter. The only time I ever met you was in Disney World. I have been informed that you may want to purchase a few Girl Scout Cookie boxes for the troops, fighting overseas. Your donation is greatly appreciated by the men and women sacrificing their time and lives for our country. Do feel free to purchase other boxes for yourself, friends, family, coworkers, and other people in your life.

I would like to give you some information on my selling and my troop. I belong to troop 22918. We are a minuscule, but mighty troop of five people. I always sell the most boxes of anyone in my troop. My goal is 300 boxes because that is the number of delectable Girl Scout Cookie boxes I sold last year. I hope you purchase a few boxes from my website. The link is below.

Lastly, I would like to tell you about the cookies, for some of the descriptions use false advertising (note: I am rating all the boxes on a scale from 1 to 10. Ten being best, 1 being worst). Savannah Smiles are like sweet lemon wedges with just the right balance of sweet and sour. This cookie gets a 7 for it's Devine taste. Next is the trefoil. It is a plain butter cookie with pairs well with any hot drink. I would give it a 6 because alone, it is sort of bland. The Do Si Do is peanut butter sandwich. I give it a 5 for unoriginal bland flavor. The Next cookie is the Samoa. I give it a 9 for its AMAZING flavor!

The next cookie is a Tagalog. If you don't like peanut butter, than don't buy it! I give it an 8 for the chocolate/ peanut combo. Next is the thin mint. I give it a 9 for the delectable chocolate/ mint combination. Then come the s'more cookie. If you have a wild sense of adventure, try this. No one has tried it, so I cannot rate it. Last and yes, least is toffeetastic. It is a bleak, flavorless gluten-free wasteland. It is as flavorless as dirt. I give it a 1.

Notice how none of the cookie boxes are a 10? There is a reason for it. The real 10 is donating a box. It helps strike a spark in the treacherous live of those making America safe. Please honor them by donating a box.

Let's recap-

I love being honest with my clients
The Girl Scout Organization can sometimes use false advertisement
These are all only my opinion

Savannah Smile:7
Trefoil:6

Do Si Do:5
Samoa:9
Tagalog:8
Thin Mint:9
S'more:??
Toffeetastic:1
Donating a box overseas:10
Please buy soon.

Before we can dive deeply into the psychology of truth, let's get one thing clear: Charlotte didn't and still doesn't think any of this is funny. But her potential "client," Jason Mendelson, sure found it amusing—as well as inspiring.

THE PSYCHOLOGY OF HONEST SALESMANSHIP

As a venture capitalist and cofounder at the Foundry Group, Jason Mendelson has developed an effective way to find new business success stories before they go viral. Before that, he worked as a senior consultant at Accenture, as a corporate and securities lawyer at a worldwide law firm, and he authored a few books on business and venture capital. He gets hit up every day by cold calls and emails asking for his time and money. As Mendelson tells it, that's why Charlotte's outreach was so showstopping.

"My first reaction was that, as a venture capitalist, my entire life is built on (people) asking me for money or for time," Mendelson told me. "In the most charitable situation they're giving me the best look of themselves, and in the worst case they're out-and-out lying to me. As a VC, cutting through the BS is the most important part of my job description. And here was Charlotte, laying it completely out. It was one of those emails where you could read the tone. There was a sincere honesty and she didn't even get the humor in it. Her parents had to teach her what was so funny and so amazing about this. She only knew one way: 'Be honest with my clients.'"

In truth, we'll never know exactly what her cookie-sales strategy was in terms of consumer behavior, buying psychology, or customer relationship management. But none of that matters. What matters is what we can learn from her approach—the approach that eventually led to her selling a record-breaking 26,806 boxes of Girl Scout cookies.[4] That bears repeating: in less than two months, Charlotte sold almost thirty thousand boxes of cookies. Even the "gluten-free wasteland" variety.

But those thousands of boxes started with a single customer relationship between Charlotte and Jason Mendelson. It was not only honesty that struck the venture capitalist but also the idea of one-to-one selling. He was floored by the fact that she was "creating a mutually beneficial relationship immediately, instead of saying, 'I want something from you.' She was treating me as a client before I even bought anything yet," he marveled. "It's a master class in sales. If all the companies I deal with were that good, we'd have much more successful companies," he quipped.

> In less than two months, Charlotte sold almost thirty thousand boxes of cookies. Even the "gluten-free wasteland" variety.

Unfortunately, we seem to exist in a time when getting our to-do list done outweighs thoughtfulness, which is perhaps how Pepsi and Dove went astray. "We get so overloaded with what we have to get done . . . with email, phone . . . texting and everything," Mendelson noted, "[that] we've become a nation of executors and not necessarily *thinkers*." But thoughtfulness, especially in today's hyper–politically correct environment, is vital to business survival. Even regardless of society's norms, people want to receive empathy, caring, and some level of thoughtful, personalized attention from those who communicate with them. Instead, we routinely get spammed by bots and cold-called by people halfway around the world with a fake phone number. Charlotte took the opposite tack. "There are multiple parts in that letter where she empathizes with me by providing an honest review," Mendelson pointed out, "by treating me as a client, by trying to do something *for* me."

As a venture capitalist, Mendelson is awash in ineffective entrepreneurs who reach out to him and misspell his name, give him form letters, spam his email, and otherwise act in thoughtless, discourteous, and impersonal ways. On the flip side, one smart entrepreneur once sent Mendelson a set of new drumsticks as a door opener when the entrepreneur saw that Mendelson had broken his at a local gig the night before. Like that drumstick-giving founder, Charlotte approached Mendelson in a one-to-one way, and that's part of what made her pitch so effective despite today's pressure to make everything scalable. He noted, "Entrepreneurs are extremely thoughtful with the strategy of business, and thoughtless with the strategy of fundraising, getting to the *people* behind the funds."

Remarkably, Mendelson admitted that although he and Sean were lifelong friends, he and Charlotte had met only once. But here was Charlotte, happy to go directly to the source and establish a direct relationship with a man she only knew as "Dad's rich friend." Mendelson donated fifty boxes. He later went back to donate more, though, as he saw what happened when another one of McCourt's contacts, Mike Rowe, saw Charlotte's letter.

"Truth in Advertising" is the title of the video blog post in which Rowe held up Charlotte's letter to Mendelson and read it aloud to his audience, producing ten million views and kicking off a media firestorm that resulted in several news articles and television appearances. Apparently, truth is so rare in business that all Charlotte had to do was provide a bit of it in her cookie review, and she was consequently able to successfully crash her Girl Scout cookie website with all the traffic she received. If you're a salesperson looking to grow your revenues, you've got to at least pause and ask why this worked, and if it could work for you, too. It certainly helps to understand why Charlotte felt compelled to bash her own products in order to sell more of them in the first place. When I asked her, I was surprised to learn that her reasoning was as old as commerce itself.

First, Charlotte was an eleven-year-old disillusioned by big business. When I asked her why she thought honesty was the best policy in selling cookies, she told me that she hates when she buys products that are advertised to work well, only to have them unexpectedly break or fail to live up to their promises. It happened frequently, she said, opining that even the Girl Scouts organization didn't explain their products to Charlotte's own satisfaction and standard for honesty. So she reasoned that she might as well be the one to correctly advertise her cookies.

Second, Charlotte always had her end goal in mind: sell as many cookies as possible so she could get some to the troops. And, she reasoned, wouldn't the troops want the best cookies, instead of the mediocre or even "flavorless" ones? Indeed, Charlotte wanted her *end customers*—those risking their lives for their country—to have the best product she could possibly deliver.

As logical as her arguments seem, I'm admittedly frightened to think about what her analysis means for our society. How have we gotten to a place where business is so dishonest that it prompts an eleven-year-old girl to adopt such a bold strategy to sell some cookies? As a champion of strategic honesty myself, I had to ask Charlotte a burning question: *Why do you think more businesses are* not *honest with their customers?*

"Because they think it'll sell them more," she said simply. "They think 'if we get [the product] out sooner before other companies can . . . it will be better for consumers.' What they should be doing is focusing more on the product than the sales, instead of focusing on the sales and leaving consumers 'stuck' with the products." Her startling mastery of business language aside, Charlotte's business advice seems simple enough: be honest and focus on creating exceptional products and services, and they'll essentially sell themselves.

> Charlotte's business advice seems simple enough: be honest and focus on creating exceptional products and services, and they'll essentially sell themselves.

Reflecting on Charlotte's brave sales technique, Mendelson said, "I hope that something sustainable comes out of this"—that people everywhere take note of some basics of interpersonal communication that we seem to have forgotten. When I asked him to sum up his experience, he said simply, "Give before you get. She gave me information, [and even] humor, even though she didn't even know it. Giving before you get is a really powerful way to live. If more people were like that, the world would be a better place."

HOW TO USE HONESTY TO WIN MORE SALES

As someone involved in sales, you may or may not have control over the product you're selling, but you can certainly control the benefits you're touting. The thing is, even without Charlotte's story, we know that honesty works. Think about the last time you were being sold something and the representative said something like, "You know, I'd go with this cheaper option over the more expensive one. It's half the price, you get almost the same benefits, and if you add the warranty for another couple of dollars, it'll be the best of both worlds." Chances are you appreciated their candor and thoughtfulness as you said to yourself, *Well, at least they're honest!*

> Being honest—about what you're selling, how you're selling it, and what buyers want out of the buying experience—will lay the foundation for an exceptional outcome every single time.

We appreciate honesty; we recognize it and praise its use. In fact, honesty is the very first sales tool you should reach for as you attempt to engender trust between you and your customers. So when applying this principle, ask yourself, *How can I use honesty to create a trustful relationship, faster?* Whether you're selling a home, a car, public relations services, a welding machine, or insurance, the premise is the same in the mind of your buyer, who's only searching for the best option (for them, not for you). Being honest—about what you're selling, how you're selling it, and what buyers want out of the buying experience—will lay the foundation for an exceptional outcome every single time.

When we do anything outside of being honest, we sacrifice trust. Maybe it won't hurt your sales today, but it will tomorrow. Look at what the automotive industry did to itself by using tricks instead of truth for decades. Charlotte could have told Jason Mendelson that every box of cookies was delicious and that trying them all was the only sound choice to make. She would have sold a few boxes of cookies, but she would have given up an opportunity to change the selling game, deepen a key relationship, earn the adoration of the media, and sell cargo planes full of treats. Charlotte learned what we must all deeply understand: honesty opens the door to innovative outcomes.

> Charlotte learned what we all must deeply understand: honesty opens the door to innovative outcomes.

IT ALL COMES BACK TO THE HOURGLASS OF HONESTY

Throughout this book, we'll occasionally come back to the framework I discussed in chapter four, The Hourglass of Honesty, to see how it applies universally. My hope is that if you take only one key strategy from our time together, it will be that applying the three levels of honesty (community, others, self) will get you most of the way toward your goal—in sales and more.

Charlotte and the Level of Community

Because of her brilliance—or perhaps completely by accident—Charlotte struck an honest chord with the *community* at large. A few days after the 2017 inauguration, our society was in disarray, struggling to cope with a new reality filled with both real facts and alternative ones. As Charlotte's father tells it, "Charlotte's letter was objectively honest, and it didn't matter what side of the political divide you were on. I think that's why people embraced it so immediately and so powerfully." Fake news was gripping society, and into that storm of events walked an eleven-year-old girl with both an undeniable this-is-how-I-see-it attitude and impeccable timing, because the community was in exactly the right frame of mind for Charlotte's honest message.

Charlotte and the Level of Others

Amazingly—or perhaps ironically—Charlotte also honestly addressed the *others* around her. In this case, her "other" was her prospective client, Jason Mendelson. She was honest and transparent *about* why she was pursuing him (his financial ability to buy cookies, of course), and she was honest *with* him about what he should and shouldn't buy.

Charlotte and the Level of Self

Finally, Charlotte was honest with herself, choosing to stay true to her own personal beliefs about the quality of her products, regardless of what anyone else might think or how many boxes of cookies she might actively deny her clients by persuading them against certain options in her product suite.

The Bottom Half of the Hourglass

From the Hourglass of Honesty framework, we know that's not where the story ends. Once Charlotte aligned the first three levels of honesty, that's when the fun really started. The honest letter she wrote influenced *others* around her—including Jason Mendelson, her parents, Mike Rowe, millions of fans, and a record-breaking number of buyers. And when that happened, she influenced the *community* around her. She bent the world toward her mission of helping people, consequently sold a Herculean number of cookies, and helped those troops overseas get a little taste of home.

Wild success notwithstanding, the honest journey of a truth-telling preteen isn't as smooth as one might hope. When her customers saw her honest sales letter, people laughed a lot, smiled, and bought cookies, and heartfelt thank-you letters poured in from active military members, veterans, and military families. But she also received a lesson about the cynical nature of human beings, with some individuals accusing her of plagiarizing a letter that must have been written by her parents. The disapproval didn't just come from strangers. Charlotte sensed a hint of jealousy and cool indifference from her peer group of Girl Scouts, despite Charlotte's success benefitting the group as a whole. As I probed into how she felt about her fellow Scouts' lack of excitement, she looked down sheepishly. A few moments later, perhaps not entirely honestly, she reassured me, "I don't care."

Caveat emptor: honesty does work. But leadership, just like innovation, can trace a lonely path. It reminds me of some of our corporate clients over the years. Many knew something had to be done, and some knew what to do, but few were willing to put their necks out and *do*, because, to be blunt, finding clarity among the bullshit means helping everyone else recognize they're stuck in a pile of shit. And people don't like that. But I'm sure that's not you; you're a doer. Brave enough to tell your prospects how it is and earn their respect for it. And if that's true, remember Charlotte McCourt's ability to break sales records while helping troops overseas—a girl who figured out how to have her cookie and eat it, too.

———— QUESTIONS FOR HONEST REFLECTION ————

1. What's going on in the world or in your industry right now that can help point you toward a more effective sales approach?
2. What do you think made Charlotte's approach so successful, apart from her simple honesty?
3. How might you immediately apply her approach to something that you're selling?

CHAPTER 6

Marketing: The Undeniable Power of Courageous Candor

And How It Can Make Your Pizza Taste Better

I magine the following . . .

You've worked all your life to become CEO, and you've spent years leading a business with a recognizable brand name and global footprint. Now that you're ready to retire, you're looking forward to riding out the last few months without rocking the boat too much, except perhaps the literal one you're thinking of buying to enjoy your much-deserved sailing off into the sunset.

Which is why you're ready. You're ready to stand up in front of your board of directors at your final meeting and announce one unwavering truth: *our product sucks.* What do you think would happen next?

WE'RE BETTER THAN THIS

Just as the financial crisis hit, Dave Brandon, the departing CEO of Domino's Pizza, announced to the company that their product needed an entire overhaul. And to add insult to injury, he approved a massive marketing campaign that would put his replacement, J. Patrick Doyle, directly in the crosshairs of potential catastrophe. When the board of directors signed off on the otherwise mundane transition of its CEO, I have to believe they never anticipated the departing CEO's "unusual" recommendation for securing the future of the company.

The strategy Brandon approved was simple: go on national television and tell America that Domino's pizza—you know, the flagship product for which it is named—is terrible.

You might think this would be a firing offense. "Heads are going to roll," you imagine people murmuring at the water cooler. Yet Brandon wasn't fired ahead of schedule. And Doyle, the incoming CEO, didn't back away and decide to play it safe. Instead, he embraced the challenge and, just a year after his appointment, went on national television as scheduled to take a sledgehammer to his company's brand image.

"This," Doyle announced in his television commercial, pointing at a pizza that looked like it had been riding in the back row of a Six Flags roller coaster, "is *not* acceptable. Bryce in Minnesota, you shouldn't have to get this from Domino's. We're better than this."[1] And so began what would become one of the greatest marketing stories of the last decade.

Although Doyle played the front man as CEO, the Domino's Pizza Turnaround—as it's affectionately called—was masterminded by then Chief Marketing Officer Russell Weiner, who at the time of this writing has unsurprisingly been promoted to president of Domino's USA. As a torchbearer for organizational honesty, I desperately wanted to understand how in the world anyone was able to convince a multibillion-dollar company to go on national television to slam their own product.

"I remember when I first came here," Weiner enthusiastically shared with me. "It was September 2008. Our stock was maybe $2.80 . . . the business was not doing well, our franchisees weren't making money, we were losing market share, and things were not good." As usual, out of desperate times comes some creative thinking, along with some obvious truths that could no longer be ignored.

Weiner knew that only objective truth could get Domino's moving in the right direction again; otherwise, he would risk accelerating the organization toward the status quo of being an also-ran pizza company with no hopes of innovating its way out of a tough spot. In times like these, many leaders are inclined to get their top people together and brainstorm a variety of creative solutions. But Weiner recognized that simply brainstorming among executives would only continue to turn up the same opinions, biases, and beliefs that had landed Domino's in this position to begin with. Instead, he needed to get at the *facts* so the company could form a new growth strategy based on what it objectively needed to do to dominate as a world-class pizza restaurant franchise. That's why, in the months following his arrival, Weiner and his team sought to uncover their organization's *true* strengths and weaknesses, as defined by the only opinions that mattered: those of Domino's customers. As Weiner notes, "We got curious about ourselves, and we promised to listen to the strengths and opportunities" that the customers would (loudly and openly) share.

"Very quickly we found out we had a product problem . . . we were a pizza company, and customers were complaining that the pizza should taste better. We also had a brand problem—and to see how big of a brand problem we had, we swapped products in competitors' boxes." When Weiner's team did taste tests of Domino's pizza presented in competitors' boxes, they found that people actually liked Domino's pizza better in a non-Domino's box than in a Domino's box, proving to Weiner that the Domino's brand was having a negative effect on the customers' opinions and experiences.

Ouch.

Given the substantial evidence that Domino's had both a product problem and a brand problem, the question before the company was, how would Domino's begin to change the tide? To make matters worse, Weiner knew that the world was changing in the midst of the financial crisis . . . that trust was eroding quickly, and that anything Domino's might say to its constituents could fall on deaf ears.

After a year, Domino's had made its pizza taste significantly better in response to all the feedback, as further tests showed. But Weiner was still unsure how he could convey with any measure of trust the message that Domino's pizza had, in fact, improved. When Weiner sat down to write a brief to the creative agency, he remembers Googling the phrase "new and improved." At the time, Google returned 46 million results—far too many to overcome with any sort of marketing campaign that touted a "new and improved" pizza. (If you've ever wondered about branding your own product as "new and improved," please don't. Today, you get more than three quarters of a billion results.) The question—for you now and for Russell Weiner in 2009—was how to break through that clutter.

It turns out that the timing of the financial crisis couldn't have been better—if not for the banks, then for a bunch of pizza joints. "At that point, back in 2009, banks were going under and car company CEOs were flying out to DC and asking for bailouts. People were losing their homes, and there was tension in society," Weiner recalls. People across America were feeling like some of the strongest pillars of society had been built on quicksand—that there was no one to trust, because no one was telling the truth. In that moment—the moment in which the folks at Domino's Pizza got brutally honest about what their customers were going through as a society—the light bulb turned on, and Weiner realized the opportunity in front of him.

"What we realized at the time was the tension within our own brand. We're a pizza company, and we've been hiding the truth that our pizza doesn't taste very good. We had the opportunity to break the societal tension while breaking our brand tension. While we were only a small little pizza company, not the bank or a politician or the government, we thought that if we ourselves act the way that society wants everyone to act, maybe we could catch the tailwinds of that bigger, societal tension working in our favor." In other words, Weiner and his team got brutally honest about the *community*, and correctly identified the societal wave upon them.

Spotting the trend, however, was only the first of many obstacles Domino's would face writing its own turnaround story. Once it was willing to be honest in general, it had to figure out what it would be honest about. It had to discover what its purpose would be, and to strategize how it would create lasting change in an organization that could properly participate in the zeitgeist of the time.

For those of you who remember the Domino's of olden days, you might remember the "You Got 30" campaign, in which Domino's heralded its thirty-minutes-or-less guarantee. If your pizza didn't arrive in thirty minutes from the time you ordered, you got it for free. Though iconic and effective at the time, by 2008 the campaign had been running since the late 1980s, and Weiner recognized that its relevance was waning. "When I was in college," Weiner remembered, "getting a pizza delivered to your door was pretty special." But things changed. Today, of course, you can get virtually any food delivered to your office via Grubhub, movies delivered to your phone via Netflix, and toilet paper delivered to your home via Amazon.

Recognizing this change, executives in 2009 might have been tempted to ask, What's the next form of delivery? However, Weiner and his team recognized that the world had forever changed and that delivery could no longer be the company's unique selling proposition. That's why Domino's did a critical exercise in its early days to dive into who it was at its best, and who it needed to be going forward. When Weiner and his team asked those questions, they realized, "We *delivered*, yes, but we didn't *just* deliver. Delivery was a tactic . . . but what we did emotionally for customers is that we *over*delivered." It was "the *emotion* of *over*delivery that really made us special, and that had nothing to do with physical delivery per se," Weiner said. In other words, Domino's recognized that it is, at its core, a company in the business of overdelivery.

Not delivery.

Not even pizza.

Armed with new insights and data, Weiner and his team solved the simple problem of how to overdeliver again, and that's when they realized *Domino's Pizza can overdeliver by being honest and transparent when nobody else is.* So they launched a new campaign that showcased how the company overdelivers in surprising ways.

"When we launched the campaign, we came up with a tag line on all our ads: 'Oh yes we did,'" Weiner remembered. "Our feeling was, when people see what we say and also what we *do*, it'll change their opinion of us so much that they'll say, 'Wow, did Domino's really just do that?' And our answer is, 'Oh yes we did.'"

Lest we bury the lede too far, Domino's Pizza has been the fastest-growing restaurant in America for the ten years following its declaration of honesty. Since the campaign launched in 2010, Domino's has focused on creating even more "Oh yes we did" moments—like developing custom vehicles to deliver hotter pizza, taking care of potholes to keep its products from bouncing around on its way to your doorstep, and providing insurance against saucy accidents that might prevent your dinner from reaching your plate. As Weiner notes, "The bigger the 'Oh yes we did' idea ends up being, the greater return we see either directly on sales or on the brand halo."

On January 4, 2010, just after beginning to publicize its turnaround efforts, Domino's Pizza stock closed at $8.68 per share. By June 22, 2018, the stock had exploded to close at $292.39 per share, creating a 3,268 percent return for shareholders. Compared to the S&P 500, which grew roughly 143 percent over the same time period, Domino's stock return outpaced the index's by nearly twenty-three times.[2] And, as a reminder just in case you've forgotten, the pizza brand created a 3,200 percent return by telling America that its product was *terrible*.

DOMINO'S AND THE INVERSE TRIANGLE

As odd as Domino's strategy might seem, it's as effective as it is logical, and it's the very same strategy that our agency has used for years. The framework behind this strategy is what we call the *Inverse Triangle*, which is a simple way to understand the flow of information in a transparent world. See, it used to be that executives had to have all the answers. They had the best information available, the best high-level overview of the organization, and often the most breadth and depth of available insights. Because of their ability to *see* the organization— its strengths, weaknesses, opportunities, and threats—executives were best positioned to push strategy down from the top, through managers, and on to frontline employees. Then, those employees would push from-the-top decisions and initiatives on to customers, and sales and marketing would push those initiatives on to prospective customers.

But, as we know, the world has changed. Executives no longer have the best sight and—by extension—*foresight* compared to what's now available. In fact, I would argue that in some cases, executives have some of the *lowest* organizational insights of all. Why? Two critical reasons: first, executives are the furthest removed from the customer. And, as we saw with Domino's Pizza, the customers have most of the answers that the organization needs in order to innovate, market, and grow. To test this assertion, ask, Who has the least in common with a twentysomething recent grad who orders Domino's Pizza three times per week? Answer: the sixty-something executive making millions per year, living in a wealthy suburb in a ten-thousand-square-foot home. Second, executives have more inherent biases than arguably any other constituent in an organization, because their consistent successes don't teach them as much as failures would. Success breeds a false sense of security that lulls high performers into thinking that their prior recipe for success will continue to work ad infinitum, which is exactly how organizations get stuck in the status quo.

> Success breeds a false sense of security that lulls high performers into thinking that their prior recipe for success will continue to work ad infinitum, which is exactly how organizations get stuck in the status quo.

Instead, the Inverse Triangle framework gives us an information flow based on the shifting balance of power and the new way that transparency has allowed for faster, clearer information to move from one place to another.

As Weiner and his team learned, the best way to source ideas in this day and age isn't with an executive brainstorm but with a bottom-up approach to gathering information and insights: first from customers

The Inverse Triangle

and prospective customers, then from frontline employees, then from middle managers, and, ultimately and lastly, from the top executives.

This approach has helped my agency gather the right ideas from the (arguably only) people who matter: the people who take out their wallets and pay money in exchange for a product or service. By conducting focus groups, interviews, and surveys of customers and frontline employees, my team and I have been able to pass valuable insights back to our executive clients. And, perhaps unsurprisingly, we almost invariably see that the executives' own insights and assumptions at some point diverge from what the customers want and how the customers feel. In many cases, we use what we find to create marketing campaigns that resonate perfectly with the end consumer. Sometimes, however, we run into executives who simply can't let go of the status quo and make room for important, objective realities. For example, a client once brought us in to revamp the organization's communications strategy, since members had been consistently complaining that the communications weren't clear or valuable in their current form and delivery method. I remember conducting one focus group with employees. Inside of ninety minutes, they had developed a cohesive solution to improve productivity, morale, and, most importantly, the ability to deliver important content to members. When I presented these findings to leadership, they nodded knowingly and assured me they couldn't possibly spend the resources to refresh that particular system—even though that opportunity is what they hired us to find, and even though they would have eliminated hours of wasted employee time each week, and even though communicating important information to members is the organization's entire purpose!

Weiner understood this phenomenon, which is why he spent his entire first year as the Chief Check Your Opinions at the Door Officer (my creative spin, not his actual title). "You need to let yourself know that your opinion means nothing," Weiner asserted, "just like your CEO's opinion means nothing. The only thing that matters is the opinions of your customers."

To make sure Weiner would cut through the typical boardroom bullshit of "I'm the boss so I know best," Weiner and his team did a lot of work interviewing their own executives to understand their biases. He wanted to be able to go back to them and say, "You may think you're right, but we tested your hypothesis and we can say, with a 95 percent confidence level, it won't work, according to our own customers. We can do it, but our customers are telling us it won't work."

That's powerful stuff, and it helped Weiner back his insights with the cold hard facts—data that could statistically show both the truth about the company's product and the best path for moving forward. "To deny this," Weiner warned, "was to say that you're smarter than the data. In that case, there's no winning—if you can't succeed when the facts are on your side, consider it good that you found that out." In other words, consider it a good thing if you discover you might be working with someone diametrically opposed to the truth; you might not want to stay long.

WHEN MARKETING INTERSECTS WITH INNOVATION

Although this book is divided into sections so you can see how to use honesty in sales, marketing, innovation, and so on, my hope is that you recognize how intertwined these functions truly are. If you can use honesty in your organization at all, you won't help but use it everywhere—and by the way, that's how you'll earn the most explosive, industry-dominating results.

> Domino's didn't achieve a 3,268 percent ROI with only a handful of cars or a brutally honest ad. The company transformed. Starting from the simple feedback it got from customers, Domino's has now become a digital innovation company, identifying every single opportunity that exists for being better at overdelivery.

To that end, Domino's has simply continued on creating "Oh yes we did" moments. While its competitors are focusing on promotions-of-the-month, Domino's is building custom delivery vehicles.[3] Weiner and his team recognized that if delivery (i.e., *over*delivery) is so important to Domino's, then every piece of their delivery process should be given exceptional care and attention. To date, Domino's only has about a hundred vehicles, so your odds of seeing one are, admittedly, slim. "But it doesn't matter if you ever see it in person," Weiner insisted. "All that matters is that we did it, we tried. Even if we failed, that's more newsworthy than if we put something else in our crust. When we think of innovation, we don't think of new products [anymore], we think about an 'Oh yes we did' moment."

Of course, you and I both know that Domino's didn't achieve a 3,268 percent ROI with only a handful of cars or a brutally honest ad. The company transformed. Starting from the simple feedback it got from customers, Domino's has now become a digital innovation company, identifying every single opportunity that exists for being better at overdelivery. For example, you might have used the Domino's Pizza Tracker, which lets you know where your pizza is on its way from the local store to your front door. This is good for you, but it's *very* good for Domino's: the Pizza Tracker has helped Domino's track, in real time, how well its teams are performing, where bottlenecks might exist, and where opportunities are lurking for even more efficient operations.

Genius.

Yet it all started with a simple commitment to honesty. It started with the company doubling down on its promise to make its product better. And it put its money where its mouth is—visiting the homes of its customers to do before-and-after taste tests, *and* recording them on camera, *and* transparently publishing those videos. Domino's exposed its focus groups, shared real-life customer stories, and thrust Doyle out into the spotlight as the scapegoat—or hero that he would eventually become. Domino's did all that because it needed its customers to believe Domino's and believe *in* Domino's.

DOMINO'S AND THE HOURGLASS OF HONESTY

In the Domino's story, you've probably already spotted the Hourglass of Honesty. First, Domino's got honest about what was going on in the industry and in society at large (delivery of food was becoming the norm, and the financial crisis was ripping apart consumer trust). Second, Domino's got brutally honest with others—its customers—and let their honest feedback objectively guide the company to the right solutions. Domino's improved the taste of its pizza, improved the customer experience with new technologies, and elevated its entire brand image by being completely transparent about prior shortcomings. Not to mention, Domino's also got honest with its executive team's biases to make sure that the execs would be open enough to see the insights bubbling up to them from their customers. Finally, Domino's got honest with itself—it could no longer rest on the laurels of its past performance but instead needed to transform into a technological pizza powerhouse that didn't just deliver but overdelivered. With an honest mind-set and a truthful assessment, Brandon, Doyle, Weiner, and the entire Domino's

Pizza team only needed bravery and commitment, and the rest, as they say, is history.

"The biggest thing I learned," Weiner shared, "wasn't a marketing lesson at all . . . it was a leadership lesson. When I got here, I was the CMO and reported to the president of Domino's USA, who reported to the CEO. When I pitched the idea of the turnaround, the CEO at the time, Dave Brandon, already knew he was going to retire in a few months. So he had nothing to gain with this campaign and everything to lose. He could've just said, 'We're new and improved,' and played it safe, and we would've been up a few percent [in sales] and nothing would have happened. But he approved it—and even still, when people look at the campaign, his replacement [Doyle] and I got a lot of the credit. But to me, having the guts to approve this and the ability to trust your people and trust the data [against] your opinion, that's the leadership lesson."

> How could you fail by honestly telling your customers that your product sucks and that you're going to do better, then actually following through and improving? Isn't that common sense?

Then, of course, there's the marketing lesson, and it's the same one Charlotte McCourt learned: Be honest and transparent, and people will thank you for it by buying your products and services.

Ultimately, Weiner learned that the most important thing a leader can do is trust his or her people—trust the insights that arise from using a tool like the Inverse Triangle. "You need to be able to say, 'Bring me these facts, and we're going to act on them,'" Weiner said in summary of his experience with Brandon and then Doyle, as each leader opted for brutal honesty instead of what most perceived to be the "safer" option. "When you're a leader," Weiner continued, "you can't be an expert in all areas, but what you can do is empower your people to empower *themselves* by dealing with facts."

If your takeaway so far has been that you only need to apologize to your customers and promise to do better next time, you'd only be one-tenth of the way there. Plenty of CEOs have apologized over the last century; few have committed to redeveloping the very identity of the businesses, and even fewer have committed to doing so with the highest levels of honesty, transparency, and accountability. Unfortunately, taking bold and honest action requires risk, and it could hurt. But, in hindsight, how could you fail by honestly telling your customers that your product sucks and that you're going to do better, then actually following through and improving?

Isn't that common sense?

"What we did at the time was like it says in *The Art of War*," Weiner concluded, comparing Domino's declaration of honesty to what Sun Tzu says of taking an island. "You win by blowing up the bridge, so your troops will fight to the death."

Domino's Pizza's leaders, franchisees, employees, and shareholders agree: honesty is a strategy worth fighting for.

—— QUESTIONS FOR HONEST REFLECTION ——

1. Domino's Pizza learned that it's in the business of "overdelivery." So what business are *you* really in?

2. How can you use the Inverse Triangle framework to improve the communication flow within your organization?

3. Who in your organization might be holding on to beliefs that are inconsistent with the beliefs of your customers? How can you help everyone in your organization get on the same page with those customer insights?

CHAPTER 7

Finance: Investing Like Buffett in Long-Term Honesty

And Training for a Marathon, Even If You Sprint

Our world has rules about finance and accounting. We're not allowed to cook the books, like Enron, or misreport earnings, like . . . well, countless companies. It should be eminently obvious that honesty and finance should be tied tightly together in an unbreakable bond.

Of course, given the financial crisis of 2008, we all know that's not the way it is. Since that time, it's been difficult to assign blame to any one party. Was it the money-hungry banks that wanted to create more loans? The regulators who didn't do enough to protect consumers? The ratings agencies that said it was OK to bury subprime loans into otherwise highly rated debt instruments? Homebuyers with pie-in-the-sky dreams but cupcake-sized credit? I have another idea: the honest culprit of the 2008 financial crisis was simply our short-term thinking about business finance and investing.

IF YOU WANT LONG-TERM SUCCESS, BE HONEST ABOUT WHAT IT TAKES

Sadly, a powerful group of Wall Street influencers may be working to prevent honest change: analysts and professional investors who exclusively focus on quarterly results and consistently downplay companies that can't show that their quarterly investments will produce quarterly profits. For a publicly traded company, even those ranked by the JUST 100, taking care of all stakeholders—employees, customers, communities, and so on, in addition to shareholders—can take too long. Or worse, caring for all stakeholders can be seen as an investment that exists on an incalculable time horizon in the eyes of short-term investors. Who's left to look up at the long-term consequences of a systemic issue when everyone is busy looking down at their next few profitable steps?

In a world where short-term profits are everything and looking for long-term sustainability will get you angry questions at your investor meeting, it's not difficult to see how a financial crisis would inevitably arise. So how do we get honest about what it takes to create sustainable long-term business success instead of focusing on the short term to our own collective peril?

There is one successful businessman and shareholder of myriad companies who just so happens to be obsessed with long-term financial thinking. We can look to him for guidance. You may have heard of him; his name is Warren Buffett.

Buffett likes quarterly reports just fine as an investor interested in the performance

> In a world where short-term profits are everything and looking for long-term sustainability will get you angry questions at your investor meeting, it's not difficult to see how a financial crisis would inevitably arise. So how do we get honest about what it takes to create sustainable long-term business success instead of focusing on the short term to our own collective peril?

of his stock holdings, but he has consistently stated that the ritual of providing quarterly guidance is "a very bad practice" and a "game" that puts CEOs in the impossible position of estimating business performance in a ridiculously short window. Jamie Dimon, CEO of JPMorgan Chase & Co., shares Buffett's concerns, saying that quarterly forecasts can "often put a company in a position where management from the CEO down feels obligated to deliver earnings and therefore may do things they wouldn't otherwise have done,"[1] like take dishonest shortcuts to avoid a stock-crashing catastrophe.

Here's some disheartening proof: in 2008, Verizon lost over $10.6 billion in its employee pension fund during the financial crisis, which left its pension plan underfunded by over $2.6 billion.[2] In other words, Verizon had less money than it needed to ensure the company could pay the pensions of every employee to whom it had made that retirement promise. And yet, in 2008, despite losing more than $10 billion, Verizon recorded a net *income* on its pension obligations in the amount of $341 million.

How is it possible to lose billions of dollars and still record a net gain? Without going too much into the complexities of corporate accounting, the basic premise is this: an accounting rule allowed companies to record an "expected return on plan assets" instead of recording the actual performance, and then gave companies the ability to record the expected return number as an *operating* income or expense that could positively influence the bottom line. When companies could use the expected return, less interest on the obligation, to influence the operating income or expense from quarter to quarter, they had little incentive to think long term about building up pension reserves to insure against future volatility, like we saw during the

Quarterly forecasts can "often put a company in a position where management from the CEO down feels obligated to deliver earnings and therefore may do things they wouldn't otherwise have done."
—Jamie Dimon, CEO of JPMorgan Chase & Co.

financial crisis. Fortunately, the accounting rule recently changed here in the United States, which might help companies make different forecasting decisions to insure their obligations over the long run.[3]

Unfortunately, the phenomenon of short-term thinking isn't confined to the enterprise sector. When the agency I cofounded was unable to grow a client's business, it was sometimes because the client was afraid of enduring short-term adjustments in the name of long-term success. This fear prevented those execs from taking the kind of bold action that Domino's and Charlotte McCourt took. Instead, they chose to remain dishonest about what was going on around them in favor of the status quo, even if it meant their staid organizations were slowly being put out of business. On the contrary, clients who were willing to pursue the truth and embrace the honest need to evolve achieved extraordinary results, gained unexpected acclaim and prestige, and positioned themselves for long-term success while their competitors were forced to play catch-up.

SPRINT'S LONG GAME: HOW TO USE HONESTY TO CREATE LASTING PROFITS

Every honest CEO in the world agrees that long-term performance is better for business than short-term success alone; yet our departments, organizations, and even stock market are set up to embrace short-term thinking (no wonder we end up with long-term ill effects, like climate change). To understand how we can begin to embrace a long-term mentality, I turned to Dan Hesse, former CEO of Sprint. Hesse managed to take a telecom company that was hemorrhaging customers and turn it into a strong competitor that gave investors a roughly 30 percent higher return than the roaring S&P of the post-financial-crisis era and a nearly 50 percent higher return than Sprint's telecom competitors. That's a decent outperformance, but it becomes downright heroic when we consider that, when Hesse inherited Sprint in 2007, the company was weeks away from filing for bankruptcy. The Nextel merger had left Sprint with an older network that consistently dropped calls at a time when every provider was racing to capture customers by luring them with better call quality. Sprint skirted bankruptcy for a time, until Hesse forced Sprint into a potentially catastrophic situation when he decided that the entire infrastructure needed to be overhauled and the aging Nextel technology would have to be shut down.

Going into that impossible decision, Hesse had already helped Sprint rise to become the most improved company in the United States out of all forty-seven industries listed in the American Customer Satisfaction Index.[4] Sprint had gone from last to first in the telecom industry for customer service, and pretty soon it was onboarding customers faster than anyone else in the industry.[5] "But," Hesse admitted to me, "we knew from a long-term point of view that our network wasn't going to grow with us. There had been lots of mergers and none of our networks worked together, and we knew we didn't have the bones. We needed to rip out the entire network and start from scratch, which would take two years of construction."

For most CEOs that's a death knell, because the short-term-focused analysts on Wall Street would only see nosediving profits as the company poured money into a yet-uncertain future. Even though we know that investing in the long term is honestly the best business decision to make, a J curve of losses happens when we decide to take short-term pains in exchange for long-term gains.

Buffett would agree. His method is to buy and hold stocks for incredibly long periods of time, and to do little else during that time but sit back and watch all the frenzy happen while his companies keep chugging along, compounding tidy profits.

Netflix knew this, which is why Netflix decided to blow up its movies-through-the-mail business to build a hellaciously expensive streaming video platform. "Netflix's business results took a dip and they took a lot of crap for a while for going off in that direction," Hesse pointed out. As we learned earlier, if Carl Icahn had believed in the power of long-term thinking, we might have been talking up Blockbuster instead of Netflix. And, just as Reed Hastings and company did with Netflix, Hesse made the long-term investment in Sprint because it was honestly what the business needed if it were to survive past Hesse's tenure. It wasn't the move that would make him personally wealthy in the short term. It wasn't the move that would satisfy the analysts on Wall Street or the pundits on cable news. As Hesse admitted, though, "You'll never get to the promised land unless you're willing to take the dip, and that takes a lot of courage for a CEO to think that long term. But a lot of being honest and doing the right thing is about taking the long-term view."

> When investors can come in and out of a stock within a matter of seconds, we can't expect everyone to take a long-term view while their investment portfolios sag before their eyes. That's actually why Buffett keeps the price of Berkshire Hathaway's stock so high; he wants people to invest and stay for the long term, right alongside him.

Unfortunately, our system isn't set up to think long-term. When investors can come in and out of a stock within a matter of seconds, we can't expect everyone to take a long-term view while their investment portfolios sag before their eyes. That's actually why Buffett keeps the price of Berkshire Hathaway's stock so high; he wants people to invest and stay for the long term, right alongside him. The long-term mentality is *that* important to his understanding of what makes a business successful. If we think he's at all correct, it means that, as business leaders, we have a serious responsibility to think like Buffett instead of like short-term investors—whether it means rebuilding a network infrastructure, investing in a bold-but-honest marketing campaign, or perhaps starting that side hustle you dream of but can't seem to work on in the short term for your own long-term benefit.

HOW COURAGEOUS LEADERS DERISK THEIR INVESTMENTS USING HONESTY

No matter what you're investing in—a new business, a new product, a new future for your organization, or yourself—you can greatly derisk any investment by gaining more of the right kind of knowledge. When leaders go wrong, it's usually either because they've already decided on a subconscious level that it's easier to drift along with the status quo than truly innovate, or they've convinced themselves that they need near-perfect information before moving forward. The truth is, none of us ever have the absolute perfect amount of information. Instead, we have to be honest enough to know where the right information lives, and know when enough of the right information is enough.

Hesse had no guarantees that his strategy would work. Given Sprint's aging infrastructure, it was only a matter of time before the wireless giants swooped in to eat his lunch. Faced with certain (eventual) death or uncertain life, he chose to invest in the future of Sprint and give it the best possible chance for survival. In some ways, Hesse was lucky to be forced to act by the impending doom staring him in the face. Even so, lesser leaders might still have chosen to ignore the threat. Unfortunately, disruption—like death—is coming for us, whether we can visibly spot it or not.

So how do the best leaders know when to move forward? First, they properly assess that creating long-term success means innovating, changing, and investing in the future as a matter of habit. Then they derisk their decision by getting just enough of the right knowledge to be confident. Typically I find that the clients we work with already have the insights they need, or they're just a few key conversations away from getting the right insights. The right insights are usually locked up in a question we repeat to ourselves but never stop to answer. The answers are usually stuck in a belief we tell ourselves but never fully explore to see whether or not it's true.

For example, in my own case, it took my business partner and I years to figure out an odd paradox we would encounter in some prospective clients. Our favorite clients hire us to act as their CMO, in which case we work together to mine the insights, create the strategy, and fully execute the growth plan. But sometimes we'd also get requests to act as a fulfillment house for marketing projects, like producing collateral, blogging, creating social media content, and more, which was also just fine with us. But here's what we found: prospects who were only interested in us producing marketing content verbally expressed their interest in quality but actually wanted more, fast, cheap, and *then* quality, *in that order*. The truth was hiding in plain sight for us—in our conversations, in our prospects' buying habits, and in our prospects' questions. All we had to do was set aside our bias about putting quality first and then get honest about what we were hearing. That's when we realized we had an opportunity to evolve.

From there we made the decision to invest in a new platform—Stradeso, a company we grew out of our agency, which became its own business. We moved confidently forward because we had the right information. At the *community* level, organizations of all types and sizes need more and more content, quickly and affordably and of a respectable quality. On the level of *others*, VPs of marketing, CMOs, consultants, entrepreneurs, and agencies have a problem: they can't get marketing content without going through an HR headache and hiring *someone*, be it another agency, a freelancer, or an employee. Finally, we only needed to get honest with ourselves and be willing to look at ourselves as something other than a marketing agency. Suddenly we were able to see that we could create a technology solution to give customers the combination of benefits they needed: *more, fast, affordable, quality*. It would have been far easier to do nothing, remaining solely a marketing agency and continuing to live in our comfort zone. Instead, we took on some short-term pain investing in a new technology in order to create a long-term organization that will (hopefully) continue thriving in the gig economy.

By the way, if it works, it'll put our agency out of business. And that's exactly the point.

HOW SMART COMPANIES USE HONESTY TO POSITION THEMSELVES FOR FUTURE SUCCESS

If you want to position your organization for future success, the key isn't just to embrace honesty. Instead, it takes embracing honesty *before you're forced to*, because if you let your competitors get there first, you aren't leading and likely never will.

Case in point: America's Test Kitchen, which started as a New England cooking magazine in 1993 and evolved into a global brand with almost twenty television seasons in two branded shows, three magazines, more than twenty cookbooks, a variety of websites, over five seasons of radio shows, a cooking school, and seven Emmy nominations (including one win in 2012). One of America's Test Kitchen's secrets is that it does not accept advertisements from the same companies it reviews—which is virtually every company that makes cooking-related products. This stance instantly kills an entire revenue model over which most entertainment brands would salivate. Instead, this honest brand staunchly avoids conflicts of interest, creating videos of employees smashing pans, torturing whisks, and otherwise beating the hell out of their cookware to give honest reviews to their ardent fan base. The result of creating long-term trust instead of grabbing at short-term profits is perhaps best exemplified by the four million routine viewers and seventeen thousand volunteer home cooks who help America's Test Kitchen find "the right way" to cook, as defined not by them but by their own fans.

Building economic models for the long term is common sense but far from common practice. And it's up to us to recognize that our innate tendencies will lead us astray. We're wired for protection, which forms the basis of our fight-or-flight response. It's easier to do nothing and slowly wither away than take bold action to survive a far-flung future that we can sometimes barely picture. But then again, things are different now. The future is rushing toward us much faster these days, and globalization, automation, real-time communication, and other markers of the twenty-first century will only accelerate our urgent need to keep pace.

> We're wired for protection, which forms the basis of our fight-or-flight response. It's easier to do nothing and slowly wither away than take bold action to survive a far-flung future that we can sometimes barely picture.

For now, beware short-term promises. "This is why we have so many bad feelings toward companies, and why it's often difficult for the CEO to do the right thing," Hesse explained about the still-prevalent short-term quarterly focus. "I can guarantee you that long-term benefits are the last thing that any activist investor is focused on and wants the CEO doing—things like focusing on employees and customers. They are interested in profits—very short-term profits in very small windows of time, and there's a tremendous amount of pressure there."

Luckily, we may not have to wait very long for this shift from short-term to long-term thinking to prevail. "In speaking with some of the world's top business leaders," President Trump tweeted in August 2018, "I asked what it is that would make business (jobs) even better in the U.S. 'Stop quarterly reporting & go to a six-month system,' said one. That would allow greater flexibility & save money. I have asked the SEC to study!"[6] With more and more CEOs and one Twitter-happy president joining Buffett's call to arms, it's only a matter of time before we put an honest end to short-term thinking for the benefit of long-term success.

——— QUESTIONS FOR HONEST REFLECTION ———

1. Do you and your organization have a clear picture of what your business should look like many years from now?

2. Have you heard of any spectacular ideas for innovation and growth within your organization that have been killed by managers who are only focused on the short term?

3. How might you begin to collect a list of long-term projects and create an action committee to review, select, and execute on those projects that are vital to your long-term success?

CHAPTER 8

Management: How Audacious Authenticity Built an Empire

And How Puttin' on The Ritz Can Help You Dominate

What makes the difference between ordinary management and great leadership? Is it that great leaders never accept the status quo, while ordinary managers cling to it? Is it that great leaders plan for long-term success, while ordinary managers fret the short-term? Or do great leaders plow forward toward the truth, while ordinary managers obfuscate the facts if it serves their individual purpose?

The honest way is not the easy way. Executives fat with bonuses, corporate perks, and overinflated egos simply don't have the incentive to "take a risk," which most of them define as changing any aspect of a business beyond a one-degree shift. Domino's could have "improved" its pizza recipe. Sprint could have "improved" its network. But neither did. Instead, they blew shit up; they hit the reset button because they knew that they couldn't avoid their customers forever, and their customers' feedback was too clear to ignore. Those executives used honesty as a weapon to create truly innovative growth, reminding us how powerful honesty can be . . . when we're willing to embrace it. Indeed, the embracing-it part seems to be the challenge. As soon as you see the truth, knowing what to do about it typically comes quite naturally. In my experience, just as the Inverse Triangle shows, your people—customers, employees, peers—already know exactly what to do.

> Domino's could have "improved" its pizza recipe. Sprint could have "improved" its network. But neither did. Instead, they blew shit up; they hit the reset button because they knew that they couldn't avoid their customers forever, and their customers' feedback was too clear to ignore.

Unless you're managing robots, managing people means managing emotions. And that holds true whether you're managing up, down, across, or even leading your customers, or kids, or dogs. The Inverse Triangle seems like a dangerous prescription, not an active management technique at all but instead a way of leading only by reflecting, guiding, and coaching. That seems completely at odds with the traditional management structure. I mean, why bother having a hierarchy if the winning technique isn't to manage and dictate but instead to inquire and reflect? It's becoming more generally accepted wisdom today that giving up the command-and-control technique paradoxically allows many of today's greatest leaders to create outstanding results in their industries. As these leaders show us, we must learn how to stop "managing" and start asking the right questions that empower people to perform better. If you believe that a great idea can come from anywhere, then you also must believe in creating systems that allow ideas to sprout and grow without inhibition. And when we work in that kind of honest, idea-meritocratic way with all stakeholders, we create an environment where we can "wow" people. Wowing people, when done the right way, tends to be a good thing for the bottom line.

So how can we adapt our organizations to fit this new model? It turns out there is a place where you can go to learn just such a thing: your closest Ritz-Carlton.

THE RITZ-CARLTON: WHAT AN HONEST MANAGEMENT CULTURE LOOKS LIKE

The Ritz-Carlton started as a restaurant chain on ocean liners in 1905. After changing hands in a series of expansions and contractions in the hotel industry, The Ritz-Carlton Boston and its brand name were purchased in August 1983 by Boston-based developer William B. Johnson for a mere $75.5 million.[1] At the time, a couple of Ritz-Carlton locations existed with a hodgepodge of licensing deals and no controls over the brand. (As an aside, there used to be The Ritz-Carlton Chicago [A Four Seasons Hotel] in what must have been the world's best example of brand confusion.) Johnson assembled a new development team of four, one of whom was the visionary hotelier Horst Schulze. Over the span of just a few decades, Schulze unified the brand into the luxury powerhouse it is today, with ninety-seven hotels and resorts in thirty countries around the world, forty thousand employees, and the lowest employee turnover rate in the industry.

> We must learn how to stop "managing" and start asking the right questions that empower people to perform better.

The Ritz's Version of the Golden Rule

The Ritz-Carlton's most brilliant cultural achievement is its Gold Standards—a masterful collection of its mission, vision, values, and core beliefs, which it shares with religious fervor across its thousands of employees. They have much cooler names for these elements: The Credo; Motto; Three Steps of Service; Service Values; The 6th Diamond;

and The Employee Promise. At the very heart of its Gold Standards is a startling commitment to the men and women who come to work every day at a Ritz-Carlton property. In fact, the Gold Standards are designed for the sole purpose of creating an extraordinary culture that produces extraordinary customer experiences. In that order.

Take its Motto, for instance: "At The Ritz-Carlton Hotel Company, L.L.C., 'We are Ladies and Gentlemen serving Ladies and Gentlemen.' This motto exemplifies the anticipatory service provided by all staff members."[2] Couple that with its Employee Promise: "At The Ritz-Carlton, our Ladies and Gentlemen are the most important resource in our service commitment to our guests." To understand how The Ritz's culture produces industry-leading results, we need to take special note of the subtle logic that The Ritz uses in working *backwards* from its ultimate goal of serving customers: *In order to produce extraordinary customer experiences, the company has to* first *produce extraordinary employee-leaders*—its "Ladies and Gentlemen," who are not subjugated to customers but are on superior footing, listed, importantly, *first*.

Employees come first; customers come second.

How many companies can you think of that proclaim themselves to be "customer-centric"? It's true that many put their *customers* first (or at least they try). But the problem is that those well-intentioned companies have skipped over the most essential group of "others" they have: *their own employees.*

On the contrary, The Ritz-Carlton realizes that managers and executives honestly have no direct control over the outcomes of the business. Notice I said, "direct" control. Instead, the receptionists, customer service representatives, maids, chefs, and the rest of the frontline employees *do* have direct control over the outcomes of the business. Every minute of every hour of every day inside a Ritz-Carlton property, frontline employees heavily influence the experiences of The Ritz's customers. As we've already covered in the Inverse Triangle, this is why those frontline employees are the most important asset any company will ever have. And this is why The Ritz-Carlton puts those employees first, *even above their own customers.*

How The Ritz Uses Authenticity as a Management Technique

After years of seeing leaders roadblock their own organizations by exercising a command-and-control style, I've developed a framework for The Ritz's management technique. I call it *Waterfall Culture*. A Waterfall Culture is a culture in which every layer of the organization has one major responsibility: to empower the next layer of the organization with everything it needs to do its job exceptionally well. To some, this may seem like an obvious way to structure an organization. Unfortunately, to most, the workday is chock-full of politics, backstabbing, meddling, illogic, circumventions, and woeful inefficiency.

And that's on a good day.

> A Waterfall Culture is a culture in which every layer of the organization has one major responsibility: to empower the next layer of the organization with everything it needs to do its job exceptionally well.

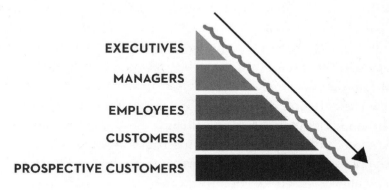

Waterfall Culture

Waterfall Culture is more than just empowering your people through your mission, vision, and values. Rather, Waterfall Culture is about proudly publicizing that your employees are not only important; they are the *most important*. That they rank above the customer is a critical distinction. I've seen countless organizations inadvertently develop harmful cultures by following a traditional customer-first dogma. I once witnessed a culture that put so much emphasis on pleasing the customer that it allowed employees to skip over protocols, fail to communicate, and even push each other aside in their frantic customer service. In turn, the daily frenzy created ill will, disrespect, ruinous values, and the systemic degradation of employee satisfaction—even though the customers were oblivious to the internal turmoil. In the long run, the best employees left and the company stagnated—all in the name of serving customers.

Organizational mandates are a dangerous thing. In defense of that organization, it's easy to see how a well-meaning directive, *take care of the customer at all costs*, could turn into a bloodbath, where everyone is stepping over procedures and processes to achieve the goal. The Ritz understood this intrinsically, which is why an employee-first approach made so much sense. If employees come first, employee processes come first. If employees come first, their information and insights come first. If employees come first, no one else does—not the customers, not the managers, and certainly not the executives. In such a world, micromanagement doesn't even make sense.

The Ritz figured out long ago that insights yielded by frontline employees could transform their business, even before they gained access to the dashboard-style technologies that we have today for business information and analysis. The Ritz kicked it old-school, with employees keeping note cards on them at all times to record customer preferences, and holding small-team scrum meetings each morning at which the frontline employees reported on any important issues. When you funnel well-timed data points through consistent processes like The Ritz's, you can derive exactly the insights you need to make critical, executive-level decisions. Yet inefficient micromanagement infects even the most well-meaning managers, who would ironically do better to simply do less. I'm sure you've seen it, too.

Surely, old habits die hard. Thankfully, more and more companies are putting time and energy into developing a superb culture in which people have the guidelines for behavior but the leeway to perform, so they don't have to be controlled. The internet is saturated with articles, listicles, infographics, and ebooks on the subject of how to develop a corporate culture, which is why we're not going to explore "how," because I believe that misses an important step. Instead, we're going to ask the more fundamental, and honest, question: *Who?*

If we start with *who*, interesting insights begin to appear. For instance, "who" is directly responsible for customer satisfaction? The frontline employees, of course. And "who" is responsible for the satisfaction of frontline employees? Well, logically, it would be their direct managers. "Who" is responsible for the satisfaction of the managers? The executives, of course, which creates a flow of responsibility that looks like this figure depicting a Waterfall Culture.

Within the Waterfall Culture framework, each layer of the organization is responsible for the happiness, well-being, and empowerment of the next layer (notice I didn't say "control" of the next layer). That means there's no question as to which people are responsible for which roles and responsibilities. Furthermore, this framework accurately mirrors the way communication must flow within a transparent organization in a transparent world, as we learned with the Inverse Triangle. Except Waterfall Culture flows in reverse. You see, *information* must flow from customers through employees and managers and toward executives, flipping the typical hierarchy triangle. However, care, attention, tools, empowerment, and leadership must all sequentially flow from the *top* to the *bottom* of the traditional hierarchical organization. Thus each management layer will always have everything it needs to do its job exceptionally well—with nothing more, nothing less, and no doubt as to "who" is responsible for whom.

Where, then, does this leave a leader in charge of the advancement of the entire operation? If we look at the most successful leaders of our time—people like Howard Schultz, Steve Jobs, Jack Welch, Warren Buffett, Jeff Bezos, and countless others—we find they have all formed a similar habit. Not only is it simple and effective but we already have a name for it: *Management by Wandering Around*, or MBWA for short. Although it's been credited to Hewlett-Packard and even to Abraham Lincoln as a winning technique, MBWA became a popular modern-day term in 1982 when management gurus Tom Peters and Robert H. Waterman Jr. highlighted it in their book, *In Search of Excellence: Lessons from America's Best-Run Companies.*

In a true Waterfall Culture, just as in MBWA, the leader wanders through the ranks, from customers to fellow executives, to make sure that the two streams are flowing appropriately (information from employees to executives, and empowerment from executives to employees). As an independent eye of sorts, the leader has the opportunity and responsibility to collect insights from every source and sprinkle them throughout the organization. In fact, one of the most valuable insights a leader can deliver is from prospective customers back to the top executives, providing invaluable data that paves the way for important strategic changes and pivots, just like Russell Weiner did at Domino's. This unique positioning is precisely why we see many CEOs in a high-level sales capacity—in part because they have unique perspectives on the entire organization, which allow for a holistic and compelling sales pitch.

> If we look at the most successful leaders of our time—people like Howard Schultz, Steve Jobs, Jack Welch, Warren Buffett, Jeff Bezos, and countless others—we find they have all formed a similar habit. Not only is it simple and effective, but we already have a name for it: *Management by Wandering Around,* or MBWA for short.

Note, however, that I don't support MBWA as an excuse to micromanage, which so often is the case within middle layers of an organization. In fact, some have rightfully argued (and I've seen firsthand) that MBWA can foster a culture of anxiety, distrust, and a pervasive feeling of always looking over your shoulder. Instead, Waterfall Culture presumes that (a) everyone is empowered to do their job to the best of their ability, (b) every management layer is responsible for ensuring that everyone has the tools to do so, and (c) every individual knows exactly what their priorities are and what they must do to achieve "success," however it's defined. The last part is key; without a measurable performance metric, politics prevail. No wonder why so many cultures turn political. Instead, at The Ritz, politics are replaced by processes and procedures, like carrying the 12 Service Values on a laminated card and conducting scrum meetings like the fifteen-minute Daily Line-Up with a rigorous agenda. Altogether, The Ritz's cultural norms and procedures make for an odd mix of near-militant group work coupled with a surprising amount of individual autonomy to perform.

Empowered Employees Come from the Hiring Process

Of course, the Waterfall Culture type of system could never work for an organization unless it finds the perfect ladies and gentlemen to serve other ladies and gentlemen in the first place. To create effective teams, The Ritz-Carlton ingrains its employees deeply with the identity of The Ritz, starting the moment a candidate applies for a position at a hotel. Only after rigorous, values-based testing over a multi-week period will a candidate be selected to continue into the training program. The initial training program is twenty-one days long and includes a mandatory mastery of The Ritz's Gold Standards.

As Judith Crutchfield, former senior director of quality for The Ritz, once noted, "Only some 2 percent of applicants survive the vetting process to become a Ritz-Carlton Lady or Gentleman."[3] That makes The Ritz over three times more selective than most Ivy League undergraduate programs. As Crutchfield revealed, "The company is less interested in luxury hospitality experience and most interested in one's *attitude*," and a rare type of winning attitude at that.

How different is that from the normal hiring process? Well, imagine if your company didn't hire on experience—at all. Is that something your current HR function could even entertain? Yet in today's world, where information is ubiquitous, it makes perfect sense. As a Ritz-Carlton doorman once recounted, "I can teach someone how to serve people, but I can't teach them to love people."

Hiring around core values has had some incredible second-order consequences. For instance, turnover at The Ritz is far lower than the turnover at competitors' hotels—just about 20 percent vs. the industry average of a whopping 73.8 percent, according to the Bureau of Labor Statistics.[4] The Ritz achieves such a low rate by indoctrinating each employee into its culture over a multi-month training process, starting with the Gold Standards and progressing to the 12 Service Values, which every employee carries with them on a laminated card. Then comes one-on-one training, role-playing, and "a follow-up orientation that seeks to meld the philosophical with the practical," as Crutchfield describes, which sounds more like a PhD curriculum than the onboarding process at a hotel.

It's clear that The Ritz-Carlton's entire system of success is built on the premise that if you transfer a strong brand identity to employees and hold them accountable for that identity, they in turn will take care of the customer in exactly the standard that is required . . . or their failure will be so obvious that parting ways becomes an unavoidable, logical outcome. When it comes to providing individual autonomy to perform, The Ritz empowers and entrusts its employees so much that every single employee is authorized to spend up to two thousand dollars to meet or exceed the needs of a customer—no further approval required. That's how much The Ritz trusts its values system and its ability to hire around its core identity—an identity that depends on the sustainability of its Waterfall Culture. It's a brilliant internal system that has direct, measurable, and incredibly positive effects on the customer—even if, in this case, our "who" isn't the customer at all.

"We are superior to the competition," Horst Schulze once asserted, "because we hire employees who work in an environment of belonging and purpose." Schulze understands how a culture cascades from one level to the next, and he's brutally honest about what encourages employees to go the extra mile for customers. "You cannot deliver what the customer wants by controlling the employee," he warned. "Employees who are controlled cannot respond caringly. You need superior knowledge and real leadership, not management. Because of this, we specifically developed a selection process for leaders; we don't hire managers."[5]

USING THE HOURGLASS OF HONESTY TO MAKE A GOOD CULTURE GREAT

When The Ritz's corporate director of culture transformation told me the brand's story in the ballroom of the Boston location, I couldn't help but think of the irony of its success, uniquely putting employees ahead of customers. While many brands out there are still struggling to reach, attract, and retain both customers *and* employees in the twenty-first century, organizations need only use honesty to light the way, starting with a deep analysis of "who" matters most and then giving their people the right tools to wow customers. As an example of one such clever technique, the next time you walk into a Ritz-Carlton, take note of how you are greeted. Take special note of the body language of the people with whom you're speaking. Chances are—as they have been taught—The Ritz employees you encounter will mirror your own body language: if you stand with your hands clasped, they will, too. If you come off as casual in your body language, they will mirror a casual demeanor. In essence, they are mirroring your behavior so that they reflect *your* value system, which in turn will make *you* feel most comfortable.

Mirroring is just one clever tactic for creating brilliant customer experiences, but if you ask me, their use of brutal honesty is the most stunning technique of all. To see how, let's go back to the Hourglass of Honesty.

Honest with the Community

At some level, Schulze recognized that the community at large, the hospitality industry, had a big, yet-unsolved problem in its horrendous employee turnover rate. And he noticed a simple, self-evident truth about exceptional customer service: you can't be of much service as an organization if the customer experience is delivered by entirely different folks each and every time. He recognized that solving for that one problem—turnover rate—could dramatically change the way things were done in hospitality and give the new standard-bearer an unprecedented competitive advantage. In other words, Schulze looked at his industry and didn't just accept the way it was; he got honest about what needed to change and then he set out to change it.

Honest with Others

By using its clever mirroring strategy and making every customer feel completely at ease, The Ritz inspires its customers to relay their wonderful experiences to the next layer—prospective customers—through extraordinary word of mouth (both in-person and digitally through social media and review sites). This is all made possible by The Ritz's commitment to being honest about *others*—its employees—and empowering them with tools like mirroring and a strong identity to help guide their everyday actions.

Contrary to what seems to be the common practice, disempowering micromanagement just doesn't cut it anymore. Employees, with their digital-nomad status and gig-economy side hustles, have tons of options as to where to spend their time and devote their energy. If they aren't allowed to actively participate in their jobs—unencumbered by bureaucracy, supported with logical systems, and empowered by purpose—they'll never remain loyal to fulfilling the organization's mission. The Ritz knows that if it wants to compete for the best leaders, it must lure them with the right foundation for success, which means offering a purposeful organization with the perfect balance of strict identity and generous autonomy. Because the truth is, at our deepest level, we are all trying to figure out who we are and how we do our best work. And when you work for The Ritz, you—their most precious leader—get the identity and autonomy to explore both.

Honest with the Self

As we look at the third step of the Hourglass of Honesty, being honest with oneself, the time came for The Ritz to be brutally honest with itself, just as it came for Domino's, Sprint, and the other organizations in this book. For me, that's when this story really gets interesting and ultimately proves the power of honesty to achieve industry-leading innovation. When Schulze and his team became brutally honest with The Ritz as a brand, they realized something very important: The Ritz-Carlton wasn't a *hotel* company at all. It was a *hospitality leadership* company.

Soon after Schulze took over as COO, his fellow executive, Leonardo Inghilleri, developed a separate branch of The Ritz-Carlton called The Ritz-Carlton Leadership Center. The Ritz-Carlton Leadership Center, which officially opened in 1999, is a global provider of leadership consulting based on The Ritz's industry-dominating, award-winning processes. In the words of the Leadership Center itself:

> As global consumers demand higher levels of service, personalized experiences, and deeper engagement with companies, the legendary customer and employee practices of The Ritz-Carlton allow our clients to develop incredible advantages in the market. Our clients acknowledge that personal, intentional, considered service is a competitive differentiator that transcends industry, and The Ritz-Carlton Leadership Center is an unequaled partner in the journey to refine and innovate service excellence.

Through consulting, enrichment courses, and customized learning services, The Ritz-Carlton Leadership Center uses its exceptional tenets to instruct businesses in every industry about how to openly, transparently, and honestly serve customers in the twenty-first century. As you can imagine, the center has thrived throughout the last several disruptive decades. It's no wonder that The Ritz-Carlton has been featured on the top Zagat lists for dining, hotels, *and* service. It's not surprising in the least that The Ritz became the only two-time recipient of the Malcolm Baldrige National Quality Award in the service category. Nor is it hard to imagine that more than fifty thousand executives from companies around the world have flocked to The Ritz-Carlton Leadership Center to be trained in its principles of service.

How do you grow your hotel company from a few disparate locations into a global leader in less than thirty years, dominate your incumbent competition, and become the best hospitality brand in the world? You don't. Instead, you honestly assess "who" you really are—in The Ritz's case, a *hospitality leadership company*.

It turns out that there isn't any competition among hotel chains that are also hospitality leadership companies, which automatically sets The Ritz in a class of its own. It was an "honest to greatness" strategy that couldn't fail—unless, of course, it hit a typical, opinion-laden roadblock. But did that happen? When Inghilleri told his team that The Ritz was in fact a hospitality leadership company and not a hotel company, did his fellow executives look at him like he had five heads or insist he get more sleep? Or did they take an honest look at what they had built, realize who they were, and embrace their honest identity?

They obviously chose honesty, and that's how the Hourglass of Honesty played out. The Ritz got honest about the issues in the hospitality industry; changed its "others"—the employees—by empowering them to be leaders instead of managers; and willingly embraced its honest identity as a *hospitality leadership* company instead of clinging to the status quo. In the process, The Ritz won unprecedented awards, earned worldwide acclaim and credibility, serviced global industries, and absolutely dominated its competition.

Innovative though it was at the time, we can now look back and say that the key to success was quite simple: just be unabashedly honest.

──── QUESTIONS FOR HONEST REFLECTION ────

1. What is one thing about your industry that you accept as "just the way it is," but could actually be addressed and improved to your advantage?

MANAGEMENT: HOW AUDACIOUS AUTHENTICITY BUILT AN EMPIRE

2. To what extent does your organization use a command-and-control system vs. a Waterfall Culture, and how might you be able to change from the former to the latter?

3. Does your organization inspire you to discover who you are, what you stand for, and how you do your best work? If not, how could you create new processes that balance a strong identity with generous autonomy, just as The Ritz does?

CHAPTER 9

Communication: How Honest Feedback Led to Billion-Dollar Greatness

And How One Radical Company Hedged Its Bets with Honesty

I f you ever had a doubt about whether honesty can make you money, then this one's for you.

Look, I get it. I've worked on behalf of leaders from car dealers to Warren Buffett, start-ups to Fortune 500s. Being honest is hard. No one likes to stick their neck out. As my business partner says, "Few play to win . . . because most play to not lose." It's sad. Frustrating. It lulls us into a sense of complacency and protectionism, where just getting by becomes the singular focus and focusing on small wins becomes the goal.

But that might be costing you. Actually, I know it is, and now you can know that, too. Because all those little wins will never help you achieve your big goals—you know, the ones you've been suppressing for years, like that billion-dollar dream hiding under your bed that you're afraid to check on because it might be growing mold.

Yet if you believe that simple is beautiful, it doesn't get much simpler than the story of how one guy from Queens, New York, became a billionaire . . . just by being honest.

"Before I begin telling you what I think, I want to establish that I'm a 'dumb shit' who doesn't know much relative to what I need to know."[1] Thus begins billionaire Ray Dalio's recounting of his life's work in his 550-plus-page tome, *Principles*, scribed as a series of "principles" he used to create his industry-dominating success. Arianna Huffington noted, "Ray Dalio shares the unconventional principles of life and work that turned this ordinary middle-class kid from Long Island into one of the most successful people of our time—and that can be used by anyone to achieve their own goals."[2]

Dalio is the owner of Bridgewater Associates, the world's largest hedge fund in recent years, which manages about $160 billion in assets. Since its founding in 1975, Bridgewater has earned more than a staggering $50 billion for its clients, putting it in the top spot on the list of hedge funds worldwide in terms of net gains.[3] Indeed, Dalio has an uncanny ability to dominate his field—and he does it by honestly assessing the world around him, the people around him, and himself. His prowess has led to a four-and-a-half-decades-long run to an estimated personal net worth of $17.4 billion since starting Bridgewater in his midtwenties from a two-bedroom apartment in New York City.[4]

But to understand exactly how he did it, we must go back to Huffington's assessment that Dalio used "unconventional principles," which transformed him into a success. Those unconventional principles can be summed up by two important tenets of Bridgewater's thick culture: *radical truth and radical transparency.*

Go figure.

BRIDGEWATER'S PRINCIPLES OF COMMUNICATION ARE MORE "LOGICAL" THAN "RADICAL"

I recall listening to a keynote speaker in Ft. Lauderdale just after *Principles* had been released. The speaker waved his arms in the air furiously as he yelled to the crowd, "Do you know what this means? A CEO who wants people to tell him when he's wrong? That's a big deal . . ."

We can all agree that Dalio is, for all intents and purposes, a genius—at least a financial one. But for that speaker to make *such* a big deal out of being honest, and for Huffington to say that using radical truth to live and work is so *unconventional*, well, that's honestly sad. It's sad principally because Dalio's principles are no more brilliant than they are basic; no more visionary than they are obvious. At times, his assertions like "systemize your decision-making" border on clear logic, utter sense, and even absurdity that such simplicity could facilitate such massive success.

This is the time to wheel out that favorite quote about how common sense isn't always common practice.

Because I am a crusader for honesty myself, Dalio's principles rang like music to my ears, the sound of which probably resembles the delicate notes of depositing billions of dollars in your bank account. But, I'll have you know, Dalio rode the struggle bus once just like the rest of us, and he's not shy about honestly admitting his greatest blunder. In 1982, he forecasted a severe economic recession—publicly, on national television—only to see the market bounce back and then soar against his judgment call. Having laid in his investment strategy according to his incorrect assumption, the misstep almost ended his career. He was forced to lay off employees and even borrow a paltry four thousand bucks from his father just to keep his new family afloat. It was, he wrote, "like a series of blows to the head with a baseball bat."[5] Yet he didn't give up; instead, he let his mistake be a springboard for change. He vowed to cast his emotions aside and double down on the twin goals of deeply analyzing historical trends and never putting himself in a position to be that wrong again.

> Dalio's principles rang like music to my ears, the sound of which probably resembles the delicate notes of depositing billions of dollars in your bank account.

Most of us can surely relate. I've certainly committed my share of egregious business decisions, some of which cost me millions and still haunt me to this day. Like Dalio, I've tried to use them as learning experiences. Like any leader-in-training, I've tried to build new habits to prevent those mistakes from swamping me again. Dalio, however, has taken this idea to the edge within his entire culture, defying what Huffington would call *conventional* wisdom and going beyond what most leaders today would even consider. In his own words, he decided, "I just want to be right—I don't care if the right answer comes from me." So, he reasoned, "I learned to be radically open-minded to allow others to point out what I might be missing."[6]

Dalio put in place four rules—principles—that would guide his life and his company from then on:

1. Seek out the smartest people who disagreed with me so I could try to understand their reasoning.
2. Know when not to have an opinion.
3. Develop, test, and systemize timeless and universal principles.
4. Balance risks in ways that keep the big upside while reducing the downside.

No one should be surprised to hear that Dalio got back on his feet (that's putting it mildly) after establishing some good habits around his own biases, like having the people around him give him the honest truth at all times. In turn, that gave him the power of being right about what was going on in the "community" (in his case, the state of financial markets), honest about how "others" (his colleagues) could help him forecast more clearly, and honest about the "self"—with his own limitations as leader. After getting this last, personal piece into honest alignment, he went on a multidecade run to become the multibillionaire thought leader of our time, changing not only the hedge fund landscape but also the role of honest communication in achieving massive success.

A LOOK BEHIND THE PRINCIPLE OF TELLING IT LIKE IT IS

Dalio's true genius was that he didn't stop at using honesty to improve his personal leadership abilities. Instead, he spent his career creating a company culture where smart people can be honest with one another, seek truth instead of comfort or conformity, understand when people are believable, and factor in their believability when assessing the validity (or not) of their opinions. He took his own belief in systematic thinking and made it mandatory throughout his company, so that as business decisions compounded over time and over his entire team, they would be unaffected by personal biases, ego, and other killers of success. Instead of leaving his people to act on a whim, he maniacally pursued a culture of radical truth: "Being honest," Dalio stated simply, "prevents confusion and misinterpretation."[7]

But Dalio hasn't chosen a usual foe; he fights age-old instincts for self-preservation by creating a culture that assaults people's beliefs at every turn. "People have trouble embracing reality and dealing with it," Dalio explained, "which can lead to an inaccurate synthesis of who they are, what they want, and what it will take to achieve their goals." It's the achieving part that is important to his organization, which is why his culture demands the eradication of "ego and blind spot barriers" that might prevent his people from being able to objectively see the truth. The pursuit of objective truth exists at the heart of the entire Bridgewater culture, which vehemently opposes leaning on the opinions of a handful of individuals as most companies do. As you can imagine, in a hedge fund concerned with quantitative performance, straying from the objective truth could be disastrous.

> He took his own belief in systematic thinking and made it mandatory throughout his company, so that as business decisions compounded over time and over his entire team, they would be unaffected by personal biases, ego, and other killers of success.

Dalio's enemies to organizational honesty, which he's spent a lifetime snuffing out of his organization's interpersonal communications style, are both "a fear of being wrong and the feeling of negative emotions associated with that—embarrassment, anger, defensiveness, etc." Dalio, perhaps the best psychologist who never was, identified early in his career that people don't typically operate out of the logical part of their brain (their "higher level") but instead allow themselves to be guided by emotion (their "lower level"). This one human condition prevents many leaders, teams, and organizations from using honesty to thrive. Bridgewater, however, refuses to accept our hardwiring. Instead of letting ego, fear, and emotion drive Bridgewater's decision-making process, employees are required to use Vulcan-like logic and test assumptions, just as one would approach math equations, to win in the financial markets.

To fix a culture stuck in the "lower level you," Dalio recommends what every other organization in this book has figured out: "Write down . . . principles, talk about them, debate them, and continuously iterate. Without clear principles," he warns, "you have many people who are working toward different things and have different values." As Domino's Pizza and The Ritz-Carlton codified their own cultures, Bridgewater has codified radical truth and radical transparency into a series of tools: personality assessments to assess culture fit; norms like recording most meetings;[8] feedback mechanisms like the "Dot Collector," which employees use to rate each other on adhering to certain principles; and objective analyses like the Baseball Card, which serves as a snapshot of an employee's strengths, weaknesses, and skills. These tools, among many others, serve as a GPS to his high-performing culture. Employees use these tools to develop a directness in their communication with one another, where open debate about what's right thrives, and constructive feedback on the fly isn't only expected—it's demanded.

> Instead of letting ego, fear, and emotion drive Bridgewater's decision-making process, employees are required to use Vulcan-like logic and test assumptions, just as one would approach math equations, to win in the financial markets.

These tools keep Bridgewater's culture aligned with Dalio's unique views—the views that, by the way, have produced outsized performance in a difficult industry for decades. Personality assessments, systemized feedback mechanisms, and software to track and diagnose issues as they occur are just part of the "suite" of tools that Dalio has created over time, which he is now preparing to share with others who want to develop similar cultures built on radical truth and radical transparency. Dalio understands that the pursuit of truth requires a truthful environment where people feel comfortable telling it like it is, because without that expected level of candid conversation, we can't hope for fact to triumph over opinion when opinions are so much easier to offer.

THE DOWNSIDES OF A RADICALLY TRUTHFUL AND TRANSPARENT CULTURE

What I love most about Dalio's story is that it's enough to prove that honesty matters—nay, that it is a central tenet of achieving game-changing, industry-dominating, literally billion-dollar success. But even Bridgewater's pursuit of truth isn't immune to a few startling headlines that may give us clues as to whether Bridgewater's culture should be our standard for excellence in business.

For instance, Dalio himself admits that 25 percent of Bridgewater's 1,500 or so employees don't last more than eighteen months.[9] That level of turnover is massively expensive for recruiting and training, which Bridgewater willingly sacrifices in the name of its core principles of radical truth and radical transparency. In addition, probably due to those who enter the culture and end up in culture shock, some former employees have taken to review sites to give their own accounts of the truth, with one former employee describing the company as a "cauldron of fear and intimidation."[10]

Despite Dalio's best efforts, it seems that most people don't like to be told the truth about their weaknesses—as evidenced by the 25 percent of people who *think* they're honest with themselves and others, get all the way through Bridgewater's lengthy interview process,[11] overcome its multiple personality tests,[12] complete the boot camp on Dalio's principles,[13] and end up in a coveted spot in the world's largest hedge fund . . . only to leave within eighteen months. Not too shocking, considering that we live in a society where being "nice" is far more socially agreeable than being "honest." Very few of us are raised to speak to people directly and bluntly, as Dalio would have it. Marvel, for instance, at the next time you ask someone how they are. They'll reply, automatically, "Good" or "I'm fine." Is that true? Maybe, maybe not, but we've conditioned ourselves to produce automatic responses, not share too many of our personal thoughts, and come across as generally likable and agreeable. And sometimes, honestly, we don't want or need the full truth. Consider the warning from Martin Whittaker, CEO of JUST Capital, who said, "Not everybody wants real honesty. If I'm a passenger on an airplane and the pilot's really honest with me, do I want that? 'I've never seen storm clouds like that before' is not something you want coming over the intercom. That's where leadership comes in. Honesty can drive trust, but trust is probably more important than honesty."

But to Dalio, trust and honesty go hand in hand. At Bridgewater you trust your comrades *because* they are honest and direct. Nonetheless, employees want out—in droves. And the ones who get out sometimes turn into some devilish headlines, like the *New York Times*'s sensational clickbait: "At World's Largest Hedge Fund, Sex, Fear and Video Surveillance."[14] Such internet monuments serve as blemishes reminiscent of Tom Brady's Deflategate. Is it radical truth? Or is it the inevitable stone-slinging that any best-in-class leader should expect to incur?

Those who depart leave clues about a performance-based culture that can turn into a psychological roller coaster of radical truth, with one former employee reviewing on Indeed.com:

> Bridgewater's unorthodox culture becomes a second full-time job. Employees there spend more time rating, judging (and demeaning) each other, than they do on actual work. Employee's thinking abilities are constantly judged and assessed by peers and superiors who have no qualifications or background in psychology, analytical psychology or social & behavioral sciences. Yet, this kind of subjective feedback is given by under-qualified individuals that ends up getting memorialized on record, that may or may not impact things like grades, ranking and compensation. The principles and ideas on

paper look ingenious; however, when put into practice, they tend to fail in a spectacular way.[15]

Another simply summed up, "Thin-skinned people who want to be coddled don't survive long . . ."

Depending on the corporate culture(s) into which you've been indoctrinated to date, perhaps Bridgewater sounds to you like a magical land where everyone's candidness breeds self-awareness, personal epiphanies, and extraordinary leadership development. Conversely, perhaps you're petrified of being scored and ranked on a daily basis, with your blunders publicly exposed for all to see and analyze. Wherever you fall on the spectrum, though, we must return to that mother of truths: a radical dose of honesty produces financial results, as shown by Dalio's creation of a winning, industry-dominating business with a flood of applicants that arrives at his company's gates every day. Perhaps his overwhelming economic success just happens to be correlated with honesty, and not caused by it. Perhaps he built a culture that eliminates personal biases and organizational blind spots, and his firm happened to achieve financial success, and it's just a big coincidence. But if you believe that, you also have to believe that there is no value in learning from the thoughts, ideas, and experiences of your colleagues. You have to believe that your best hope for success is "your way or the highway," because you're never wrong. Hey, I have a big ego, too, so I'm not saying that can't be true. All I'm saying is that with billions of dollars on the line, I'd want to make damn sure that we got to the right answer—and if your money was on the line, I bet you'd want that, too.

There's also the question of whether radical truth and radical transparency work well when billions are on the line, but don't function as well for non-finance departments and their less quantitative personality types. For instance, Bridgewater's legal or compliance departments likely flourish under radical—and necessary—truthfulness, while their events team may not find epiphanies in overanalyzed, ego-bashing feedback saying the hamburgers were overcooked by two degrees at this year's holiday party. And then there's that other obvious downside to feedback, which is the quality of the source. When someone gives you feedback of any kind, it might or might not be true (depending on whether they are believable or not), and it might or might not be helpful (depending on whether they are mildly intelligent or not). So perhaps there's a grain of salt to be had here. But to me, the real kernel of truth in brutally candid feedback is to understand *how* other people think and *how differently* other people see you vs. how you see yourself. If you can observe and analyze enough of those opinions without wanting to run away from all those assaults on your worldview, you'll eventually get to the objectivity at the bottom of all that subjectivity . . . and that's where real personal growth is.

All that said, regardless of whether radical truth and transparency could improve your team's performance or you're feeling somewhat less radical these days, the objective facts remain that the largest hedge fund in the world has absolutely dominated—for lengthy periods of history—while using honesty as a competitive advantage.

The key, according to Dalio, is actually within your own self-assessment—in other words, it's imperative that you, as an individual, properly ask and assess what's true and then match it as objectively as possible to the consensus of others in a transparent way. "Transparency assures that people see things directly so that they can form their own opinions about what is going on," Dalio wrote. "It's difficult to BS someone when they get to see things for themselves."

Dalio's utopian version of a high-performing culture sees that no opportunity slips through the cracks, no ego gets to put opinion over fact, and nobody is immune to being held accountable. Notice that the premise isn't about living *your* truth, which is oh-so-popular within our entitled society these days; in fact, it's quite the opposite. Dalio's technique is about living the *objective* truth, no matter how difficult it is for you to confront it. That's what has kept Bridgewater thriving all these years—not the presence of a financial wizard but depending on truth no matter what challenge the organization needed to overcome.

To Dalio, his is a natural way of life for anyone who wants to achieve anything, and he would recoil from an employee assessment that is overly kind as quickly as most would recoil from being told their last month's worth of work was an abhorrent mess. "One of the goals of our culture," he added, "is to put people in the position of needing to reflect openly on their own weaknesses and have forthright conversations with others about them. Doing this helps them become more open-minded and see things more objectively."

Or it helps people entrench further into their blind spots and believe more firmly in their own ego-driven "syntheses," as Dalio calls them. I'm referencing that curious psychological phenomenon where people arrive at the conclusion that *everyone else must be crazy, 'cuz it sure ain't me!* Trust me, I've seen this entrenchment in leaders (I use that term lightly) of all types of organizations, and I bet you've seen it, too. So I entreat you to consider the following inexplicable paradox: With billions of dollars on the line, Dalio prefers to have a team of people obsessed with finding the correct answers based on logical facts, devoid of personal or organizational biases that could lead them astray, yet few leaders even think to embrace such a level of honesty in their own organizations. Instead, cultures—and their bottom lines—suffer because of ego, a lack of candidness, a lack of clear communication, and a resulting lack of accountability.

> The premise (at Bridgewater) isn't about living *your* truth, which is oh-so-popular within our entitled society these days; in fact, it's quite the opposite. Dalio's technique is about living the *objective* truth, no matter how difficult it is for you to confront it.

CREATING A CULTURE OF HONEST COMMUNICATION TAKES AN HONEST EFFORT

If 160,000,000,000 reasons aren't enough to convince you that honesty has a significant role in achieving greatness, I'm not sure what will. The truth is, no one can force you or anyone else to embrace honesty. Honesty is a quest; it's a journey that Dalio was forced to undertake early in his career and then decided to drive into his culture, which in turn helped him innovate and dominate his industry. As Bridgewater's people get honest about what's going on in the world, candid with each other in the pursuit of objective truth, and honest on an individual level with what they know and don't know, they get into honest alignment and create the powerful ability to spot industry-leading opportunities. When everyone pledges to illuminate each other's blind spots, they stitch together a domination machine that no dishonest organization can hope to match.

The debate on direct feedback, it should be honestly noted, is far from won. Researchers have done extensive studies on the value of positive vs. negative feedback, with many scholars finding that enforcing positive feedback is far more helpful psychologically (i.e., to our big-ass egos) than accosting someone with negative feedback, which invokes their fight-or-flight response. My assessment is this: positive reinforcement seems like a wonderful tool for teams that you, as a leader, need to keep happy, open, and satisfied if they are to pass you the insights you need. But let's not kid ourselves: the reason positive reinforcement works is *because* of our delicate egos. We should at least agree that directness is more efficient, if nothing else, and perhaps especially so for executives whose key decisions can make or break an organization's future. I'd like to think that in the name of efficiency, I'd rather be told what I'm doing wrong as soon as possible so I can fix it, just as I experienced in my figure skating days (where I never seemed to do anything right, come to think of it)—though I suppose I'd have to ask those around me if I'm as appreciative of direct feedback as I think I am, or if I am, in fact, closed-minded AF. Search for self-awareness notwithstanding, for me and for Dalio, it's a matter of time; there's nothing faster than going directly to the issue and solving it. Perhaps it's the entrepreneur in us, since we naturally play to win instead of playing to not lose. But if you want to be a true leader in business, leading is winning. Otherwise, what's the point?

Of course, that's my opinion, right? You get to define your own leadership style however you want. Your success will ultimately stem from deeply understanding yourself; you don't want to end up in Dalio's culture if confronting your weaknesses scares you to death. Some people love knowing about their weaknesses and exploring the root causes of mistakes, while others will never examine their weaknesses and risk upending everything they've believed about themselves since the beginning of time. That's why, as Dalio explained, "we end up with a lot of people who leave quickly and a lot of people who wouldn't want to work anywhere else."[16] Those who stay inherit the ability to question everything and everyone—even the big boss himself—to ensure that every possible perspective is stated and explored. The cultural pursuit of objective truth makes for a continuous testing ground for weeding out the dishonest and rewarding the truthful (and the thick-skinned). When I asked Dalio if he's done a good job at assembling a team of people in his organization who are all fundamentally honest, he replied, "Every company has some dishonest people; however, it's much more difficult to be dishonest at Bridgewater than it is at most companies, because of the ways we have radical truthfulness and radical transparency."

> Positive reinforcement seems like a wonderful tool for teams that you, as a leader, need to keep happy, open, and satisfied if they are to pass you the insights you need. But let's not kid ourselves: the reason positive reinforcement works is *because* of our delicate egos. We should at least agree that directness is more efficient, if nothing else.

Thinking that you're truthful and transparent is one thing. And *hearing* the truth from your peers—that your work this month sucks—is one thing. But being able to use that brutal feedback as a constructive exercise in self-improvement (without it crushing your soul) is something else entirely. If you can stomach it, though, that feedback represents a massive opportunity for more effective communication, productivity, innovation, and profits. Not to mention, you get to discover the real you—one of the most wonderful gifts we can receive, in my humble opinion.

The upside of the 25 percent of Bridgewater employees consistently leaving after eighteen months is that those who remain are absolutely committed to radical truth and radical transparency. As another former (but apparently content) employee wrote:

> It was hard for me at first to adjust; but, in my opinion, every company should be run the same as Bridgewater. The culture was simple if you understood what the goals were. Just getting to the best information possible, the best possible outcome, the best results require ULTIMATE truth, transparency, and not letting your emotions get in the way of constructive criticism. There is more to it than that, but there was a set of 200+ principles that employees are to understand and try and live (or at least work) by those standards. These principles make sense. For example, principle #9, *Trust in truth:* While truth, itself, may sometimes be scary (like you are bad at something), it won't change reality and it will allow you to deal with it better. It always leads to the best outcome. This may seem a simple, obvious concept, but it's not in reality. People who are one way on the inside and believe that they need to be another way outside to please others become conflicted and often lose touch with what they really think and feel. It's difficult for them to be happy and almost impossible for them to be at their best. Thinking solely about what's accurate, instead of how it is perceived, helps [employees] be more straightforward and focused on important things.[17]

So what are the important things in your personal and professional life? If Dalio's right, then all you have to do to achieve your best results is embrace honesty.

Simple, obvious, honesty.

——— QUESTIONS FOR HONEST REFLECTION ———

1. Do you have an objective list of ways your organization could improve? How might you begin to share those opportunities and begin to illuminate your organization's blind spots?

2. How can you solicit feedback from your colleagues to ensure that you're continually improving your own leadership abilities?

3. In what ways might dishonesty be getting in the way of achieving your top priorities—personally and professionally—and how can you take deliberate action to think and act more honestly?

CHAPTER 10

Innovation: Saying No to the Status Quo

An Unlikely Story about Moral Mortgages

Rocket Mortgage FAQ:
Q: Is Rocket Mortgage easy to use?
A: Yes.

Q: Can I really just push a button and get one?
A: No.

Q: Then why is it your slogan?
A: "Push multiple buttons" doesn't sound as good.

So went one of the television ads for Rocket Mortgage—arguably the most important and necessary technological advancement the mortgage industry has seen since . . . well, ever.

For those of you who don't own a television, or who have lived under a rock, or who have lived under a rock without a television,

143

Rocket Mortgage is an app-based mortgage application process backed by Quicken Loans, which as of the time of this writing is the largest mortgage lender in the United States.

When I first saw Rocket Mortgage debut its "Push Button, Get Mortgage" simplicity, the millennial in me celebrated. The truth is, in the technologically advanced world of the twenty-first century, there is simply no excuse for going through the traditional, unbearably arcane and tree-killing process of getting a mortgage. I feel about mortgages the same way I feel about voting: if the phone knows who we are, can take and verify all our personal information, and can communicate effortlessly and at lightning speed with whatever zeros and ones it needs to produce an outcome, then why in the world wouldn't we use this wondrous technology to solve these inefficient systems? The trouble is, as I like to warn clients and teammates alike, *Don't bring logic to a gun-fight*, because that's an easy way to get yourself killed.

But, unwilling to cling to the status quo, Quicken Loans somehow pushed through the industry's old-school ways and completely transformed the way we get a mortgage. In the process of overtaking Wells Fargo as the number-one mortgage lender in the country, Quicken credits its Rocket Mortgage product for helping it claim the throne, given that 98 percent of the company's mortgage volume accesses the Rocket Mortgage platform during some or all stages of the mortgage process.[1]

Naturally, I wondered how the privately owned Quicken Loans— battling against mighty, publicly traded, mortgage-providing giants like Bank of America, Wells Fargo, Chase, Citi, and U.S. Bank—was able to innovate and dominate its industry. I suspected, and indeed hoped, that Quicken Loans might help me prove the connection between organizational honesty and industry-dominating innovation; however, I never expected to find how deep that connection proved to be once I dove into the inner workings of the Detroit-based enterprise.

Unsurprisingly, I found, in a nutshell, that the late Peter Drucker must have been talking about Quicken Loans when he remarked, "Culture eats strategy for breakfast." One doesn't have to look very long or hard inside the Quicken Loans organization to see the thick, principled manner of its corporate culture, which champions the art of innovation in every layer of its operations and decision-making.

Sound familiar?

WHAT MAKES A CULTURE OF INNOVATION?

As Quicken itself admits, "There is no secret sauce," but there are ingredients. Quicken calls its ingredients "ISMs," which are "ideals we live by . . . more to do with who we are than what we do."[2] The ISMs are promises—to each other, to clients, and to the communities in which Quicken operates:

1. *Always raising our level of awareness.*

   As Yogi Berra said, "You can see a lot just by looking." Keep your head up. Look. Be curious. Notice what is actually happening around you. Really notice. Listen. Listen to your clients. In fact, listen to everyone. Everything starts with awareness. Being alert. Being awake. Tuning in to the frequency. It's a perpetual choice to both stay aware and raise your level of awareness. Our future, growth, innovation, and success start with the thousands of eyeballs of our team members. That's you.

2. *The inches we need are everywhere around us.*

   If a company does one big thing better than their competition, it becomes fairly easy for their competition to level the playing field: they can just imitate that one thing. But if a company does thousands of little things better than anyone else, they become nearly impossible to imitate. We call those thousands of little things "inches." We'd never be able to foresee all the things that should be noticed or improved. Instead, we drive a culture that motivates our team members to find the inches we need all around us. We are all empowered to find the opportunities to make an impact everywhere; one inch at a time, these inches all add up to greatness.

3. *Responding with a sense of urgency is the ante to play.*

Urgency is your inner compulsion and drive to get things done in a timely yet thoughtful manner. On this team, we return all phone calls and emails the same day. We're on the lunatic fringe. We're obsessed with answering inquiries ASAP. Not just to clients and partners, but to each other! There's no other way, and no other option. Urgency motivates us to ensure we communicate all news fast, both good and bad. We take care of things, especially our clients . . . NOW!

4. *Every client. Every time. No exceptions. No excuses.*

Clients don't care how much you know until they know how much you care. Could it be any clearer? A great company is built one client at a time. If you AMAZE every client every chance you get, then they are satisfied and so are you. There's no feeling good around here because 90 percent of our clients were satisfied. Every client means 100 percent of our clients, and not some of the time. Amaze them EVERY TIME. No exceptions. No excuses!

5. *Obsessed with finding a better way.*

Our never-ending mission is to find a better way for every process and everything we touch. If it's good, let's make it great. If it's great, let's take it to an even higher level. Don't settle for less. In fact, don't settle at all. Finding a better way is not something we do on the side or when we get the time. Rather, it's a key priority for every one of our team members. It's our passion . . . our way of living . . . our obsession. We don't just work IN our business—we work ON our business.

6. *Ignore the noise.*

We've found it's not always skill and long hours that lead to greatness. It's also the ability to ignore the noise. Noise could be from naysayers, something going wrong, sun in your eyes, ball took a bad bounce, dog ate your homework, someone cut you off on the way to work, etc. A lot of things that seem serious at first glance turn out to be noise. Will you allow it to keep you from winning? The noise may fluctuate in volume, but your determination to press on in spite of it (ignore it!) will make all the difference to you and our Family of Companies. There's not a human on the planet who does not experience noise. The winners have developed an ability to ignore it and press on.

7. *It's not about WHO is right; it's about WHAT is right.*

There is no place at our company for typical corporate arrogance. WHO is right (or WHO is wrong) is irrelevant and inconsequential to WHAT is the right decision or best outcome for the issue at hand. All decisions should be made with a single motivation: the right or best decision for our clients, team members and company. Think about how much a company compromises itself by basing decisions on WHO is in favor or against something instead of WHAT is the best and right decision. The WHAT trumps the WHO in our shop.

8. *We are the they.*

There is no "they." We are the "they." Just open minds and an open culture rooted in trust. The leaders within the Rock Family of Companies trust you to make decisions, and, if you make an honest mistake, it's OK! We trust you will learn from your mistakes. It's a foreign concept to most organizations, but for us, it's crystal clear.

9. *You have to take the roast out of the oven.*

A wise man once said, "Taking longer to make a decision doesn't increase your chances of making a better one." Perfection is not the goal when it's time to make a decision. Focus instead on constant improvement and innovation. Overanalyzing can kill an idea and make you miss an opportunity. Don't fear failure. If our environment did not tolerate failure, then innovation would die, creativity would die, and eventually, so would our business.

When there's a decision to be made, there are three possible outcomes:

- You make the right one—Great!
- You make the wrong one—Hopefully you learn something valuable from it.
- You make no decision—You haven't made the right one, and you haven't learned a thing.

Always make new mistakes. Make decisions. And, when you believe that roast is pretty much done, pull it out of the oven.

10. *You'll see it when you believe it.*

Nothing significant in this world has ever happened without someone believing in it first. It's only the passive observers of life who say "I'll believe it when I see it." We take the opposite approach, and lead with our hearts and minds. We know the truth: If we truly believe in something, we can—and will—affect the outcome. If we believe in ourselves first, we dramatically increase our odds of success. If we believe it can happen, then it will.

11. *We'll figure it out.*

We don't need to have all the answers before we take on a project or launch a new and innovative idea. We have faith that when it comes to some of the details, we'll figure it out along the way. If we wait to cross every "t" and dot every "i" before proceeding with an idea, concept, or improvement, then we wouldn't make much progress at all. It's our belief in each other and ourselves that gives us the confidence to find new solutions to keep us moving forward. Sometimes a game-changing project will be held up because of a small detail that doesn't matter. Should we solve for the exception and delay the launch of a project that could otherwise make a huge impact? No! Instead, we take the roast out of the oven and figure out the exception as we go. That's how we roll. We know that building something new or creating something special is messy, and that greatness doesn't always come in nice, tidy packages. This is an advantage, not a hindrance. As long as we continue to love the idea and trust the process, then we truly believe we'll figure it out.

12. *A penny saved is a penny.*

Your uncle's advice, "A penny saved is a penny earned," is the worst financial advice in history. Choose to value your time. Invest it chasing pennies, and you will find pennies— and pennies never add up. Invest it in ideas, improving your skills, innovation, developing your talent, design, marketing, and technology, and your return will be more than just pennies. Stop wasting your time with the silly pursuit of pennies. Instead, invest your valuable time creating dollars. The choice is yours.

13. *Numbers and money follow; they do not lead.*

Money and numbers are a measurement of actions. They don't have value in themselves. They are neither the ends nor the means. Ironically, the vast majority of those who chase money will never end up with much of it. Instead, chase the great ideas. Chase the design, engineering and development of the product. Those who are motivated by building, improving and developing unique ideas and knowledge are the ones who acquire wealth.

This also applies to individuals. Invest in developing your skills, knowledge, and creativity. Become an expert. Pursue your vision with uncompromising passion, and become the best. Numbers and money follow successful accomplishment. Become great at something or build something great. Chasing numbers and money first will leave you chasing your tail.

14. *We eat our own dog food.*

Tying the threads and leveraging ideas and connections within our Family of Companies is what it's all about—that's what we mean when we say "eating our own dog food." The basis of all wealth is found in the strength of relationships. Create them. Seek them out. Build upon them. Be loyal to them. If your level of awareness is high, you will find an endless amount of "dog food" around you. The more you give to these relationships, the more you will get from them. So start giving—now.

15. *Simplicity is genius.*

Sometimes the "intellects" of the world believe that if it's too simple, it can't be good. Nothing could be further from the truth. Simplifying things in this fast-moving, complicated world isn't just good—it's GREAT. Simple design. Simple process. Simple communication. When we communicate with others, we cannot assume they know exactly what we know. You are you, and they are them. We must start at chapter one, not chapter five. Simplicity doesn't just clarify; it creates wealth in the process. Because if there is anything in this world that everyone can agree upon (outside of the "intellects," of course), it's that simplicity makes things better for everybody. That's why simple is something we strive for in everything we do. All day. Every day. It's as simple as that.

16. *Innovation is rewarded. Execution is worshipped.*

Ideas are fundamental to who we are. We encourage them. We love them. But ideas alone don't mean much. It takes both ideas AND execution to make things happen. Great ideas get you to the fifty-yard line; outstanding execution gets you into the end zone.

17. *Do the right thing.*

The high road is not a shortcut. Stick to the highest standard of integrity, without compromise. Character is what you do when no one is looking over your shoulder! Doing the wrong thing is never worth it. How can you go wrong doing the right thing? Remember, eventually three things always come out: the sun, the moon, and the truth.

18. *Every second counts.*

You will always invest your time somewhere doing something. As long as you are alive, it's not a choice whether you invest your time or not; the only choice is what you will do with it.

Time, not money, is the most valuable commodity of all. Time can never be replaced. Never trade significant amounts of time for small sums of money. How will you invest the 31,536,000 seconds you are gifted each year? Choose wisely.

19. *Yes before no.*

It's critically important that we live the culture of YES. This does not mean that every single idea, question, suggestion, or recommendation will ultimately be met with a big thumbs-up. It means that we respond to all curiosity with the mindset of YES first. Our bias is to the YES side of life. This is in stark contrast to the too common approach of an automatic NO to any expression of an inquiring mind. Saying NO is easier, but the status quo is not our favorite state. We live in the land of growth, possibilities, ideas, innovation, positive impact, and results. The only path to that place is through openness to the unknown. So YES before NO, and NO only if we have done the work and exhausted all the potential of YES first. In other words, KNOW before NO.

When I first investigated Quicken, I came armed with the question, *How did Quicken Loans ever come up with Rocket Mortgage?* The answer: with everything Quicken believes in, there is no universe in which it could have failed to develop a new mortgage technology and fallen behind its competitors, competitors that you and I both know don't have belief systems anywhere close to Quicken's. What strikes me are the little things: acting with a sense of urgency, saying yes before no, putting emphasis on *what* is right over *who* is right.

Those last two are particular afflictions that scar the business world. The challenge is clear, the tactics are doable, yet the organization just can't *move*. Why? The dictator-in-charge has created a culture of saying no, relishing in the status quo, and controlling every decision with their own personal biases instead of honestly assessing the objective merit of new ideas and acting with the urgency that innovation requires.

CREATING AN ENVIRONMENT WHERE INNOVATION THRIVES

With Quicken's remarkable values in hand, I reached out to Jay Farner, the CEO of Quicken Loans, who's so proud of his culture that he was more than happy to share his insights about it so others could learn.

The ISMs started as a loose set of guidelines that came out of the values of Quicken's founder, Dan Gilbert. As Farner said over the phone en route from one busy engagement to the next, eventually "we had to take the time, if this is the core of who we are, to package them up in a way people can understand them, and relate to them, and make them comfortable, so people knew that honoring these guidelines was something we really believed in. If you slap something up on a one-pager and don't give it time and attention, people won't see that it's something you believe in." Farner explained that early on, Gilbert realized "that most companies focus on *what they do*, and you can't do anything good if you don't first focus on *who you are*." When you're confident about who you are, that identity gives employees a framework to operate in, just like The Ritz's Waterfall Culture. "We take our team through training sessions and talk about who we are. That gives them a lens to make good decisions," Farner explained, "and they run all decisions through that lens."

> Innovation—the art of looking ahead to the future and developing products, services, and systems that will help your organization succeed over the long term— is a character trait, not a pursuit.

While some popular thinking recommends starting with *why*, the leaders in this book and I agree that starting with *who* makes a lot more sense. Innovation—the art of looking ahead to the future and developing products, services, and systems that will help your organization succeed over the long term—is a character trait, not a pursuit. Innovative leaders create innovative outcomes, and becoming an innovative leader is not only possible but *formulaic*, as long as you're willing to start with honestly assessing who you are, documenting what you believe in, and using that basis of *identity* as a starting place for innovation. I mean, think about it: if you don't know *who* you are, how the hell are you supposed to know *why* you're doing what you're doing?

In the aptly titled "It's Who We Are—Not What We Do: Ideas Are Supported by Belief" video on YouTube,[3] one Quicken employee recounts how she presented ideas to her boss, only to be abruptly cut off. "Go do it, and tell me about it later," she recalls her boss saying. I'd estimate that most bosses would indeed cut off their direct reports' ideas—usually in order to squash them, not to *encourage* their development without *proper sign-offs* (whatever that means). With a culture of people who all deeply understand who they are individually and who they are organizationally, Quicken's managers feel confident that their people will make sound choices that will lead to successful outcomes—if not this time, then at some inevitable point in the near future.

Quicken's founder started with only twelve ISMs in 1985 when the company was founded; they expanded and evolved over time. Farner said ISMs get formally changed through a diligent process and are only added when an idea is already bubbling up through the ranks as a modus operandi. "If we see that trend continue over a significant period of time, we'll add an ISM," Farner noted, "and sometimes we'll take an ISM away if we think it's not as relevant, or even if it's so ingrained in our culture that it's not going anywhere, so we can remove it safely."

> The slow, methodical process of building a culture of innovation takes patience, which is why Quicken depends on both a formal and informal process to keep its culture of innovation strong.

The slow, methodical process of building a culture of innovation takes patience, which is why Quicken depends on both a formal and informal process to keep its culture of innovation strong. Formally,

Farner explained, his Z Team—named after one of Quicken's original leaders, who sadly passed away from cancer—is his executive leadership team, which actively discusses culture at every single meeting. They talk about how it's going, if there are any opportunities for improvement, and what, if anything, has been bubbling to the surface from the organization at large.

But perhaps even more importantly, Quicken's people—the emphatic backbone of the company—are all informally responsible for maintaining the cultural code, day in and day out. If trends arise, it is everyone's responsibility to flag those trends and ask about modifying, adding, or deleting ISMs accordingly. And like most entrepreneur-led organizations, those ISM decisions are juried by the guardian of the ISMs, founder Dan Gilbert, who has a firm belief that if Quicken has great people who know who they are—as individuals and as an organization—success will take care of itself.

DESIGNING THE FUTURE REQUIRES LONG-TERM THINKING

As Sprint's Dan Hesse noted, quarterly constraints can put a damper on such long-term thinking, since creating a thoroughbred culture full of the right people takes time, energy, and a long-term mind-set. That's why it may not surprise you to learn that Quicken Loans is a privately held organization that doesn't have to report to Wall Street. To date, Farner has been with Quicken for almost a quarter century, and Dan Gilbert has been with the firm since its founding in 1985. "We're not thinking about what happens next quarter," Farner admitted, "we're thinking about what happens three to five years from now, because our mission is to make an environment in which people can grow and communities are positively impacted . . . that creates a situation where we're always pushing for what's next." If you want to innovate and lead your industry, the idea of innovation must permeate your culture and create the same sense of urgency that Quicken deliberately highlights in its ISMs. "I won't call it fear," Farner continued, "but I will say there's an entrepreneurial spirit that creates the feeling that if we're not creating something new, we're not doing our job."

Just as Dan Hesse and Warren Buffett believe, the executive team at Quicken is all about taking the long-term view, which is a pursuit that echoes within every "honest" leader out there who has managed to remove all traces of corporate bullshit and replace it with simple ideas like taking care of people, letting them pursue innovation, and creating an environment to foster both. To Farner, that means forgoing duct-tape solutions and opting to always play the role of disruptor. "Whenever there's a problem or opportunity presented," he explained, "the question we ask is, *How do we change that completely? How do we eliminate that?* It's never about how we adjust the process slightly" to maintain the status quo.

> "I won't call it fear, but I will say there's an entrepreneurial spirit that creates the feeling that if we're not creating something new, we're not doing our job."—Jay Farner, CEO, Quicken Loans

This notion of rejecting the norm and establishing new protocols is critical to a company's growth. It's the art of the mythological phoenix: living purposefully to destroy and re-create in a never-ending cycle of *how do we become better?* I should know—this catalytic mind-set is how we launched our newest company, a technology platform, out of our communications agency. For years our vision was to disrupt the marketing industry, but we never stopped to ask ourselves how we could possibly accomplish that vision by *being a traditional agency.* Once we opened up our blind spot, we realized that we needed to completely change the way we did things if we truly wanted to change the way things are done. Pairing that internal insight with the external insights of listening to what customers wanted, we developed the ingredients to innovate. Mind you, innovating meant deliberately trying to put our existing platform business right out of business. But if we don't face the truth, someone else will do it for us, right? And I won't lie: admitting those truths staring us right in the face was hard. But once we accepted it, knowing what to do with the truth was relatively easy.

THE FLAWED DIAMOND AND THE EXECUTIVE MIRROR: ALLOWING INNOVATION TO SHINE THROUGH

Lest you think Quicken fosters a free-for-all every day where employees run amok, worry not. The company has a critical, guiding question for its innovative decisions: What's our superpower? If Quicken doesn't have a real advantage it can use to make a particular idea work—a superpower for that situation—then it will often forgo an idea because the team (honestly) assesses that other companies can and will execute better than Quicken will. In a company where innovation is rewarded and execution is worshipped, innovation often hinges on this litmus test of whether Quicken believes it can execute or not. Because, take note, it *will* execute when the idea is right.

That's not to give leaders everywhere an excuse to kill the ideas of their people; in fact, the companies I've seen that innovate and dominate hold beliefs almost identical to Quicken's "yes before no" and "it's not about *who* is right, it's about *what* is right." Take, for instance, the cultural code of entrepreneurial banker Vernon Hill, founder of Commerce Bank. In his world, it only takes one person to make a "yes" decision, but two people to say "no." Committed to doing what is right, Hill thought of bank branches as retail stores and placed a premium on customers' needs. While other banks were pushing customers to the banks' "less costly" online service options, Hill did the opposite, giving customers a phenomenal in-store customer experience with longer banking hours, friendly staff, and the full suite of services in-store. He even welcomed dogs into his banks, because, duh, lots of people own a dog and often take Rover along to run bank errands. With such a huge emphasis on giving customers what they wanted (instead of what was cheap and easy), Hill grew Commerce Bank from one branch to 470 between 1973 and 2008, delivering investors a staggering 23 percent compound annual return for three decades. Being honest about what your customers want—and thus telling them "yes" instead of "no"—makes a difference.

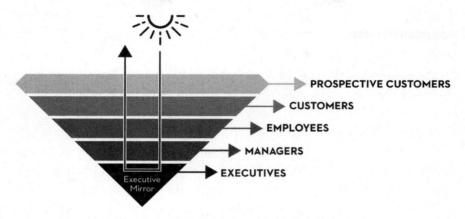

The Flawed Diamond and Executive Mirror

Gilbert, Farner, and Hill all recognize that their roles aren't to innovate, per se, but to create innovative cultures that in turn create innovative products that handily dominate industries. To help illustrate why this style of management produces industry-leading results, consider a framework I call the *Flawed Diamond*, as shown in the Flawed Diamond figure.

The idea is simple and relates directly to the Inverse Triangle. The reason a diamond sparkles so brilliantly is that light passes into the diamond at the top, reflects and refracts off the shape of the stone, and then returns out through the top of the diamond, having been split into its array of colors just like a prism. When the diamond is properly shaped and—most importantly—doesn't have any flaws in it, the diamond shines brilliantly in a dazzling rainbow of color.

As we saw with the Inverse Triangle, the flow of information and communication has forever changed. When we look at the new flow of information, it looks an awful lot like a diamond: information and insights pass from the top, in this case starting with the customers. They filter through employees, middle managers, and finally to executives. Then it's up to executives to decide what to do with the information.

The executive role, in this equation, has fundamentally different responsibilities than before. Whereas before an executive had a responsibility to create information and insights and *push it down* through the organization, now the executive has a responsibility to *absorb* and *reflect* that information so it can become a weaponized asset to the organization, its people, and its mission. Essentially, just like a good diamond has no flaws to interrupt the reflecting light, effective executives today must be honest with themselves, get out of the way of their people, and eliminate any barriers to this flow of information, time, energy, ideas, and innovation within the organization.

I call the new executive role the *Executive Mirror*, which describes how executives today do well when they act like a filtering mirror—taking in information and insights, deciding which pursuits accurately reflect their culture and mission, and then allowing that "light" to pass back *up* through the ranks—to middle managers, back to employees, and finally back to customers in the form of innovative new products and services.

Notice I say, "which pursuits accurately reflect their culture and mission," not "which pursuits the leader *feels* or *thinks* is the right one." Most organizational leaders embrace the latter, while the leaders at Quicken Loans, who say yes before no and allow their employees to run with ideas, choose to act as filtering mirrors to their people, ensuring that the ISMs are upheld and the mission is being appropriately pursued.

> In essence, Buffett gives his CEOs a code to follow, leeway to innovate just as Quicken gives to its employees, and the encouragement to act like owners empowered to take bold action for the long term.

Industry-beating investor Warren Buffett unsurprisingly uses the very same framework in his companies. "At Berkshire," Buffett said in his 1998 shareholder letter, "we feel that telling outstanding CEOs, such as Tony [Nicely of GEICO], how to run their companies would be the height of foolishness."[4] Instead, Buffett hires wonderful CEOs to do their jobs and knows that his own role is to let them run unconstrained, even though Buffett's technically their boss. Instead, he focuses on making those CEOs (who are essentially Buffett's employees) as effective as possible by eliminating "all of the ritualistic and nonproductive activities that normally go with the job of CEO," like reporting quarterly guidance. He then gives each CEO "a simple mission: Just run your business as if: (1) you own 100 percent of it; (2) it is the only asset in the world that you and your family have or will ever have; and (3) you can't sell or merge it for at least a century." In essence, Buffett gives his CEOs a code to follow, leeway to innovate just as Quicken gives to its employees, and the encouragement to act like owners empowered to take bold action for the long term. Are you picking up a theme here? If you ask me, anything else is just plain dishonest—about how the business world really works, about what your others are really feeling, and about your own strengths and weaknesses as a leader.

"In this environment of freedom," Buffett wrote proudly, "both Tony and his company can convert their almost limitless potential into matching achievements."

INNOVATION IS AN ACT OF OMISSION

Find the right people, put them in positions to succeed, and then get out of their way. Innovation isn't a thing your organization does; it's what naturally occurs when roadblocks vanish so the right ideas can emerge, just like that bright-ass diamond. It all sounds so simple, yet few organizations allow for this sort of flow. Instead, egomaniacal managers put up giant roadblocks while asserting their whims and staking their territorial boundaries. The fact that Berkshire Hathaway follows our more honest philosophy speaks volumes to its effects; the fact that Quicken is *set up* like a Flawed Diamond (sans flaws) clearly shows that it was only a matter of time before Quicken created Rocket Mortgage. When companies have forward-thinking, honest cultures, innovation and domination are *inevitable* . . . as not only Quicken Loans but also Domino's Pizza, The Ritz-Carlton, and Bridgewater Associates attest.

"In other cultures," Farner told me, "people may be nervous to share ideas that may be disruptive or different; here, you're probably more at risk bringing an idea to the table that's only a slight adjustment, and you're safer bringing ideas to the table that are disruptive." And in true Flawed Diamond style, Quicken brings thousands of interns into their culture every year so that, in Farner's words, "we can stay up on what matters to them . . . and let them ask questions like, "Why does it have to be so hard to get a mortgage? Why can't I just get it right now?"

In fact, those last two questions are exactly where "Push Button, Get Mortgage" came from. It came from Quicken's community of "intrapreneurs," who were keen to ask "dumb" questions and create the next level of thinking that Quicken needed to keep pushing boundaries. Quicken puts not only its employee time but also its money where its mouth is, routinely launching new companies led by employees who come up with great ideas. Farner's message to innovators is simple: "If you bring your great idea, you get the platform from Quicken to go build that idea. Instead of people having to go build a business on their own, come leverage the strength of our platform and come build it here!" Farner knows that if he can get his people thinking entrepreneurially all the time, Quicken will get first dibs on any innovative ideas that have the potential to move Quicken forward into the future.

> Farner knows that if he can get his people thinking entrepreneurially all the time, Quicken will get first dibs on any innovative ideas that have the potential to move Quicken forward into the future.

Not enough can be said about the inverse relationship between innovation and roadblocks. Every single management layer of every organization has a responsibility to be a gatekeeper; unfortunately, most take that responsibility as a license to kill instead of a license to empower. The ideas are there—right there in front of every manager. But the decision every gatekeeper makes about which ideas live and which ideas die directly relates to the structure and culture of the organization. Fortunately, implementing a better structure can eventually transform a risk-averse culture. Any organization can gain unprecedented competitive advantages by simply having a consistent, dedicated forum for tossing around new ideas. Such a forum needs to incorporate multiple management layers so that no one person gets to nix an idea because of politics, bias, risk aversion, or even personal opinion. When one gatekeeper can't block industry-dominating insights, the entire organization wins. Not to mention, employees will rejoice knowing that their direct manager can't squash their vision, steal it, or otherwise prevent well-meaning insights from benefitting the greater good.

I asked Farner what leaders, managers, and employees in organizations large and small can do to help grease the wheels of innovation within their own industries. "I have these conversations all the time," he admitted, "because we're always making changes in our organization and we're always dealing with challenges. Nothing is ever perfect, so acknowledging that reality and embracing the fact that every day you wake up you get to make a difference is the starting point. Don't try to boil the ocean, just start. Start making a cultural revolution within your small team and start there."

> "To create, sometimes you have to have patience and you've got to be committed to a longer vision, and that can be really challenging for leaders."
> —Jay Farner

In all the industries and clients I've worked with, what I've never found, ever, is a lack of ideas. But *oh!* have I found roadblocks preventing the execution of those ideas. Everyone wants to innovate, but few want to adopt the experimentation and patience that innovation requires. "To create, sometimes you have to have patience and you've got to be committed to a longer vision, and that can be really challenging for leaders," Farner asserted. "They're forced to hit such immediate results, while they're not able to invest in long-term strategies and transformational goals, and it's unfortunate." He trailed off, "Maybe that's the world we're living in today."

But it's not the world Farner and Quicken Loans are living in. May the mortgage world be on notice: if you're unable to get honest about what it takes to develop a truly innovative organization, Quicken Loans is coming for you. And there's no need to guess how they'll do battle.

They're sending rockets.

———— QUESTIONS FOR HONEST REFLECTION ————

1. Look again at Quicken Loan's ISMs. As you read each one, ask yourself, How do their beliefs compare with mine, and compare with those of my organization? Which set of beliefs—Quicken's or mine—is more honest?

2. How can you start small, within one team or department, with a program to encourage new ideas and execute on them?

3. What roadblocks might be getting in the way of innovation at your organization? How might *you* be a roadblock to new ideas, and what can you do to make sure you're not accidentally getting in the way?

CHAPTER 11

Leadership: The Underappreciated Quality of Supreme Ignorance

And How Being a Big Dummy Can Help You Outsmart Your Competition

could barely hear the blunted notes of a microphone in the distance, paired with the every-so-often flash of light that would whip through the hallway in some shade of theatrical glow. It was surprisingly quiet in the guts of a New York City theater near Broadway—remarkable, given the hustle onstage just one flight up and the bustle of the city beyond.

It was Advertising Week New York, and I had been waiting for a good half hour before I heard a rumbling down the hall. Within seconds, a parade of people streamed in—makeup artist, stylist, assistant, event personnel, and more. Chief among them, Bethenny Frankel.

She barely paused to say hello to the writer in the corner who was there to do a story for his online column in *Inc.*, but I confidently strode forward and introduced myself. She lingered just long enough for an affirming handshake and a hurried smile before she was promptly whisked to a chair in front of a wall of mirrors, where her team descended on her to conduct the transition from on-the-road Bethenny to onstage Bethenny.

She had recently come off the set of *Shark Tank*, an unlikely place for someone who made a name for herself on reality television as a Real Housewife of New York. And yet, as she shared the ups and downs of her career with me, it became clear that her place among today's best business gurus was almost predestined from the start, and for the most honest of reasons; in fact, Bethenny is known for her brutal honesty and unapologetic authenticity, on air and off. I'm wholly confident that those characteristics were highly valuable to reality television producers hungry for conflict. But those traits in and of themselves weren't what struck me most about Bethenny, nor can they fully describe how a person with no prior business experience could start the Skinnygirl Cocktails brand, grow it, and exit for a reported $100 million, ending up on the cover of *Forbes* magazine.

In fact, Bethenny was quite honest with me that few of her career moves were strategic, or even planned at all. Instead, she seemed to rely on an effective cocktail of gut instinct, belief in self, and perseverance.[1] Oh, and one other inescapable truth she holds most dear, which I sum up thusly: *Ignorance is power; knowledge is bliss.*

Bethenny lives by one simple rule: if you don't know what something means, ask—immediately. "I'm just really honest about those things," she admitted freely and without any glint of ego. "When I don't know something, I don't pretend."

Sure enough, twenty minutes after we spoke, she went onstage near Times Square and blatantly interrupted one of her peers—disrupting the entire rhythm of the panel—to grill him about a marketing term she didn't know. Hers is a humble and simple method that has allowed her to capitalize on her strengths while minimizing her gaps in knowledge.

THE NO. 1 TRAIT OF TODAY'S MOST SUCCESSFUL LEADERS: KNOWING NOTHING

Coincidentally, hers is the same honest leadership trait that we've seen in many of the other leaders written about here. "Whatever success I've had in life," Ray Dalio wrote on the first page of *Principles*, "has had more to do with my knowing how to deal with my *not* knowing than anything I know."[2] Perhaps the self-admission of befuddlement is highly correlated with financial gains. To wit, I often think of Nate Silver's quote in *The Signal and the Noise*: "One of the pervasive risks that we face in the information age is that, even if the amount of knowledge in the world is increasing, the gap between what we know and what we think we know may be widening."[3]

Do me a favor and read that one twice, 'cuz that's some eye-poppin' truth right there.

Even Russell Weiner of Domino's Pizza aptly noted, "Too many people think, 'I'm right and my CEO's opinion is wrong.' You're each dealing with facts and forming different opinions." And that's just it: if we can't parse opinion from fact and agree on objective reality, we can't possibly transform into the evolved, innovative, industry-dominating leaders we know we can be.

> If we can't parse opinion from fact and agree on objective reality, we can't possibly transform into the evolved, innovative, industry-dominating leaders we know we can be.

As I shamefully recounted earlier, whereas I used to assume that a lack of *intellectual processing power* was the culprit behind many a leader's shortcomings, I now posit it was simply a lack of honesty. More accurately, it was the extension of a lack of honesty, which, when it comes to leadership, is better described as a lack of *self-awareness*. I've seen it in clients large and small, rearing its head whenever we help them confront an uncomfortable truth about their customers, their teams, their products, or their business models. One of the best (or worst) examples was one former client who looked at a report we pulled from Google Analytics and said the results were so inconsistent with what he "knew" to be true that we must have forged them! Trust me, if I had that much power with Google, I'd likely have a very different (and higher-paying) job.

There's plenty of living proof that dishonest people can, and do, succeed in building profitable businesses. However, I implore you to consider that it takes something more—much more—to become an industry *dominator*, a magnet for *innovation*, a respected *leader*. That difference is the honest art of *self-awareness*, otherwise known as being brutally honest with yourself.

Many don't realize that Warren Buffett's self-proclaimed greatest mistake was the acquisition of Berkshire Hathaway itself—the textile operation he purchased in 1965 that would serve as the bedrock of his empire. Buffett considers it a misstep because he clung to the downward-spiraling textile industry, which showed inexorable signs of never returning to its former glory, despite knowing the objective truth. "A recent *Business Week* article stated that 250 textile mills have closed since 1980," Buffett wrote in his shareholder letter in 1985. "Their owners were not privy to any information that was unknown to me; they simply processed it more objectively. I ignored Comte's advice— 'the intellect should be the servant of the heart, but not its slave'—and believed what I preferred to believe."[4]

Of all the advice I give my coaching clients, my favorite is this quote (my own, of course) about leading a business: *entrepreneurship is 10 percent about business, 100 percent about people, and 1,000 percent about the self.*

No, I wasn't a math major, but I assure you the math in that quote checks out. That's why many leadership organizations like the Entrepreneurs' Organization and Young Presidents' Organization focus on *personal* development as well as business development. No group can advance faster than its leader, which makes personal development simply essential.

THE JOHARI WINDOW: THE BEST FRAMEWORK FOR EXPLORING YOUR INNER LEADER

When I joined the Entrepreneurs' Organization and became part of its more than twelve thousand members worldwide, I learned about a framework called the Johari window. The Johari window is a simple technique that helps us become aware of our blind spots and come to know what we don't know. The psychologists Joseph Luft and Harrington Ingham created it in 1955 (combine the "Jo" in Joseph with the "Harri" in Harrington and you get "Johari"). The framework comprises four quadrants or panes that look like a window.[5]

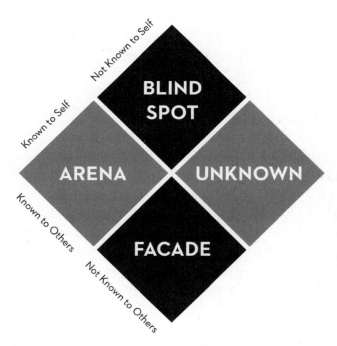

The Johari Window

The panes, or quadrants, offer four combinations that describe the state of any characteristic you possess, depending on who recognizes it.[6] The combinations are as follows:

1. *Known to others and known to self.* This quadrant, called the "arena," describes everything that is known by everyone. For instance, you might know you are dependable, and others might know you are dependable. You recognize your ability, and so do others. Most of the elements that make up our personalities fit into this quadrant.

2. *Not known to others but known to self.* This quadrant, the "facade," describes things that are essentially your secrets. For instance, others might not see that you are fearful, but you might know you are fearful. In this case, fear is a trait you don't share with others, for some reason or another. All of us have elements in this quadrant, whether we want to admit it or not—things we fear, things we're ashamed to admit or share, and so forth.

3. *Not known to others and not known to self.* This quadrant, uncreatively called the "unknown," contains elements of ourselves that we haven't yet recognized. However, no one else has recognized them, either, making them simply unknown to everyone. These are characteristics that may come out over time as we mature, for instance, but in the meantime they aren't obvious to others, and therefore aren't necessarily helpful or detrimental to us as leaders.

4. *Known to others but not known to self.* The "blind spot" is the most enlightening quadrant of the Johari window. This quadrant contains elements that others know about us but we are not yet able to see, admit to, or otherwise recognize. For instance, you might truly believe that you are not afraid, while everyone else can see that you obviously are. All of us have elements in this quadrant to some degree or another, and it is *this quadrant* that we should focus on most as leaders in a constant state of personal development.

Beware the Blind Spot

What lies in the blind spot is what can hurt you the most, so that's the quadrant we must particularly focus on if we want to improve as leaders. Characteristics that live in the blind spot prevent you from success because they aren't in alignment with the truth. For instance, if everyone widely recognizes that you are unreliable, they will most likely respect you if you admit you are unreliable and take steps to correct that characteristic. If, however, you absolutely refuse to accept that you're unreliable, that delusion creates distrust between you and everyone else, because everyone else already recognizes the truth of your situation. These types of tensions arise within leaders who are not self-aware and wreak havoc on an organization's ability to make progress. For instance, the leader who believes she is giving, when everyone else disagrees, will always resent her people for not being grateful, when in fact they are trying to help her be more fair. The leader who believes he is strategic, when everyone else knows him to be reckless, will always criticize his people for being too risk averse, when in fact they are trying to save him from making mistakes. The leader who believes she knows better, when everyone else knows she doesn't have the necessary knowledge or skill, will try to tightly control her people, when in fact her people would perform far better if they were simply allowed to do their jobs without interruption.

> The trick is to first recognize that you even have a blind spot (hint: we all do). Then you must honestly identify which of your characteristics reside in that blind spot.

These unfortunate scenarios play out all across the business world every day. All of them are fully avoidable, and they all stem from the honest truths living in our blind spots. The trick is to first recognize that you even have a blind spot (hint: we all do). Then you must honestly identify which of your characteristics reside in that blind spot. Only by first recognizing these elements can you even begin to honestly address and improve upon them, which puts you back in a trustworthy position with those around you.

Self-Reflection Forms the Foundation of Effective Leadership

Since I learned about the Johari window, I think about it all the time—often second-guessing myself on what truly lives in that quadrant and what doesn't. But although that has led to some *very* uncomfortable truths about myself, I know all that self-reflection is necessary if I want to improve my life. As Socrates said, "To know thyself is the beginning of wisdom."

> Many of the executives I've coached have ended up making drastic changes to their businesses and lives after realizing that they weren't quite aligned with their passion, or their target market, or the product or service they were selling. And once those Tetris blocks clicked in to complete the business puzzle, it was like opening up the dam on their top and bottom lines.

After years of coaching leaders, I've seen firsthand that while Socrates's assertion yields truly game-changing amounts of business value, those personal insights can get locked up in the biases to which we so inexplicably cling. Many of the executives I've coached have ended up making drastic changes to their businesses and lives after realizing they weren't quite aligned with their passion, or their target market, or the product or service they were selling. And once those Tetris blocks clicked together to complete the business puzzle, it was like opening up the dam on their top and bottom lines.

I once had a client who was struggling to open a specialized manufacturing company, but everywhere she turned she hit a roadblock. Faced with difficulty at every turn, she was about to give up when she came to me. After we dove deeply into her experiences and her passions, she told me about how much joy it brought her to improve manufacturing *processes* and help up-and-running manufacturing companies make their people and machines more efficient. When we fleshed out what a manufacturing process improvement business might look like, she realized that *that* kind of business was in complete alignment with her abilities and the customers' needs, and she opened that business the very next day.

After identifying the need for change, my clients inevitably express *relief*, because on some honest level, they knew something was out of alignment in their business or life all along and they just didn't have the right tools or enough motivation to take a bold new tack. A leader's instincts are often strong (that's how they became the leader in the first place), so you can often begin to illuminate what's lurking in your blind spot simply by stopping to listen to your own gut feelings. Just make sure you check those feelings against the perspectives of those around you so you come to an objective realization instead of a subjective one. Just as it is impossible to be your own psychologist, deep self-reflection isn't nearly as effective when done alone. For me, it took joining the Entrepreneurs' Organization, learning about the Johari window, and being placed in a Forum of other entrepreneurs to even begin to illuminate my many, many blind spots. There are eight of us entrepreneurs in my Forum, and we meet once a month to vulnerably and honestly share what's *really* going on in our lives and businesses so we can help each other see the invisible blocks that might be holding us back. The process requires a type of honesty and a form of direct feedback that's not for everyone, as Ray Dalio's culture shows.

If you want to become a better leader, you must master the art of realizing you're a no-good dirty liar. Most importantly, you must come to terms with the fact that you're mainly lying to yourself, and in a shocking number of ways. As Martin Whittaker, CEO of JUST Capital pointed out, "I think honesty with oneself is crucial . . . it starts out with an honest assessment of yourself and an awareness of one's own strengths, weaknesses, how you learn, what your natural risks and derailers are. All of that feeds into the way you act and what kinds of relationships you have with those around you . . . [and] that's what drives performance."

HOW PERSONAL BIASES AFFECT A
LEADER'S PERFORMANCE

What do a leader's blind spots and biases have to do with the performance of their business? Well, consider what I've observed over the past dozen years helping clients grow. When we created marketing campaigns for clients of our agency, the clients who were confident about their *who* and open to their *how* enjoyed results more like Domino's, because they remained open about what was honestly going on in the world around them, what their others were saying, and how they needed to adapt. When clients had little to no preconceived notions about how they wanted their marketing to look and feel, we were able to dig into their insights with fresh eyes and employ every available relevant growth strategy on their behalf. Over time, the process of open exploration yielded increasingly more knowledge, insights, and effectiveness. As a result, those open-minded clients got a fantastic return on their investments; they hired us to do a job and then gave us the freedom to do it with their partnership. Meanwhile, other clients saw a drastically reduced return on their investments because they already had all the answers to their growth challenges. They were either convinced of their superior marketing abilities, or they knew exactly what their target markets wanted (because they firmly believed *they, themselves,* were the target market), or they wanted to micromanage every piece of the process, right down to the very last shade of chartreuse in their ads.

Sadder still were the few clients who received what we would consider to be clear indications of, let's say, "unfavorable" market responses to their products or services but who were thoroughly unable to accept the market's wisdom in favor of their own. *What do you mean people think my baby's ugly? Those people must be visually impaired.* A few, unwilling to make strategic changes, eventually became one of those ugly business-failure statistics.

As Warren Buffett says about communicating to Berkshire Hathaway shareholders: "We will be candid in our reporting to you . . . the business facts that we would want to know if our positions were reversed. We owe you no less. Moreover . . . we also believe candor benefits us as managers: The CEO who misleads others in public may eventually mislead himself in private."[7] Unsurprisingly, I agree with Buffett: lying to yourself as a leader is even more egregious than lying to others. I should know . . . I've been lying to myself ever since I can remember, but I'll take solace in the fact that at least I'm working on it.

I can only suspect that the firm, confident leaders who insist they know it all also get up on top of their homes to tell the roofer how to lay down their shingles and get under the kitchen sink with the plumber to instruct him or her on how to fix the leak.

Sarcasm notwithstanding, cognitive biases prevent organizations of all sizes from evolving, growing, thriving, and *profiting*. Sadly, some of the largest (and least innovative) organizations we've worked with are often the most dysfunctional, led by a leader who either hasn't heard of the Johari window or, even worse, couldn't care less what's in it. Unfortunately for these leaders, they need to embrace the truth if they want to emerge from their sales plateaus and begin claiming unprecedented industry growth and profitability once more.

> "The CEO who misleads others in public may eventually mislead himself in private."
> —Warren Buffett

THINKING OUTSIDE IN CAN PREVENT YOU FROM MAKING CATASTROPHIC MISTAKES

Some of the best thinking on biases in leadership has come from South African–born Willie Pietersen, who served as CEO for brands such as Seagram USA, Tropicana, Lever Brothers Foods, and others. I had the pleasure of meeting Mr. Pietersen a few years ago and listened in nodding approval (more like emphatic head-banging) as he explained poor business leadership as a lack of what he calls "outside-in thinking." According to Pietersen, thinking outside in is all about thinking of your business from the customer's point of view instead of looking at your business from your own, internal point of view.[8] Yes, you're right: this is pure, unadulterated logic at its best, "and yet," Pietersen points out, "most organizations lament that they are not good at it." What makes it so difficult?

He identifies four reasons to explain the gap between who organizations aspire to be and who they are in reality: human psychology, misleading advice, organizational barriers, and confusion between strategy and planning. As you no doubt know by now, "human psychology" lies at the heart of our struggle with honesty and is also at the heart of why organizations stall and sometimes drift downward into oblivion. Pietersen's analysis is this: even though organizations *know* that their customers' opinions are paramount, as Domino's Pizza proves, many organizations still attempt to understand their customers from the inside out—through the lenses of their own personal biases instead of objectively, through the customer's eyes.

"Really, it is a process error," Pietersen submits, "compounded by human nature, which [in this case] is the tendency to discuss or gossip about internal issues" instead of coming to honest terms about an organization's external, customer-centric issues. Instead, the important data, wrapped up inside the heads of the customers and recognized most clearly by the frontline team, takes effort to obtain and humility to seek, and therefore remains in the blind spot.

Pietersen has seen throughout his career that the typical "inside-out mind-set is pervasive . . . it is the natural default condition. This is where we find comfort and security in a world we know and enjoy [but] the truth of the matter is that outside-in thinking is an unnatural act. Without a forcing mechanism, it hardly ever happens." Think about how wrong Ray Dalio could have continued to be if he hadn't created a culture around him that would force the most objective truths to the surface to guide Bridgewater's financial decision-making. Think about what would have happened if Domino's Pizza had never thought to *truly* ask its customers what they thought about the pizza—and ensured that the execs believed what they heard. Instead of asking customers, leaders usually inflict themselves with Pietersen's second sin, "misleading advice," by adopting their own thinking as gospel and only accepting information and guidance that fits within what they already know is true.

Pietersen's third outside-in miscue is with "organizational barriers"—essentially, good old-fashioned silos in which one department has no idea what the others are doing. Silos pervade organizations everywhere—and they'll directly block any organization's ability to honestly assess the customers' needs and address them as a unified team. Think about what would happen if The Ritz's teams performed differently depending on which location you walked into because they had no way of sharing best practices? All their cultural efforts would go up in proverbial flames. Across the companies with high-performing cultures we've examined so far, the leader of each has worked tirelessly to ensure that their teams work cohesively under one honest set of cultural guidelines instead of acting disparately.

Finally, Pietersen notes, it's far easier for us to check boxes than think outside them, which is why many leaders commit his fourth offense, "confuse strategy and planning." Many an organization heralds their strategic planning process, but the truth is, strategy and planning are two very different pursuits. "Strategy," Pietersen describes, "is about doing the right things. It harnesses insight about the external environment to make the most intelligent choices about where to compete and how to win the competition for value creation. It is quintessentially outside in."

> Many an organization heralds their strategic planning process, but the truth is, strategy and planning are two very different pursuits.

Meanwhile, planning, by contrast, is about "doing things right. It flows from the choices made in the strategy process and provides orderliness, discipline, and logistical rigor. Its purpose is not to create breakthrough thinking, but to produce predictability through forecasts, blueprints, and budgets. Its orientation is largely internal."

Planning is simple; it does not disrupt the status quo. It does not challenge *who* you are as a leader, who your organization is, and what painful truths might be lurking in your blind spot. Our natural inclination as humans is to avoid truth and embrace comfort; to that end, Piet-ersen notes there is evidence suggesting that strategic planning initiatives "produce 90 percent planning and only 10 percent strategy. Planning then becomes a substitute for strategy, and over time such companies will lose the ability to think and act strategically." This is exactly why we transitioned our agency from providing "marketing" to providing "stra-tegic communications for growth." And it's also why we created a new tech company to put our agency entirely out of business. In both pivots, we realized that executing on the status quo might simply not have been enough to create sustainable growth for the long term, especially if the organization honestly needed an overhaul to its business model.

IGNORANCE IS POWER; KNOWLEDGE IS BLISS

Whether you're the leader of a Fortune 500 company, a start-up entre-preneur, or a middle manager in Nebraska, ask yourself what you could gain by admitting what you don't know.

And if you think that's too basic or too obvious a strategy for self- or organizational improvement, consider this: admitting what you don't know is exactly the strategy Toyota used to kick the American auto-makers' collective behinds in the 1980s and '90s. The car company uprooted a massive American industry using a little piece of string called an andon cord.

The andon cord, replaced in 2014 by more technologically-savvy buttons, was the physical system of ropes that Toyota rigged along its legendary Toyota Production System (TPS) assembly line. The concept was simple: if you found a defect in your part of the production line, or if you encountered some systemic problem that you thought needed fix-ing, you'd pull the string to stop the line and help would come. Toyota's executives figured that if someone found a defect along the production line, then the defect most likely came from somewhere upstream of that spot. When an employee pulled the cord, it stopped the line until the problem was found. Once the root of the problem was found and cured, and the line was restarted, the root cause of the issue was no longer a problem going forward.

Any organization that wants to consistently improve the quality and speed of its production would logically want to adopt such a system. And the system has been around for decades now, in one form or another. Yet many organizations react with horror at the mere thought of stopping the production line, whether that means literally stopping an assembly line at Toyota or pausing to fix an aging infrastructure at Sprint. Many cultures encourage short-term productivity *at all costs*, even if allowing errors actually costs the organization *more* in the long run.

Case in point: I once heard an operations professor at Columbia Business School talk about his trip to Tesla's factory in the company's early days. There, he saw an excessive number of cars waiting in the finish area to have assembly line defects repaired before sale. When he asked about the extra cost he knew such a sizeable waiting line would incur (naturally, given his role as a professor of operations), the Tesla representative brushed away his concern, saying, "Don't worry! We have the best defect repair people in the business!"

If that doesn't make you cringe, it should. Elon Musk is literally a rocket scientist, yet he had built a factory full of managers who didn't want to admit they had blind spots all over the place that were costing Tesla time and money.

What about you? What's in your blind spot? What do others know about you that you aren't willing to admit to yourself? How might those discrepancies be holding you back?

Think about your most recent work meeting. Do you have an andon cord? Maybe not a literal one, but a figurative way for you to raise your hand and say, *Hey, we have a problem here and we honestly need to address it?*

Bethenny Frankel walks around with an andon cord in her mind. Every time she hears something she doesn't know, she pulls that cord and opens her blind spot just a little bit more every time. Winding down our time together, I asked her to reflect back on her life and think of some advice for the next up-and-coming entrepreneur out there—in her thirties, living in a tiny apartment, wondering how she'll survive and thrive and make a name for herself, just like Bethenny years ago. She didn't skip a beat in answering, "I'm not some genius or anything. It's simplicity. Simplicity of the idea. Simply being passionate, determined, and honest are so important. You can get so far with that."

As she was leaving for her panel, she gifted me with one last defiant quip: "You can never assume that someone is smarter than you. Your doctor, your lawyer—they're only as good as what you give them."

It's possible she was right about me, if only because I know how dumb I truly am.

———— QUESTIONS FOR HONEST REFLECTION ————

1. What do others know about you that you aren't willing to admit to yourself? How might those blind spots be holding you back?

2. Who in your peer group or family can help you illuminate your blind spots so they don't get in your way?

3. What does your organization believe about itself, its customers, and its industry, that may not be true? How can you create an andon cord for your organization to ensure that problems get addressed and fixed?

PART III

How to Use Brutal Honesty to Achieve Massive Success

Tom felt exasperated.

He had just walked out of a dizzying, hour-long meeting with his boss and his boss's colleagues, who formed the group of managing directors responsible for promotions. Standing in the pale white hallway, he just couldn't believe what he had witnessed.

After two solid years of performance, he had been denied a raise. The rationale they'd given was BS, and he knew it. Since he'd come on board, he had delivered amazing results for his firm. He had generated more than $12 million in new sales, capturing a meaningful percentage of the local market and bringing on board a few notable clients who would help them attract even more new prospects. Tom was simply at a loss to figure out why he had been denied a promotion when he had done his duty to the firm.

Sure, he had ruffled a few feathers, but the firm's processes were too slow and his new clients would never have come on board if Tom hadn't moved quickly on their behalf, and they even admitted as much.

Nevertheless, the little "board" of managing directors had sat there and told him he "didn't exactly fit the culture," and "there's a way we do things around here." *Yes,* Tom thought as he listened in disbelief, *and if you continue to do things that way, this firm will never make it.*

———————

Have you seen this scenario play out in the workplace? Who's right?

Well, let's imagine that the group of managing directors was right— that Tom simply ticked off too many people by making decisions on his own, usurping the formal power of some managers, and deliberately skirting ironclad procedures that had been properly written, vetted, and approved. Does that make Tom wrong?

Or, let's say that Tom had figured out the objective truth, which was that clients needed faster service and the firm he worked for needed a process overhaul to position themselves to win more business and achieve their goals. Does that make the group of managing directors wrong?

No. In this all-too-familiar situation, everyone is wrong. This is a classic case where each party believes they are correct, and correctness is actually not what's at stake. What's it worth to be right if you lose a high-performing employee? What's it worth to be correct if you fail to actively confront processes, systems, and prevailing mind-sets that get in the way of innovation and growth?

It is one thing to use honest tools to get at the objective truth. It's quite another to use that truth to create an effective organization.

For you *Game of Thrones* fans who haven't caught up yet (or for those who haven't yet watched it but might), be forewarned that there's a spoiler ahead as we look at a leadership lesson about honesty from the show. In season five, Jon Snow—arguably the show's most noble character—verges on war with an unprecedented enemy he knows can't be beaten without drastic action. He reasons that the only way to win the war against this far superior enemy is to join forces with a different enemy, the Wildlings, a group of marauding clans that Snow and his people have been fighting *against* for a thousand years.

Snow's own soldiers watch in scorn as their commander opens the gates to their castle and allows tens of thousands of those Wildlings to pass unharmed. But Snow knows that he needs those clans to win the ultimate war, the war that literally means life or death for all of them. And yet, though Snow's strategy is sound and his intentions honest, he is stabbed in the night by none other than his own men.

My unpleasant point: it's one thing to be honest and pursue the truth. It's another to persuade others to embrace honesty, too.

In part two, you learned about a few honest leaders and organizations who developed innovation machines—companies that figured out how to recruit the best talent, create dominant products and services, and explode their sales. In the next four chapters we'll consider how to act politically in order to act honestly—because in a rare twist of truth, we must be honest about what it takes to pivot our organizations from status-quo followers to innovative leaders. Using honesty as a strategic technique for success in your organization—however you define it—means changing the behaviors of humans. And as long as we're changing humans and not machines, we must take the need for persuasion into account.

I routinely hear from organizations that they want to grow, but their actions speak louder than words. Typically, leaders *want* change, but without the proverbial boat-rocking. They *want* to innovate, but want to do so by doing things the same way. This is akin to wanting wealth but failing to either make more money or stop spending so much of it playing Candy Crush. It's like wanting to get in shape but failing to exercise or eat anything other than Flamin' Hot Doritos. Sincerely wanting something isn't enough. You need a plan of action, and it needs to be simple enough that you can execute on it without being fired or losing all your customers.

To get moving in the right direction, we'll look back at some of the concepts we've learned and turn them into very easy action items that you can use to create an honest-to-greatness business from scratch or transform a business you already have into an honestly great one. Consider it a sort of "quick-start guide" for how to use each tool to get traction with strategic honesty. I assure you that the tools presented here won't help you use complacency to create incremental growth, but they will help you use brutal honesty to achieve massive success. If you do nothing else but execute on these simple strategies, you will quickly outpace your competition and make it brutally difficult for them to catch up.

Caveat emptor: many of these frameworks heavily depend on each other and create the rising tide that lifts all boats. Used in a vacuum, these tools will likely, and spectacularly, fail as your employees and customers alike will decry your hypocrisy. But, when used together, they form a powerful basis for an industry-leading company that attracts the best talent, rapidly innovates new products and services, and even cuts through the clutter with sales and marketing that deliver results. I've ordered these tactics in a way that might make it more palatable for you to introduce honesty into your corporate culture, but think about your own situation and adapt as you see fit. One other note: don't overcomplicate things. Don't look for MBA-level analyses if all you need is an honest conversation. After all, isn't that why you're here spending time with lil' old me?

These next chapters will follow the Hourglass of Honesty, helping you get honest with and about your community, others, and self. As an authority in your business, you can directly implement some of these very simple tactics to begin to use honesty to achieve your goals. But sometimes you don't have the authority to make direct change, so we'll also look at some special circumstances that middle managers face, since sometimes it's not as easy as creating an executive order and enforcing it from the top. Whether you're building a multinational culture of honesty, managing both down and up to get results within your team, or even trying to create massive change in your personal life, these tactics will help you think, act, and succeed with honesty.

Finally, some of these ideas will work for you, some won't; that's because every Hourglass of Honesty is slightly different. Your community will be different. Your others will be different. You are different. But there are a few structural elements that you can put in place—like the bumpers in a bowling alley—that can help guide you toward greatness instead of ending up in the gutter. Use these tactics at your discretion or try them all to see what works for you. Adapt them freely as you see fit. And remember, this is not gospel. You and I are both human, both grappling with that existential challenge called truth. Nonetheless, I hope you'll consider some techniques that have worked for me, and let me know when you find others that work for you.

In addition to all the ideas and actions provided in this part of the book, I've created a free workbook of questions designed to help you and your team use honesty to achieve greatness. To access the workbook, go to peterkozodoy.com/honesty.

CHAPTER 12

How to Get Honest with and about Your Community

Getting honest about what's going on in your community depends on how you define your community. Typically, what I find is that leaders can quite clearly define the big, sweeping changes happening in our society—like political partisanship, new gender norms, and the general cynicism that has pervaded our culture. In part one we looked at many global ideals that are shaking up the business world, like the increase in information transparency, the rise of Conscious Capitalism, and the growth of JUST businesses. Meanwhile, I routinely see leaders get hung up on what's happening in their own industries, literally right in front of their eyes—just like Kodak failed to make the shift from film to digital. It's as if leaders become farsighted as they get more successful; excited to visualize the entire road map but blind to the herd of moose that's taken up residence in the ten yards ahead. That's why I've defined "community" more tightly as your industry and your organization at large, because that's where the biggest blind spots typically live.

To begin to illuminate those blind spots, we must seek to answer this pivotal question: Why do executives do what they do? As one professor at Columbia Business School liked to remind his class, stupidity is always a potential explanation that must be considered. But, as we've seen with CEOs like John Antioco at Blockbuster, the more likely explanation is a fundamental lack of honesty—not on a character level but on a strategic business level. Warren Buffett has another name for the dishonesty that led to Blockbuster's demise: the *institutional imperative*. When Buffett reflected on his first years after graduating from Columbia, he wrote, "I thought that decent, intelligent, and experienced managers would automatically make rational business decisions . . . but I learned over time that isn't so. Instead, rationality frequently wilts when the institutional imperative comes into play."[1] Even the great activist investor Carl Icahn couldn't resist the institutional imperative when he bet big on Blockbuster . . . and ran it right into the ground.

DEFINING THE DANGEROUS INSTITUTIONAL IMPERATIVE

What is the institutional imperative? Buffett points to four main features. First, an organization following the imperative resists any type of change that derails it from its current direction in a sort of twisted object-in-motion-stays-in-motion Newtonian law. Think, for instance, of Kodak clinging to its film-based business model despite mounting evidence that consumer preferences were switching over to digital cameras exclusively. Second, any funds that become available in an organization quickly find a use, whether it's an honestly appropriate use or not (and typically, it's not—by either a strategic or ROI-based standard). If you work in a corporate setting that uses budgets, you might be familiar with the "use it or lose it" mind-set, in which departments that don't use up their current budget won't get all of it the next year, leading to tons of wasteful activities that justify their "need." Third, leaders who insist on wearing rose-colored glasses, instead of willingly embracing the hard facts, will eventually only receive rose-colored reports from appeasing followers instead of honest reports from caring fellow leaders. Think of what would have happened if the execs at Domino's had said, "We know the pizza tastes fine, so whatever our problem is, it's definitely not that . . . so stop discussing it!" Finally, organizations following the imperative inexplicably seek to imitate their peers in every conceivable way, even though the name of the entire business game is to *innovate* and *lead*, not *copy* and *subsist*. This is how we get entire industries stuck in archaic ways of doing business, like the mortgage industry competing on rates while what was really needed was an overhaul of the whole mortgage process.

> "After making some expensive mistakes because I ignored the power of the imperative, I have tried to organize and manage Berkshire in ways that minimize its influence."
> —Warren Buffett

"Institutional dynamics, not venality or stupidity, set businesses on these courses," Buffett wrote in his 1989 letter to shareholders. "After making some expensive mistakes because I ignored the power of the imperative, I have tried to organize and manage Berkshire in ways that minimize its influence. Furthermore, Charlie [Munger] and I have attempted to concentrate our investments in companies that appear alert to the problem."

FIGHTING THE INSTITUTIONAL IMPERATIVE

As Buffett explained, overcoming the institutional imperative requires first *recognizing* its invisible grip on your organization—and its grip on you, as the leader. To that end, I offer up a simple two-step program for getting honest about what's going on in your community so you can easily recognize how to boost your leadership acumen and create a more innovative, productive, and successful organization: first, start by defining your*self*, and second, don't get misled by *others*.

STEP 1: START BY DEFINING YOURSELF

If you're not at least aware of truth, you won't recognize it. If you don't sit around a conference room table and wonder who's lying to themselves, you'll never hope to see the blind spots hiding in plain sight that are ready to make you the next Blockbuster Video or Kodak. I've run workshops where, in a few short hours, executives have brain-dumped enough innovative ideas to last them for the next ten years. Inevitably, one senior executive (usually the CEO) says to another, "Where did all these come from? We've had brainstorming sessions before, why are you only bringing up these ideas now?" And inevitably, the accused executive responds, "I've wanted to execute on these ideas for years, and I've hinted at them before, but we've never been open and honest enough for me to feel like they would be taken seriously."

This is a "safe space" issue, describing the need we all have for psychological safety, lest we toss out our private thoughts and get ridiculed, shunned, or fired. And it's closely related to Buffett's institutional imperative, where everyone simply assumes that the way it's done is the way it's done. Those habits of being—of meeting, talking, thinking— are locked up in the identity of the organization. As Willie Pietersen, former CEO of companies including Seagram USA and Tropicana, noted, if every "brainstorming" session you host only attempts creativity with insider information and restrictive thinking instead of "outside-in" insights, then you'll only get very predictable, and minor, tweaks instead of game-changing ideas. And if you host meetings like that,

> James Clear said it best: Our habits define who we are. Change the habits, change the identity.

then you're the kind of organization that suppresses bold ideas and only makes minor advancements. Period.

Now, that may be just fine with you. But the leaders in this book— think of Russell Weiner at Domino's or Jay Farner at Quicken—would probably prefer a Jon Snow death to sitting around pretending to innovate while actually just thinking of ways to appease the status quo. James Clear, in his book *Atomic Habits*, said it best: Our habits define who we are. Change the habits, change the identity. "After decades of mental programming," he writes, "we automatically slip into these patterns of thinking and acting."[2] That's Buffett's imperative. So how do we break it? How do we redefine who we are and come back to what we all want, anyway: to create and pursue new ways of achieving our goals?

Develop New Habits—and a New Identity—by Using a Culture Code

To change habits, you must design a new standard to literally force people into new ways of thinking and acting. You might have noticed that all the featured brands in this book have very strong, clear identities that build successful cultures, like the ones at Quicken Loans, Bridgewater Associates, The Ritz-Carlton, and more. Having a cultural code makes it far easier to set the standard of behavior; it gives you a physical thing to point at and say, "This is how we act. This is how we behave." News flash: If you don't tell people how to behave, they'll run amok. Have you trained a puppy? Have you raised a child? We must be honest that this is life: gray areas arise, and if we don't have a code to follow, we humans generally default to doing whatever is in our personal best interest. And I'm not talking about one of those bullshitty HR booklets that never gets enforced, with overused clichés (Game-changing! Innovative!) and mission statements more suitable for putting small children to sleep ("Our purpose is to provide low-cost, high-quality goods and services to firms all across the northeast region who want and need more innovative solutions to the . . ." *Please stop talking so I can put my head into this vice, k, thanks*).

> Gray areas arise, and if we don't have a code to follow, we humans generally default to doing whatever is in our personal best interest.

Instead, I mean *a set of simple beliefs* that gets inscribed and enforced so that everyone is rowing the boat with the same set of oars pointed in the same, right direction.

Case in point: Columbia Business School's honor code. At orientation, all business school students make this promise: "As a lifelong member of the Columbia Business School community, I adhere to the principles of **truth**, **integrity**, and **respect**. I will not lie, cheat, steal, or tolerate those who do." Columbia saw so much value in the honor code that it was nailed to the walls of every single classroom as a constant reminder of students' responsibility.

Rohit Malik was the chair of the Honor Code Committee at Columbia Business School when the code was written in 2007. Malik told me that then, and unfortunately even now, "There's a disconnect between what many of our leaders are preaching and how they're acting." The honor code reminds students to walk the talk. It reminds them that they have a responsibility to uphold certain *very simple* values in a world where, as Malik described, "we have a high degree of emphasis on material gain and external rewards, and people seem to be valued a lot for their accolades, prizes, titles, and money, rather than their principles and their values." In a nutshell, the code reminds students to be honest, both in school and in their careers long after.

A code—whether it's for students or professionals—gives people an icon to point to and say, *Hey, are we living up to this? Are we acting in accordance with what we believe?* It also shows members of your organization what the organization and you as its leader value the most. As Simon Sinek, author of *Start With Why*, noted, when people believe what you, the leader, believe, inspiration and work ethic surely follow. Just be careful to avoid hypocrisy as you create a belief system for your organization, because saying one thing and doing another will inspire your most honest, honorable people to leave you faster than you can say "honesty." Not to mention, you might get some nasty online reviews on glassdoor.com.

———

Here's what you must realize as a leader within your organization: whether your honor code is nailed to your wall or floats untethered in your mind, you own one, nonetheless. You create your own code of values every day in your words, your actions, and your habits. Because words have the power to turn into actions and actions into habits that we use to shape our world and the world of those around us, it is imperative that several key, immutable values underscore our entire purpose as leaders within any team, department, or organization: Honesty. Integrity. Doing what we say we're going to do. Adopting a set of rules for how we operate—just like Bridgewater or Quicken—and enforcing those rules so that our people know we're fair. Those organizations know who they are. Most don't. And if you're not clear about who you are and how you behave *as an organization*, then you're not getting honest about what it takes for an organization to thrive in a highly competitive world.

——— ACTIONS TO CONSIDER ———

1. Openly discuss the institutional imperative at your team meetings and remind your peers that a massively successful organization cannot, by definition, succumb to doing things a certain way just because that's the way you've always done it.

2. Get honest about your organization's identity by defining it in a culture code, using the codes in this book as inspiration (see Quicken Loans, Bridgewater, and Columbia Business School as examples).

3. Avoid hypocrisy. One of the worst offenses an organization can make is to be unfair to its people. Set a standard and enforce it.

Now, the savvy among you—yes, I'm talking to *you*—may have noticed that starting with defining yourself sounds an awful lot like getting honest with yourself. Meanwhile, this is a chapter on getting honest with the community. So what gives?

Getting honest about the community, as we've narrowly defined it in this chapter, is about fighting the institutional imperative—the inextricable pull to go along with the herd. We can fight that imperative. We must. But we can only progress to step two if we can rely on a clear identity to give us strength when we encounter big new truths that threaten our organization's very existence. Otherwise, we may properly identify what's changing in our industry but fail to bring it up and discuss it for lack of a proper process or forum (remember the "safe space" issue). In addition, keep in mind that honesty is a journey. Working this process means assembling a puzzle that is unique to your situation. All three levels of honesty dovetail together and lean on each other's insights, so keep exploring. As you discover more through these exercises, you'll clarify each level of your life and business—community, others, self—until you see a clear picture leading you forward toward success.

STEP 2: DON'T GET MISLED BY OTHERS

Buffett's not alone in his observation that organizations love to play copycat. I can't tell you how many times a client has asked me, "How can we beat the competition?" followed, without pause, by, "I know! Let's look at what our competitors are doing!" Somehow this is intuitive to many. *If I want their success, then I should do what they're doing.* But that makes no sense if you're a leader who wants to achieve *massive* success—the kind of success that, by definition, *leads* an industry. If Domino's Pizza had looked at other pizza restaurants, it would have competed on delivery instead of on *over*delivery. If The Ritz-Carlton had looked at other hotel chains, it would have made prettier rooms instead of developing a culture of leaders. If Quicken Loans had looked at other mortgage providers, it would have competed on better rates instead of innovating the entire mortgage process and conducting a digital transformation. If you're a natural follower, then we can still be friends, but this book isn't for you. If you're a leader, then *lead*—and do it by accepting who you really are, what you really want, and what it's really going to take to get there.

That's what Domino's, Quicken, The Ritz, and countless others did. They looked at their competitors only long enough to decide that those competitors didn't have a chance; they were stuck making two-degree tweaks to their "success" formula in a world with two choices—disrupt, or be disrupted (*that is the question*). Invariably, a few entrepreneur clients each year come to me for help growing their businesses, wondering why they're having so much trouble. And I have to break the news to them (honestly, of course). Their business models aren't unique.

There's no clear reason why anyone in their right mind would do business with them. There's no clear value proposition. As Mr. Wonderful would say on *Shark Tank*, take it out back and shoot it. Typically, these entrepreneurs are stuck looking around at what everyone else is doing and playing the imitation game. No matter how you cut it, that's just not an honest innovation strategy.

Meanwhile, in one of my agency's greatest marketing success stories, a client came to us and said, "Hey, none of my idiot competitors are advertising. I want to advertise." This company sticks balloons up your nose and inflates them to clear your sinus passageways so you get a more permanent solution to sinus issues. It's not exactly the most appealing thing to advertise. And yet, about two years after we started, our client stood onstage with us at their industry's national conference and proclaimed that we delivered him a 500 percent return on his investment. By selling balloons. That go up your nose.

Sure, we did a nice job and all, but his business never would have taken off like that if he hadn't been honest about his community—his industry and his organization. Organizations in his industry didn't even think about omnichannel marketing campaigns. In fact, our client knew that the doctor-owned clinics around him would never invest in marketing, so if he did, he knew he would clean up. He also realized that if he couldn't persuade the owner of the practice he worked for—a doctor—to invest in marketing, they'd end up just like all the other practices out there. Fortunately, he was persuasive, a hallmark of effective action we'll look at in chapter fifteen. What's most odd is that he was all too right about his community; instead of seeing the innovation and at least following suit, most of his competitors lamented about their patients being "stolen" and pretty much kept on doing what they were doing before, unwilling to adapt even in the face of innovation.

As another shining example of how to get honest with and about your community, consider this: we now widely agree, and plenty of studies show, that diversity greatly enhances a group's ability to think creatively and solve complex problems. Diversity is good, right? Diversity brings multiple perspectives and "fresh eyes" to a problem. When someone looks at a problem for the first time, they ask wonderfully naive questions, like when Quicken Loans's interns asked, "Why can't we get a mortgage through our phones?" And yet, I bet your latest RFP asked for vendors with very specific niche experience in your industry. You likely asked for a vendor that *specializes* in your industry. If so, consider that they'll likely approach your challenges with the same industry blinders that you wear, too.

Meanwhile, the most innovative leaders know that pollinating ideas across industries is what truly drives innovation, which is why my team and I designed our agency to work across industries from the very beginning. Getting honest about your community is as simple as realizing that many of the "truths" that we learn by following the herd are in fact self-reinforcing beliefs that we adopt as immutable laws about the way things are. But we do that at our own peril. What is going on—or *not* going on—in your organization? In your industry? In the world? Ask the questions that bring you the context you need to make sound, strategic decisions so you can avoid the institutional imperative and identify opportunities to truly innovate instead of blindly follow.

——— ACTIONS TO CONSIDER ———

1. Write down your industry's beliefs, practices, norms, behaviors, and attitudes. Work together to determine which of those industry "best practices" are in fact helpful, and which might be getting in the way of seeing new opportunities.

2. Diversify everything you can: your hiring, your vendor selection, even where you hold your meetings. If you want to approach challenges differently, change both your environment and the people in it.

3. Ask yourself one pivotal question at every strategic meeting: If we had to rebuild a new business in this industry, what would that business do and how would it do it?

Getting honest about your community means getting honest about what's going on in the world around you. And in the world around you, most organizations have no idea who they are and what they stand for. Meanwhile, entire industries hold self-limiting beliefs that get in the way of greatness. But you don't have to fall into those traps; you can define your organization's identity as an honest one that pursues massive success.

As promised, there's no rocket science here. No flashes of light from an intellectual genius. Massive success doesn't require a PhD dissertation full of complicated mathematical theories; it requires getting honest about who you are as an organization and then carving your own path no matter what your industry thinks is right or wrong. Yes, being honest is risky. Developing Rocket Mortgage sure must have been an expensive risk. Ray Dalio's abrasive culture could have doomed him to poverty. And The Ritz's opening the Leadership Center was simply ludicrous—until you realize that's just who they are, and they didn't give two shits in an outhouse what anyone else thought.

Don't we praise that? *Wow*, we say, *that person is so authentic.* Then we sit around wondering how to make our organizations more successful . . . by acting like everyone else. The leaders and organizations in this book had honest discussions about what was really going on in their industries and in their organizations, and then they went about evolving alongside those big shifts. If you think it's more complicated than that, then I implore you to consider that you might be lying to yourself.

─────── QUESTIONS FOR HONEST REFLECTION ───────

1. What are ten common beliefs held by your industry that, if proven wrong, would unlock incredible profits for your organization?
2. Does your organization have a clear identity defined by a culture code, and do all the people in the organization truly share that common identity?
3. Where does your organization get its strategy—from industry dogma, or from outside-in feedback from customers and employees? Is your organization's strategy unique, innovative, and honestly valuable?

— CHAPTER 13 —

How to Get Honest with and about Your Others

I n the last chapter I asked you to consider that creating a massively successful organization begins with getting honest about your community, especially your industry and its self-limiting beliefs. The process—using fresh perspectives to ask simple questions that lead to massive opportunities—should be obvious and intuitive. Yet organizations find it brutally challenging to be honest about the world around us, lest it upset an apple cart or two. The reason why we find honesty challenging: we're human beings.

Yuck.

We're people who walk around naturally thinking that we are right and everyone else falls into two camps: they agree with us, or they're wrong. Sadly, many consider those to be the only two options, particularly in today's polarized political climate. As long as we're dealing with people, we have to learn to get honest with and about the others around us—which, I'll admit faster than anyone, is easier said than done. But the same principles remain: honesty is an act of omission, of cutting out bullshit and letting what's true shine through. For instance, we've all heard that we're supposed to hire the best people and put them in the right seats. But instead we hire incorrectly and then make excuses about why they should remain. Or we find the right people but micromanage them and forget to let them honestly do their jobs. So what can we do? We must obliterate our self-inflicted roadblocks by changing our behaviors and the behaviors of those around us, which takes either political savvy or brutal truth, depending on who you are as an organization and how your people communicate.

A big part of getting honest about your others means getting honest about what it takes for you to get honest with them in the first place. I love nothing more than when I see mental light bulbs go off during my workshops, or when people come up to me after a keynote and confess that their mind-sets have been transformed. "That's great!" I proclaim, feeling a bit bad that their uphill battle may have just begun, because once you see the light, getting others to see it too can be a massive challenge. That's why getting honest with and about your others means setting the stage for your peers and creating the right mind-set for your team so they can evolve right along with you.

> We must obliterate our self-inflicted roadblocks by changing our behaviors and the behaviors of those around us, which takes either political savvy or brutal truth.

While we saw that "others" can mean a lot of different stakeholder groups—customers, investors, and even relatives and friends—the relationships most pertinent to creating massive *business* success are the interpersonal relationships that exist within an organization, which we'll mainly focus on here. This is because most people intuitively understand whether the product they're making pollutes a community's environment or not, and whether their service is actually good for customers or not. Yes, people lie with and about others, like customers and shareholders, but usually in a deliberate act. Instead, we'll focus on the lies that usually go unnoticed—the ones that otherwise noble people would be horrified to discover lurking in their own leadership styles—because those lies form the glue that holds organizations in place, preventing them from industry-dominating growth.

INSPIRING ACTION TAKES CLEAR COMMUNICATION

Most teams don't operate in a brutally honest environment, so just because you've had an epiphany about honesty doesn't mean everyone else has shared your journey. If you're going to ask your team to adopt honesty as a cultural mantra, you need to walk your team through *why* honesty will create the results you all desire. What are the pros of honesty? What are the cons? How will you create a safe space? Authors Kathie Dannemiller and Robert Jacobs refined a version of the formula for change that simplifies this process for us: DxVxF>R, where:

- ✗ D=Dissatisfaction with the current state;
- ✗ V=Vision for a better, future state;
- ✗ F=First steps or process to get there; and
- ✗ R=Resistance to change.[1]

Combined, if you express enough dissatisfaction with the way things are, a clear enough vision for what could be better, and a process for how things will be different, that's typically enough to overcome R, or the resistance to change that most people will feel as they're faced with jarring uncertainty.

If you have an honest discussion with your people about each of these factors, you can often win easy buy-in, especially from those who have been unhappy with some of your organization's more hypocritical tendencies. And, bonus, you'll quickly discover those members who aren't willing to embrace change and would be better suited somewhere else. But no honest change can occur on the fly, without clear communication. At some point, if you want to create a pivot point in your organization's trajectory, you're going to have to sit everyone down in a room and vulnerably admit, "OK, everyone . . . what we've been doing ain't workin'. It's time to make a shift and do it together . . ." Level with people. Be honest with them about what's not working, what could be, and how you might get there. It's what you would want if you were sitting on the other side. And usually, they already know the truth . . . all you'll be doing is finally coming around to being honest about it.

THE FLAWED DIAMOND: INTRODUCING YOUR ORGANIZATION TO A NEW CULTURAL NORM

After you introduce your people to the idea that you can do better, it's time to install new cultural norms just like the ones featured in the case studies of this book. The first concepts to introduce to your team are the Flawed Diamond and your new role as the organization's Executive Mirror (assuming you're in a leadership role).

As you'll recall, the Flawed Diamond was an extension of the Inverse Triangle, describing how the best insights no longer come from the top of the typical hierarchy but from the bottom—from prospects and customers. In the diamond analogy, your team has the responsibility to convey important ideas and feedback to management. And, as we saw with the Executive Mirror, management has a responsibility to vet ideas through the lens of the organization's identity and strategy, eliminate roadblocks to those ideas, and remove barriers to implementation.

To put this into action, first set a standing meeting for ideation, perhaps once weekly or biweekly as your schedule will allow. In the first meeting, show them the Flawed Diamond concept and introduce your team to the idea that no single member of the team—not even you—has all the answers individually. Instead, your people, together, have the

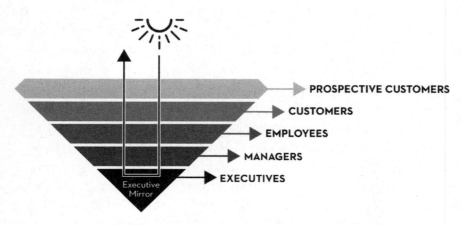

The Flawed Diamond and Executive Mirror

answers, and it's your collective responsibility to eliminate roadblocks within the organization that keep you from innovating. Help them take ownership of their challenges by encouraging them to bring solutions *along with* perceived problems, and encourage everyone to consistently be mindful of ways the organization could improve. At the start of each meeting, ask the following conversation starters:

1. What are the true pros and cons of our organization's culture? Our strategy? Our products? Our services?
2. How can we obtain more feedback from our frontline people to get better, clearer insights from our customers and prospects?
3. How might our current processes and systems be *preventing* the truth from being communicated throughout the organization?
4. What new processes and systems can we design to enhance the crucial flow of information?

Get people thinking about setting up the right *systems* for communication, and the answers will come. Answers aren't difficult to find; it's that the questions are rarely asked. Just by opening up your team's dialogue you can quickly find opportunities to gain valuable insights that are locked up in your organization. But you may find a team unwilling to share; either they're paralyzed by fear or seemingly bereft of strategic ideas. If the latter, you may have people who are incompatible with creating an innovative culture—people who are happy to take orders but bristle at the thought of making any sort of tough, strategic choices. That's a hard truth to face, but it could be a big factor holding your organization back. If the former—your people are afraid to speak up—then you may want to begin with a closed feedback system. Some people, especially in the beginning, may feel more comfortable submitting their thoughts anonymously, in which case you may want to ask your people to write down their ideas or type them up and pass them in. Once you start to generate those ideas:

- Open them up as a group, posting or writing them on a board in front of the room and debating their merits openly.
- Find a counterpoint to every point.

- ✗ Make everyone weigh in—don't let the loudest speak for the group.
- ✗ Watch for groupthink—when you see one person persuaded by the majority, circle back to them and ask them for their *honest* thoughts.

That last point is an important one. Your job as moderator—not as an idea generator—is to ensure that everyone's opinions are heard. Groups are easily persuaded by a majority, even if that majority is wrong. For a frightening look at the groupthink phenomenon, Google "Asch conformity experiment."[2] In the experiment, Solomon Asch put a group of "subjects" in a room, all of whom were insiders working with the researcher except for one real subject. The researcher showed them a card with one single line on the left and a group of three lines on the right, then asked each participant a simple question: Which of the three lines on the right is the same size as the one on the left? The participants answered the question one by one, with the insiders going first and the real subject answering at the end. The insiders had been instructed to choose an incorrect line—a line on the right that clearly did not match the one on the left. This way, the real subject heard the insiders' responses before submitting his or her own response. Despite the subjects' having clear visual evidence, Asch found that the one lone subject would go with the group's decision 37 percent of the time, even though they knew for a fact it was the incorrect choice.

> Your job as moderator—not as an idea generator—is to ensure that everyone's opinions are heard. Groups are easily persuaded by a majority, even if that majority is wrong.

That result occurred with clear, visual evidence right in front of their eyes. Imagine how it plays out when the answers aren't as clear or obvious, and the politics of job preservation mix with the human need to be accepted and liked. That's why your meetings can make or break your organization's ability to unearth insights and take action. Your meetings will either squash the truth or unearth it like diamonds from a mine. It's up to you to watch out for the sake of honesty and to avoid groupthink. Take note of when people change their opinions, and why. They might change their mind publicly, while secretly knowing the group is going the wrong way. Invite those people to speak and make it clear that the unpopular opinions in the group are the most important when it comes to approving or denying a new idea.

I can't stress enough how important it is to be honest with your others and encourage them to be honest in return. I once did a marketing workshop in New York for a group of one hundred dance studio owners from all around the world. During our honest analysis, they were telling me about initiation fees that they all seemed to charge their customers, which sometimes got in the way of earning a new client.

"And these fees . . . ?" I asked skeptically. "Your customers like paying these?"

"Well . . ." one woman admitted sheepishly, "no. They complain about those fees. But we've always had initiation fees and of course we make money doing it. Although then again we lose customers who would probably otherwise join and potentially stay with us for a long time."

"I see. So would you like to pay me an initiation fee so you can pay me more fees to teach you how to build a better business?" I asked, leading the witness.

She laughed. "Of course not," she said. "I mean, it's silly when you put it *that* way." The room grumbled behind her as they reconsidered an age-old tradition.

At the end, another owner came up to me and said, "I can't believe I've been doing that all these years. Getting pushback. Parents hate it. Why did I do that? I could have just welcomed them as new customers and avoided all those awkward conversations. I'm not going to do that anymore."

Unfortunately, those habits are everywhere, roadblocks just waiting to be blown up. And if you don't start encouraging your people to honestly question *everything* with fresh eyes, and then share what they think, you'll never even see those barriers to growth and progress.

As time goes on, and you and your team get used to debating openly, you can open the discussion floor without having to use a closed-vote system to get those ideas flowing. Encourage vulnerability and encourage the wildest and craziest ideas with enthusiasm. Take a page out of Quicken's book and try to say yes before no. And by the way, you can't help but empower your people throughout this process,

> You won't help but empower your people throughout this process, because you'll be telling them that they hold the keys to your organization's success. It's good for innovation. It's good for morale. And those process improvements may be perfect for your bottom line.

because you'll be telling them that they hold the keys to your organization's success. It's good for innovation. It's good for morale. And those process improvements may be perfect for your bottom line.

Many will read this and think, *This will never work. My people don't have any good ideas. All they'll do is use the opportunity to bitch and moan.* If that's true, do you really have the right people—people who share the organization's identity and thirst for both personal growth and organizational success? Have you been honest about how you interact with them and set the stage for honesty? I once worked with an entrepreneur who preached about open-mindedness and the value of free-flowing communication but lamented that his employees were a bunch of dummies with no good ideas. I came to listen in on one of their meetings and couldn't believe what I found: every time someone spoke up, the entrepreneur "leader" would screw up his face and physically recoil before launching into a filibuster about why that would never work. While he was carrying on, I watched his team members physically shut down; they would literally avoid eye contact, fidget with their papers, and shift uncomfortably in their seats. Personally, I found interesting insights in many of their ideas, which could have led to great solutions with a bit of empathetic, open-minded probing. Mind you, those solutions would have come at zero cost to the leader, who could have simply sat back and let his people figure out how to make him more money.

Not every leader has a blind spot this big, but as we'll see in the next chapter on being honest with and about yourself, I implore you to consider that your others might be ready and willing to help you achieve your goals—as long as you're ready and willing to truly hear what they have to say.

USING HONEST DIALOGUE TO CREATE MASSIVELY SUCCESSFUL MEETINGS

Adopting an honest culture depends on being honest with one another, just as Ray Dalio discovered at Bridgewater Associates. His radical culture of ranking and rating people might fit your own culture or it might not, but that level of "radical" isn't necessary to get honest dialogue flowing. In many cultures I've worked with, the leader has simply never asked people to be honest with their opinions and explained why it's important to be forthright; leaders assume that everyone will naturally bring forth good ideas, forgetting that job preservation ranks first in the minds of the vast majority of employees. As you saw in the example of the entrepreneur, whenever a leader assures me, "Oh, my people don't have any good ideas," I answer back, "I'm sure you're right, but even if it's a waste of time, I don't mind spending an hour speaking with them anyway." For some reason they always look uneasy when I say that.

Asking an objective third party to facilitate some early discussions can be helpful. As an independent agency that mines the great ideas of an organization's people, my team has a huge advantage in this regard by providing anonymity. Trust me, there's never a lack of great ideas when employees are given the floor to speak their minds without fear of retribution.

Honest dialogue means respectfully and empathetically sharing what could be better. It also means setting expectations so all employees know that:

- Not everything they put forth will be acted upon.
- No matter what, everything they put forth will at least be considered by the team and, if dismissed, given a logical, fact-based (*not* opinion-based) reason why it objectively won't work.
- When team members do put forth an idea that may work, they are given both the latitude to try it and the credit for having thought of it. (Remember the comment from a Quicken Loans boss: "Go do it and tell me about it later.")

These are simple rules that I see in very few organizations. Or I'll see rules like these in writing but not in practice. If leaders want to rule their organizations with iron fists and ignore the benefits of these tools, that's their prerogative . . . as long as they're honest about the massive opportunities they'll miss when ideas don't get explored and key employees don't stick around because they can't have an impact. By contrast, imagine the advantage Quicken Loans has when it goes to recruit smart people who want to work in a place where their ideas can make a difference (more on recruiting later in this chapter).

> Make no mistake: leaders have the responsibility to inspire others to *act*—not on the whims of opinionated power brokers but on the facts derived from the honest pursuit of what's true.

As a final note on mining insights and taking action, management consultant and author Ram Charan has written extensively about the failures of corporate executives to make decisions and execute—those two bread-and-butter imperatives of the C Suite burden. He posits that the root cause of failure, in corporations large and small, is a sort of false commitment to action that occurs when opinions, not facts, rule strategic meetings. When opinions rule, any actions that come out of the decision-making process "eventually get undone by unspoken factors and inaction," Charan writes.[3] "Intimidated by the group dynamics of hierarchy and constrained by formality and lack of trust," executives give lip service to ideas in order to *appear* like they are doing something, but they ultimately don't act when the time comes. Make no mistake: leaders have the responsibility to inspire others to *act*—not on the whims of opinionated power brokers but on the facts derived from the honest pursuit of what's true. As Charan concludes, "To transform a culture of indecision, leaders must . . . see to it that the organization's meetings, reviews, and other situations through which the people of a corporation do business have honest dialogue at their center."

Committing to honest, objective truth within your team isn't difficult, but it does take bravery and effort. Russell Weiner, now president of Domino's Pizza, showed incredible resolve when he did psychological assessments of other corporate executives to examine their biases before proposing new solutions. Even the ability to thoughtfully and honestly consider executive biases set Weiner on a successful path, because he knew those executives would never act on the truth if they weren't willing to accept it in the first place, especially when the facts could run counter to their beliefs.

HOW TO USE HONESTY TO SELL DOWNHILL

A few weeks ago I was talking to a client who had done an extensive audit of her customer's supposed "best" sales team members at an eldercare facility. What she found horrified her—pervasive use of customer-unfriendly industry buzzwords; unenthusiastic pointing out of dining rooms and other boring common areas; and no empathetic mentions of the *lifestyle benefits* that a customer would receive toward the end of their life.

We had worked together for several months, pivoting her business from a social media management firm to a sales consultancy. As a result, she had raised her prices significantly and was landing lucrative deals, including a recent $50,000 contract with this new, ideal eldercare client. But now, confronted with the brutal truth, she asked me how in the world she was going to tell her amazing and high-paying client that their "best" salespeople sucked and that they needed to overhaul everything.

"You don't," I told her flatly. "If that CEO gave you her best salespeople with the expectation that you would use their 'best practices' to help the rest of the team get better, then we need to be honest about her beliefs and work from there." Remember, we're being honest with *and about* others. This CEO already "knew" two things: first, that her best salespeople had best practices, and second, that she even had "best" salespeople in the first place. If my client had gone to that CEO and said, "Well, you're wrong—your 'best' salespeople are actually the worst," it would have torn apart the beliefs of that leader and given her an unexpected, massive problem. We must be honest: Most people don't want you to turn their worlds upside down . . . even when, and sometimes especially when, that's exactly what they're asking for.

> We must be honest: Most people don't want you to turn their worlds upside down ... even when, and sometimes especially when, that's exactly what they're asking for.

I should know. I had plenty of prospects over the years who came to our agency wanting to completely overhaul their marketing efforts. But when we showed them what innovative marketing looks like, they were scared off and retreated to their status quo. I really do believe these fine folks wanted to change, but their fear of the unknown and the weight of a potential metamorphosis banded together to get in the way of taking massive action. Then I got wise to the idea of selling downhill, which essentially means selling into what people already believe instead of trying to upend their entire belief systems and ways of being. When you sell downhill, it becomes much easier for you to convince someone else to see it your way because you don't make it about your way at all; you make it about *their* way.

For instance, in the example of my client who asked me how to convince the CEO that her sales team was terrible, the solution was a feed-forward framing technique I learned long ago that I now use with my clients, my friends, and even my wife (but don't tell her I said that). The phrase is simple: "I heard/saw/observed (fill in the blank), and it makes me wonder if (introduce new future state)." So in this example, instead of saying, "Hey, your sales team is terrible," you can use feed-forward framing to paint a different picture of what the future could look like by saying, "Hey, I saw that your sales team used a lot of industry buzzwords. It made me wonder if prospective customers might not know what those words mean?" In that way, you are putting ideas into the head of the person you need to convince and convert—in this case, the CEO who already has preconceptions of what is true. If you plant ideas in her mind and make them hers, and then help her come up with the answers on her own, her response will be so much more positive than if you force your know-it-all solutions down her throat.

Because not everyone works with Ray Dalio at Bridgewater. Not everyone is used to having their ego assaulted and being told that they're wrong—*especially* people who have "succeeded" and risen to authority positions. Frankly, I prefer the direct approach. It cuts out a tremendous amount of waste and allows you as a leader, as well as your organization, to move much faster. But people are sensitive. Egos are large. And if you want to be truly honest *about* the others around you, we need to accommodate the fact that they have spent years living in between their ears and believing what they already believe.

> While feed*back* forces people to go backward and assess what they did wrong, feed-forward brings people into a future that hasn't yet been lived. Therefore, no one can feel bad about something that hasn't happened yet.

While feed*back* forces people to go backward and assess what they did wrong, feed-forward brings people into a future that hasn't yet been lived. Therefore, no one can feel bad about something that hasn't happened yet. You're introducing new opportunities rather than examining past digressions and assigning blame. This makes it possible for you to fill the future with all kinds of things that could have wonderful returns and results, and—here's the best part—the hero of the entire story is the person you're selling. If you want to create a compelling sales pitch, stop trying to *change* people and start *persuading* them of what they already know—that they already have all the answers they need to succeed. You are simply there to help them, guide them, and suggest what else might come to be.

Sure enough, a few hours later my client emailed me. "Good conversation with the client today," she wrote me. "'I wonder if' got us exactly where we needed to be." David Crane at NRG and John Antioco at Blockbuster learned that getting honest is the first step, but doing something about it is the second, most critical, part, where both Crane and Antioco fell short. So if you want to get things done, consider whether using direct honesty *with* your others is the right tack, or if getting honest *about* your others—and selling downhill—might be the more effective way forward for a particular person or situation.

At this point, you have every right to be annoyed that this is a book about brutal honesty and here I am asking you to consider mollycoddling people to get them moving along in the right direction. We can't have it both ways, right? Actually, we can—because a large part of using strategic honesty with others is about setting and meeting expectations. Problems arise when there are surprises, when a person expecting truth gets the workaround, or when a sensitive individual gets blindsided by brutal feedback. As leaders, it's our responsibility to read people, be honest about what makes them tick, and be honest with them about our expectations *and* theirs.

One of my guilty pleasures, and I'm going to the highest level of vulnerability with you right now, is the reality show *Below Deck*, which chronicles the lives of crew members aboard luxury yacht charters. In the first episode of every new season, a (usually) direct-feedback type manager will meet their new crew members and set the stage for their management philosophy. Invariably, the manager will say something like, "I tend to be direct and give abrupt orders, but, really, I'm not a bitch." When they say that, I shake my fist at the heavens and shout, "WHY?" because they're missing two huge opportunities by taking that approach.

First, they set expectations too high. Now crew members are looking for the manager to prove that they're not a bitch—and every bitchy thing the manager does frustrates the staff and leads to mistrust. The manager would have fared better by saying, "I'm the biggest a-hole the world has ever seen, so watch out," and then every kind word or act would have *exceeded* expectations. Mind you, I'm defining honesty as blatant dishonesty here—as intentionally misleading people in a direction that's overly negative. So ask yourself: If someone underpromises and overdelivers, do you consider that to be a form of trust-building honesty? That answer might depend on the reverse: If someone overpromises and underdelivers, is *that* trust-building honesty?

As for the second missed opportunity, the manager misses the chance to ask their new direct reports, "How do you like to be managed? Do you prefer direct feedback, or do you prefer kind feedback?" Of course, there is no form of feedback that is overtly kind—but now you have a substitute in feed-forward. That said, even if people tell you they like direct feedback, they might be living in their blind spots, believing they want the brutal truth when in fact they're as sensitive as they come. So, as leaders, we have the responsibility to discuss and agree on management expectations to avoid surprises, and then we must honestly assess the situation as it unfolds to make sure we don't accidentally get caught in someone else's blind spot. Although this takes some thoughtfulness, patience, and practice, getting honest with and about your others' relationship with honesty can help you avoid explosive—but completely avoidable—conflicts.

RECRUITING, PRODUCTIVITY, AND INNOVATION ALL HAVE THE SAME ROOTS

Segments of this chapter follow two sides of the same coin. First we looked at how to introduce honesty to your others with a set of rules that can make meetings and interactions more insightful. Then we considered whether you need to be honest with, or honest about, the others around you so you can properly manage them to turn honesty into action. Now we must look out to the next concentric ring and ask how we can use honesty with and about others to ensure we can recruit, attract, and retain the right people to be honest with in the first place.

Honestly, there are few reasons why anyone would want to work for most organizations. In my experience, most organizations are b-o-r-i-n-g. Most are led by a dictator. Most are hypocritical. The hypocritical ones are the worst: they say they're innovative, but they shut down new ideas; they say they care for employees, but their only proof is the ping-pong table in the corner; they use sexy buzzwords on their websites about employee engagement, which ironically serve as a lighthouse to warn people away. All the concepts we've spoken about so far hinge on the important role of honesty. So let's be honest: Why would someone want to work for you, really?

One of the frameworks we've covered has the ability to transform your recruiting efforts, your productivity, and your innovativeness—and that is the concept of a Waterfall Culture.

The Waterfall Culture explains how The Ritz-Carlton was able to take a few hotels and turn them into a hospitality leadership empire. What they figured out was that each layer of an organization has one key responsibility: to empower the next layer with the right resources and support to do an exceptional job while upholding the rigorous identity and ideals of the organization. The model works because it shows that the organization values all team members, especially those on the front lines. Like the "Ladies and Gentlemen" serving at The Ritz-Carlton,

Waterfall Culture

employees in a Waterfall Culture—who come *first*—will feel more empowered than those in a top-down environment.

A more empowered employee means a more engaged employee, which is not a common occurrence at many workplaces these days. In fact, according to Gallup, just 34 percent of US workers are "engaged" at work.[4] The price of that disengagement is steep: organizations that rank in the top 25 percent of businesses for high employee engagement create earnings-per-share growth that is more than 400 percent higher than the bottom quartile. Plus, those engaging organizations also rank higher on *customer* engagement, productivity, retention, and employee health, and they garner an average 21 percent higher profitability. "The twenty-first century workforce expects to have a manager who coaches them based on their strengths," the Gallup poll concluded, noting that as millennials have entered the workforce, "this growing awareness and action of many workplaces likely explain the gradual shift upward in the percentage of engaged workers."

This is a winner-take-all situation. Create a culture where managers empower their direct reports, give them a strict organizational identity to adhere to, let them spot opportunities for innovation, and coach them to take action, and you get not only an engaged and loyal workforce but also a more effective and productive one. Who wouldn't want to join an organization like that?

Keep the following four things in mind as you create a Waterfall Culture in your organization:

1. To get the most out of your people, you must tell them why they matter. Introduce them to the Flawed Diamond framework and the idea of a Waterfall Culture so they understand their massively critical role in making the organization successful.

2. Remember that getting honest about what needs to change will mean honestly changing your people. Not everyone is a fit for a Waterfall Culture in which all employees gain great autonomy to act independently. You might need to hire new people, and it behooves you to anticipate making some potentially painful decisions.

3. Codify rules about providing support for each level of your organization. Make it clear *how* each level will support the next, *what* each level can expect from the one above it, and *why* it's important.
4. Create an andon cord, just like the one Toyota used to signal that something is wrong.

Sadly, most whistleblowers—which is what the andon cord effectively is—risk losing their jobs. But if you want to innovate, create an andon cord so people can report when there's something wrong, and reward them handsomely for using it so they can get the tools and support they need to do their jobs. Toyota had a literal cord they hung above the production line—but yours could be as simple as a dedicated part of each team meeting, or a dedicated "fixit@yourorganization.com" email address where people can report inefficiencies and offer opportunities to improve. It's a good old-fashioned suggestion box in a time when people will share their opinions *anyway*—so you may as well give them a constructive way to do it rather than taking to Twitter or Glassdoor at the expense of your reputation.

Your version of an andon cord will also break silos, because when people call out what's missing or broken, it will force everyone to analyze the upstream process and engage multiple departments. Using a type of andon cord requires that you remain open-minded to the feedback you get, giving you the long-term benefit of quickly gathering all the information you need to eliminate the roadblocks hiding everywhere in your organization. Your competitors don't do this. Be the one to actively search for those flaws in your process and then—*bonus!*—speak openly about your honest system. Share your andon cord process, market it, show it off proudly for your industry and the world to see. Then let me know what that does to your employee engagement, recruiting, and customer acquisition.

HOW TO USE HONESTY TO SOLVE A CRISIS

So far, no psychology degree required here—just an honest look at the aspirations and expectations of the others around you. Be honest with your people and be honest about what they need, and they'll reward you by reducing turnover and increasing productivity; remember, teams in the top quartile in employee engagement outperform bottom-quartile units by 21 percent in both profitability and productivity, according to Gallup.[5] But even without statistics, we know that honesty helps us alleviate problems and move confidently forward. How do we know this is true? Because that's what your family expects. It's what your friends expect. We usually forgive someone who makes a mistake and says, "Oops, I messed up. Here's what I'm going to do to fix it. Will you forgive me?" At a minimum, we say, "Well, I can at least respect that you're honest."

This bit of psychology works particularly well for crisis communications. Remember what happened when Domino's Pizza went on national television to tell everyone, "You shouldn't have to get this from Domino's . . . we're better than this." People didn't throw stones or jump on the "Domino's Sucks" bandwagon. Instead, they rewarded Domino's with respect and showered it with their patronage. Yet organizations in crisis typically default to pulling the covers up over their heads and sheltering in place until the storm passes.

Today, it doesn't pass anymore. It lives forever on the internet and seemingly forever in our news cycles, where stories of yesteryear seem to pop up like weeds—whether yesteryear is last year or thirty years ago. It's all back to how we share information, and now that we live in a near-transparent world, hiding simply isn't an option. Plus, you don't hide when you wrong a friend, do you? You tell them, "Look, I fucked up, and I'm sorry." That's the honest thing to do . . . and Domino's shows us that when we apologize and genuinely fix the problem, people usually forgive.

Imagine what could have happened after Volkswagen's emissions scandal if VW had come out with a whole set of videos showing us a behind-the-scenes look at its factories and its testing facilities; if VW had interviewed key executives, managers, and frontline employees about some of the changes the company was making to be more transparent and ensure it remained in compliance; if VW had shown the public how it was doubling down on honesty and investing in sustainable energy sources for the future so that emissions issues would become a thing of the past. What could an initiative like that have done for VW and its brand image? Would that have been too complex or difficult to execute? My hope is that you begin to see business crises—like VW's emissions scandal—not as storms to weather but as massive opportunities to innovate and dominate . . . if you're simply willing to be honest.

As I was putting the finishing touches on this book, I got a call from a dear friend and fellow entrepreneur who was grappling with his business partner over whether honesty was the right approach for their particular situation. On the phone, he described how he had insisted on writing an honest, transparent letter to his shareholders, spelling out everything that was going on as the partners requested urgent funding to help the company complete a potential sale. My friend argued that the shareholders deserved the truth, and that sharing the truth would help engender support. His partner argued that the truth would scare the shareholders away and insisted on leaving out a few big details.

Perhaps you've been in a similar situation. How much honesty is too much? Where is the line between oversharing the truth and maliciously hiding it? Ultimately, I shared two insights with my friend that I'll share with you now.

First, I asked him to consider his core values, which we'll learn more about in the next chapter. Is it in your DNA to be forthright with other people? If others were to discover, at some later date, that you had hidden information from them, and they became angry at you for breaking that trust, how would you feel about yourself and your actions? How might that dishonesty, and hit to your reputation, show up to hurt you in the future? Situations like these can end up resembling what happens when someone in a steady relationship cheats on the other. What is it that's so hurtful about being cheated on? I would argue that we are most devastated by both confronting how *stupid* we were for trusting so much and admitting how *easily* we were duped. No one likes to play the fool, and the consequences to the relationship can be devastating.

Second, I asked my friend to consider the opportunity to get everyone working toward their common goal, which he'll lose if he tries to go it alone. People can't solve a challenge if they don't know about it, which is a large part of what makes the lower half of the Hourglass of Honesty work as you get honest with and about yourself and then seek to bring that honesty to the others around you. Remember that the business technique here is to *use* honesty strategically; to wheel it out and show it off as the way to move forward, as in the technique I pointed out for VW. I didn't tell my friend what he should do—you'll learn why in the next chapter—but I did tell him what I would do: be honest, and then point out the honesty. Say, *"Listen, I'm being honest with you here because you deserve it. I trust you with it. Because if I don't give you transparency now, we all lose the opportunity to find the best way forward together. And the truth is, finding the best way to achieve our shared goal is all that matters."*

Could those investors still cause a stink? Of course. Most people react with feelings, not logic. But don't shareholders deserve transparency from the company they've invested in? Plus, if you ask most people, *hey, would you rather that I didn't tell you the truth?* they'll take a deep breath, calm themselves, and admit that honesty is indeed the best policy for solving any business challenge.

What's most interesting about being honest with others in a business crisis is that we're all in a crisis of sorts. Massive disruption is afoot. Competitors are eating your lunch. If you're not going to be honest with your others now, then when will honesty be appropriate? As long as we're human, honesty will be challenging. But if you think about it, telling it like it is might be the easiest thing of all—especially when you can see from the cases in this book that it's the most effective way forward.

——— QUESTIONS FOR HONEST REFLECTION ———

1. How might you set the stage for change by introducing your organization to the DxVxF>R formula to get the discussion going?

2. How can you create meetings that encourage people to bring forth innovative ideas and debate them openly? How can you use feed-forward to encourage positive ideation instead of accidentally shutting people down with feedback?

3. How can you create an andon cord that forces open and honest dialogue for the betterment of your entire organization?

CHAPTER 14

How to Get Honest with and about Yourself

Over the years, I've mentored hundreds of entrepreneurs to help them build seven-figure companies. It's one of my favorite types of work, because entrepreneurs have the singular authority to unstick themselves and take action. But that's the funny part: even though they arrive at my doorstep unconstrained by bureaucracy, they still allow self-limiting beliefs to creep in and put giant roadblocks in their way (as have I, mind you). I can't tell you how many times a "business issue" turns out to be some sort of cockamamie mental assumption the entrepreneur has made, which may be either partially or entirely untrue. As I've learned from their journeys and from my own: eliminate the belief, solve the problem.

CREATING YOUR VALUES HIERARCHY TO GET INTO ALIGNMENT WITH YOUR TRUE SELF

As we saw with many of the organizations in this book, success starts with who. The same rule applies to you, as a leader: when you start with who you are, you gain an operating system that allows you to navigate complex challenges using your honest identity as a compass. When you know who you really are and what you really want, you can begin executing toward your greatest self. Otherwise, you could spend a lifetime failing at something you never even wanted in the first place, which I consider to be one of the saddest afflictions of all.[1]

To get at your honest self in a more structured way, here's a framework worth pursuing if you desire to better understand who you are, what you stand for, and what might be living in that blind spot of yours. It's called a *Values Hierarchy*, and it takes your personal core values and prioritizes them to illuminate some interesting aspects of your belief system that make you the leader you are. Your values hierarchy can both guide your decision-making and even help explain some of your frustrations, since it should clearly spell out which habits and behaviors matter to you, and which you abhor.

> To make your own values hierarchy, brainstorm a list of core values that resonate with you—they could be words like "happy" and "truth," or "passion" and "speed." Really, it could be any word that can help another person more deeply understand who you are and what you believe in.

To make your own values hierarchy, brainstorm a list of core values that resonate with you—they could be words like "happy" and "truth," or "passion" and "speed." Really, it could be any word that can help another person more deeply understand who you are and what you believe in (I've included a list of five hundred core values in the appendix to help you get started). From there, pick six to ten of your top values, and prioritize them in order from most important to least important. Which ones make up your foundation? Which indicate where you're trying to go, or who your most ideal self might be?

My hierarchy starts with "honesty" and "passion," includes such personal ideals as "accountability" and "velocity," and moves upward to my top values of "service" and "enlightenment." So although I own a foundation of several critical values for which I stand, my ultimate value is helping others achieve greatness, which signifies a more enlightened life. When I encounter someone who frustrates me or doesn't work well with me, chances are that I can explain the issue as a mismatch in *values*, which I had never even thought to consider before writing out my own hierarchy. For instance, when I encounter someone who is fundamentally dishonest, or doesn't value helping others, or doesn't respect others, or generally makes decisions at a turtle's pace, I tend to cringe—and my values hierarchy tells me why. When you design your own hierarchy, you'll see other people and organizations very differently, and more fundamentally. Your values hierarchy will help you explain why certain clients work well with you, and why some never seem to click. It will help you explain why some friends drift away from you over the years, while other, newer friends jibe with you so well, and so quickly.

In fact, your values hierarchy can explain most interpersonal differences you might want to investigate—including family members, friends, significant others, partners, employees, clients, and more. Having a values match is like having a DNA match; it's both undeniable and deeply rooted in your own inescapable truth. You gain real power when you intimately know who you are, right down to the values that make up your belief system. Because when you properly get honest about who you are, as we've seen earlier, you can literally change your world—putting yourself into alignment with your best life.

Your values hierarchy will also tell you why you feel guilt, shame, or elation when you take certain actions or exhibit certain behaviors. For instance, "service" and "accountability" are higher up on my ladder than "honesty" is, which means that when gray areas arise where I'm held accountable to help someone, I might just be willing to lie. Which brings us back to chapter four, where I confessed that I used to roll over like a dog for clients who insisted on building marketing campaigns based on their personal whims instead of on their customers' feedback. I was faced with a common challenge for entrepreneurs: Take the money and feed my employees' families? Or forgo the opportunity and risk having to let good people go? Because service and accountability rank higher than honesty on my ladder, I chose to go along with those clients even though the honest thing to do would have been to walk away. Rest assured, honesty won out in the end. My shitty short-term thinking resulted in unhappy clients and unhappy team members, and I had to learn—the hard way, as usual—that if I were truly interested in serving others and being accountable, I had to admit that a business built with mismatched clients didn't serve anyone responsibly. I learned two important lessons in those years: first, that we can share values and still come into conflict if our values end up in different orders of importance; and second, that knowing my values—and their order—gives me an extraordinary tool to assess my options and choose the right actions for long-term business success *and* personal fulfillment. Oh, and let's not forget the third lesson: getting honest about what my values actually mean is really, really important.

> Your values hierarchy will also tell you why you feel guilt, shame, or elation when you take certain actions or exhibit certain behaviors.

Today, I think about my values hierarchy in almost every interaction I have. It's one of those guiding frameworks that, once completed, has accumulated more and more uses throughout my business and personal life. After more than a dozen years of helping companies grow, I can confidently tell you that countless entrepreneurs and Fortune 500 CEOs alike have failed not because of a lack of ability but because their most fundamental assumptions about their personal and organizational *identities* and *beliefs* were somehow misaligned with the truth.

UNDERSTAND YOURSELF, OR YOUR BIASES MIGHT EAT YOU ALIVE

If the leaders in this book are correct that long-term organizational performance starts with a leader's ability to be honest with the self, then exploring your values, beliefs, and biases is a supremely important step toward achieving massive success. One of the most concise summaries of our human biases comes from the aptly named book *Predictable Surprises: The Disasters You Should Have Seen Coming, and How to Prevent Them*, by

---

ACTIONS TO CONSIDER

1. Create your values hierarchy by writing down all the values you think resonate with who you (really) are.
2. Try to determine the top six to ten true core values that are most important to you. You'll know they're right when they make you happy to think about and act on, and when it makes you angry to see others violate them.
3. Put your values in order from most to least important to you and post your hierarchy where you can see it as a guide for when situations (or people) become challenging and you're faced with tough decisions.

Harvard Business School's Michael D. Watkins and Max H. Bazerman. In it, they lay out a bevy of "psychological vulnerabilities," or cognitive biases that "can lead us to ignore or underestimate approaching disasters." Their list of the most common biases includes:

- Believing things are better than they really are.
- Giving high but unwarranted weight to evidence that supports one's own beliefs, and discounting evidence that does not support those beliefs.
- Trying to maintain the status quo while downplaying the importance of the future.
- Only giving weight to things we have experienced firsthand and not properly prioritizing problems we haven't personally experienced.

Do a Wikipedia search for "list of cognitive biases." You'll find plenty that pop out when we least expect them and ruin our opportunities for success. And the pressure to succumb to our biases doesn't only come from within; external forces, like advertisers and news outlets, constantly fight to exploit our biases. For instance, one of the most powerful psychological persuasion techniques is the art of *framing*, which means presenting a certain concept in a certain way in order to sway an opinion (like the feed-forward framing technique we learned in the last chapter). The news does this all the time. If you watch two different news outlets, you'll see it: the same story, with the same facts, presented in two very different ways in order to give the facts a positive or negative inclination. We would all do well to identify the seemingly innocuous phrasing that peppers news stories. For instance, compare the made-up example of a news headline: "America Decides to Withdraw Its Military Presence and Send Brave Americans Home to Their Families" with "America Backs Out of Its Military Commitment by Withdrawing Thousands of Essential Support Personnel." Same story; two different connotations.

We do this in our personal lives, too, when we tell small children about all the fun benefits of going to the dentist while conveniently leaving out the drilling-into-your-skull part. Alternative facts are a real thing in a world where we get to make choices about which facts to present to others, which means it's up to us to look skeptically at the information coming at us to ask whether we're being led astray by those who are exploiting our preconceived notions of what's true in order to push an agenda. Most importantly, we must be honest with ourselves about how we naturally pursue facts that align with our belief systems instead of properly considering all sides and getting to the objectivity of the matter. We cling to the facts we prefer as a matter of psychological safety, and it's quite possibly the most dangerous characteristic that a true leader should never possess.

Just between us, I will let you in on a secret about how you can get the best marketing results today (or any manner of business results, for that matter). In fact, I could draw you a tidy little graph to show you what we've experienced with our clients. On the x-axis would be the amount of biases that our client has, from many to few, going left to right. On the y-axis would be the results of our marketing campaigns, from poor to great, ascending the y-axis. The graph would look like an exponential, positive-sloping curve rising from the lower left to the upper right. In other words, the more biases our clients have exhibited and imposed on us—personally and organizationally—the lower our performance on their behalf. Those clients with few biases—the ones who have used a Waterfall Culture to hand us a budget, participate open-mindedly, and give only one directive (grow our revenues or get fired)—have done exponentially better.

THE ROOT OF PERSONAL AND BUSINESS GROWTH: GETTING HONEST ABOUT YOUR BULLSHIT

In one coaching call, I was talking to a client about his "sales problem." He had created a bolt-on monitoring tool that, when installed at water utility companies, instantly saved the utility thousands of dollars each year. But he was stuck, unable to figure out how he could create a juicy, cash-flowing business on inbound requests and referrals alone.

"Why not build a sales program where you create a leads list and start cold-calling?" I asked simply.

"Oh," he assured me, "I could never do that. I hate sales calls, so I don't want to be that guy and bother everyone."

"I see," I responded. "So what you're saying is, you'll only sell to people who call *you*?"

"Yes, exactly," he replied, sure that he had gotten through my thick skull.

"OK," I began, "so what you're saying is, you'll only sell to people who are lucky enough to find out about you and then bold enough to call you?"

"Well," he wavered, "I suppose that's true . . . and as I said, I don't want to bother people!"

I pushed him. "So what you're saying is, water utilities that are lucky enough to find you and bold enough to pursue you are the only water utilities that deserve to save money?"

"W-well . . ." he stuttered.

"And that all other water utilities that aren't lucky enough to stumble upon you and brave enough to start a conversation with you . . . they don't deserve to save money?"

The line went dead. Silence . . . until he started laughing. "Well," he admitted, "I guess you got me there. I just never thought about it that way."

Brutal truth: leading is about getting the fuck out of your own way and helping those around you get the fuck out of theirs. And that's how leadership and innovation go hand in hand. Sure, you could create an innovation "division," where a handful of R&D folks are responsible for creating new products or services. But what about all the brains that come to work and think about your organization every day? They may not share your own self-limiting bullshit . . . and if you give them the ability to voice their ideas, some of that brilliance will push through even the reddest of bureaucratic tape. I always marvel at how others marvel at innovation, like it's some LSD trip that only a select few Einsteinian business mavens can achieve. But it's actually quite simple to create a culture of innovation, built on sound leadership principles that help remove roadblocks and get *everyone* at your organization thinking about how to make meaningful, lasting changes. Honest innovation starts with you, the leader—and I say that without regard for whether you're in a position of authority or not. Every person—from the entrepreneur and CEO to the doorman at The Ritz-Carlton and the manager of a Domino's Pizza store—has the power to be a leader, if only they will take on a leader's responsibility to confront and eliminate harmful biases and blind spots.

> Every person—from the entrepreneur and CEO to the doorman at The Ritz-Carlton and the manager of a Domino's Pizza store—has the power to be a leader, if only they will take on a leader's responsibility to confront and eliminate harmful biases and blind spots.

Get Honest With Yourself to Eliminate Dangerous Silos

As we've discussed, the most heinous act a leader can commit is to brush aside objective information in favor of clinging to subjective insights. Like water to a river valley, information is the flowing force for giving life to an organization. If your information can flow freely around the organization without encountering roadblocks (i.e., you), it will always achieve a higher power than if it is locked down in individual departments. By achieving a higher power, I mean that the information will serve the greatest number of people, so that those people may in turn serve customers in the most impactful, transparent, and authentic ways.

In an age where information is power, consider the amount of information that is withheld interdepartmentally, for political or other reasons, and the impact that positive information could otherwise have. When it comes to silos, make no mistake—the end loser is the *customer*, and there's an opportunity cost to your organization. When your people divert time and energy toward managing political silos, they're not focusing on the customer. When departments sabotage relationships inside or outside the organization, they not only divert time and energy away from customers but they also lose the opportunity cost of what the department could have achieved if it hadn't been engaged in such ridiculous folly. Customers—and your bottom line—lose on both ends: what is *and* what could have been.

For better or worse, those silos survive in the organization because they live in *your* blind spot as a leader. The last thing you want is for your people to develop effective actionable ideas, only to deliver them to an organization that is unprepared to act on them due to infighting, closed-mindedness, or a fundamental lack of communication across the organization. Russell Weiner, now president of Domino's Pizza, told me an illuminating story about a corporate executive who called Weiner to ask how the exec's company could gain back the trust that was lost with a recent data issue. Weiner recounted: "Everything I said I would do, he said, 'We can't do that.' It's almost like, one of the tests to figure out if what you're thinking of doing is a good idea is that it scares you a little bit . . . and part of the solution needs to be something that's big enough."

Weiner also believes that, in any brand that's been around long enough, people generally know what's wrong and what has to change. For instance, cigarette manufacturers clearly harm their customers. The problem is, as Weiner describes, "the honest thing they need to do to fix their business will certainly disrupt their business and could potentially be the end of their business." I saw this principle firsthand when my agency disrupted our model by inventing Stradeso, a company literally designed to put our agency out of business. Whether that new business does well or not, it was the honest move to make. I know the truth: if I don't disrupt my own business, my competitors will do it for me. All these organizational issues depend on your continually opening up your blind spot so that you don't accidentally become your organization's greatest weakness.

GETTING HONEST WITH YOURSELF MEANS REINVENTING YOURSELF

Entrepreneurs give us a particularly compelling glimpse into how to get brutally honest with ourselves, because founders typically operate all alone. We have no safety nets, usually no board of directors, and no managers to escalate to. Creating a business is one lonely pursuit that puts many founders in and out of despair as their businesses soar and flounder (been there, done that). And because an entrepreneur's atmosphere is so volatile, it makes for the perfect case study on personal honesty.

When it comes to silos, make no mistake—the end loser is the *customer,* and there's an opportunity cost to your organization. When your people divert time and energy toward managing political silos, they're not focusing on the customer.

After mentoring hundreds of founders, I've learned a lot about how blind spots can hide massive threats to an entrepreneur's vision. Typically, those blind spots hide flaws in the very foundation of the business—who the business serves, what problem it solves, and so on. With 100 percent control over our businesses, our actions can singularly create or destroy massive value, and it's up to us to pursue personal development so that we can each properly lead. After all, we can only grow our organizations as fast as we grow as their leaders.

I was in my early twenties when my business partner and I started our first company. My team and I started out creating $1,000 television spots for local car dealers. It was exactly as glamorous as you might imagine. And I remember thinking, *Wow . . . if we could only sell more $1,000 television spots, we'd be rich!* Apparently we hadn't stopped to do the math on how many television spots it would take to become millionaires . . . and once we did, we embarked on many painful pivots to get the business to the multimillion-dollar mark. The story goes to show how easy it was to slip into thinking that *growth* was what we wanted, when instead we needed to get honest about what even makes a successful, profitable business in the first place. To answer that, we needed to reinvent ourselves over and over again—from video production company to marketing agency to growth partner. Even that wasn't enough. As I mentioned earlier, we ended up building Stradeso, a marketing tech platform, out of GEM, our marketing agency, because we got brutally honest about how our industry was evolving; the fact that our customers' needs were changing; and how much our own model was increasingly coming under fire by the new and the innovative. Those insights, which required business-model-breaking honesty, fueled the next reinvention. It never stops, no matter what business you're in.

Speaking of, one of the best questions I ask my clients is, "What business are you in?" As we've seen, Domino's Pizza is in the *overdelivery* business. The Ritz-Carlton is in the *hospitality leadership* business. And Bridgewater Associates, I would argue, is in the *honest communication* business. None of these answers has anything to do with the industries of those companies. At my company GEM, we're in the business of *partnership*. At Stradeso, we're in the business of *turning problems into projects*.

I once asked one of my clients, the owner of a bridal store, this key question at a conference workshop.

"We're in the bridal business," she confidently responded.

I assured her that was not the case.

Guessing specificity was the answer, she asked tentatively, "Then we're in the business of wedding dresses?"

"Not quite . . ." I said. "You just told me all about how you help women feel like stars on their wedding days. You help them walk down the aisle and have their husbands-to-be say, 'Wow.' You give them that confident feeling when they're most vulnerable." After having led the witness, I asked again, "What business are you in?"

> One of the best questions I ask my clients is, "What business are you in?"

She had a light bulb moment that day and went home to build her new business—a business that provides *self-esteem*, not wedding dresses. Being in the self-esteem business opened up a whole host of strategies that her competitors weren't even thinking about, from the first interaction with a bride-to-be, to the in-store sales process, to the referral process, and everything in between. If you know what business you're *really* in, you can align everything you do to that true insight. But first you have to get honest about what your business is all about in the first place. So what business are you in?

As entrepreneurs, our businesses are extensions of us. Entrepreneurship takes time, patience, and a willingness to improve ourselves every single day. To that end, most of my work with entrepreneurs focuses on keeping them from getting caught by what's in their blind spots and helping them dig deep into their belief systems to make sure they're not leading themselves astray. That could be positive or negative; some of my clients could temper their confidence, but for the most part, most need to gain back the confidence lost from doing what I consider to be the hardest job in the world: creating something from nothing as an entrepreneur. If I've learned anything, it's that getting honest with yourself—especially as an entrepreneur—is like solving a Rubik's Cube; when you think you've nailed it, you haven't, and when you think you're far off, you're sometimes only a few turns away from getting yourself and your business into alignment with who you really are, what you really want, and what it really takes to get there.

Don't think for a second that I'm *only* talking about entrepreneurs here; leaders of every kind in every organization would do well to take the same level of ownership and honest thinking into their roles, especially if they believe that true leadership means forcing themselves into deep self-reflection about who they are and what they want. Just because entrepreneurs typically have more autonomy doesn't mean that they're the only ones who get to dive deeply into their honest selves. Arguably, if you do so in a corporate setting, you would stand out by leaps and bounds, especially if your organization values entrepreneurial thinking. Hopefully I've changed your mind a bit about what effective entrepreneurial thinking even looks like: a brutally honest effort to continually define who you are and redefine your business until who you are clicks into place with what you do. Such is the way of a successful business, and such is the way of a fulfilling life.

If you're familiar with *Shark Tank*, you know who Barbara Corcoran is. The successful entrepreneur sold her business for

> If you know what business you're really in, you can align everything you do to that true insight. But first you have to get honest about what your business is all about in the first place. So what business are you in?

millions in 2001, and since 2009 has been bidding for ideas she likes on the ABC reality TV show. A couple of years ago I worked on one of Corcoran's start-ups as part of Columbia University's entrepreneurship program, and she had a great analogy for the lows and highs of starting a business. She said the experience is like a bouncing ball: "The harder it comes down, the higher it bounces back up." Having had a few of my own tough times, I can certainly attest that the ball does bounce back, no matter how downtrodden the situation may seem. But the most important lesson she shared with me is that there's only one rule in entrepreneurship (and leadership): "Don't give up."

That, right there, is honest advice, from someone who's certainly not afraid to tell it like it is. If you never give up, the only thing left to do is constantly reinvent. Ask yourself the tough questions, like I had to do when I asked myself how we could design a new business to kill our old one. Even the largest of companies, like Quicken Loans with its Rocket Mortgage product, benefit from consistently reexamining their business model, so make a habit of continually asking whether there might be a better way to build your business (and life). Often, just stepping back to ask that question will illuminate some yet-uncharted ways to success.

─────── ACTIONS TO CONSIDER ───────

1. Get your team together to figure out what business you're *really* in—i.e., what emotional value your organization provides for customers after they've bought your product or service.
2. Revamp your strategy to align your entire business model, business development process, operations, and more to that one powerful emotional value in order to unlock your next successful pivot.
3. Commit to thinking like a reinventive entrepreneur, continually transforming yourself and your business with honesty instead of simply managing or operating within the status quo.

THE JOHARI WINDOW: HOW TO BE A DUMB SHIT IN ORDER TO ACHIEVE GREATNESS

In chapter eleven you learned about the Johari window, which is a framework for understanding that we all have blind spots—things others know about us that we don't yet recognize in ourselves. If you truly want to ensure that none of your individual self-limiting beliefs or biases get in the way of progress, you'll have to adopt the same mentality as Bethenny Frankel, Ray Dalio, Jay Farner, and more: *I don't know.*

We've all heard of the humble leader, but the idea of humility only scratches the surface of getting honest with yourself. As an example, I got humble AF when my agency lost a million-dollar account a few years ago. But the humbling experience of that singular event paled in comparison to the years of self-honesty I experienced after. That one event made me rethink everything—our business model, the people around me, the very idea of happiness itself. Shocks to the system, like losing shit-tons of money, can apparently create some deep self-exploration. But what I really learned was that waiting around for a shock to your system is like waiting to prepare for the hurricane when it's already upon you. It's too little, too late, and you've only wasted valuable time.

Furthermore, today's popular 360-degree assessments can only scratch the surface of self-honesty. While helpful to illuminate some blind spots, other issues arise. For instance, Ray Dalio would likely disagree with most executive assessments that are submitted anonymously, because anonymous feedback can skew quickly away from objective truth. Did the anonymous assessor just get their feelings hurt by the subject, encouraging them to retaliate? Is the anonymous assessor using the opportunity to vent frustrations about the subject's getting a raise ahead of themselves? Is the anonymous assessor guessing about certain character traits based only on what they see on the surface, rather than who the subject actually is? Without transparent, open debate, some assessments could skew the data. And when that data is used to assess an executive's pay, for instance, everyone might be left worse off than if those debates were brought into the light.

That's why, as we saw in the last chapter, learning to embrace honest dialogue is so much more effective than hiding in the shadows. And here's the key: if *you* aren't willing to embrace your faults, be vulnerable, and embrace honesty as a leader, you will never be able to create the type of open atmosphere that allows honesty to thrive. In other words, this whole thing starts with you—no matter whether you're the corner-office boss or not. For better or worse, there are only two ways I've found to illuminate my blind spot: first, constantly give it attention, and question, over and over again, what might be living inside it; and second, enlist the help of trusted sources around me who can help me understand which of my beliefs are true and helpful, and which are only getting in the way of my own success.

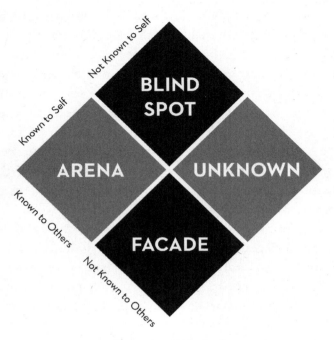

The Johari Window

Even if you didn't have the proper term for it, you've used the Johari window and peeked into your blind spot before. Think back to a time when you were forced to get honest with yourself—perhaps admitting that you didn't love that person after all, or you needed that vacation more than you realized, or you couldn't believe that you cried like a blubbering baby during that movie. You learned something deep about yourself in those moments, and it might have shocked you and even made you feel ashamed or afraid. In those honest, vulnerable moments, you will always learn something new about yourself. And if you listen closely enough to what your inner you is telling you, you just might change your life.

Active listening comes first. You can't hear what you're trying to tell yourself unless you learn to block out the noise and home in on your true identity. Remember your core values? If you're living a life misaligned with those values, chances are you're miserable. You probably know life has to be better than this. You probably feel like it shouldn't be this hard. You likely experience an uneasiness in the pit of your stomach, or a dull ache in your heart. That's when you know you're not being honest with yourself. I should know—I felt that way for years, like something was misaligned between me and my best life, like there was so much more out there for me to learn and achieve. If you want to know how to get honest with yourself, listen to yourself. Get to know you. Understand who you are and what you want. Because most people don't. Most people block their own greatness with bullshit, and there's absolutely no reason at all for inflicting that kind of pain on ourselves.

Don't be most people; instead, be honest.

With the Right Coach In Your Corner, You Can Change Your Life

I wish I could give you a tidy, five-step formula for getting honest with yourself and opening up your blind spot so you can become a more empowered (and empowering) leader. But I can only offer up a painful path. Mine would look like:

1. Wake up and realize you've been lying to yourself about the life you really want.
2. Feel like a complete idiot.
3. Surround yourself with smarter people who can help reveal your blind spots.
4. Figure out what makes people and organizations crush life.
5. Shake off fear, find yourself, and go for what you really, truly want in life.

To be clear, I don't want you to experience steps one and two, so I'll pick up at step three, which I've found to be the most effective way to get honest with and about yourself—because the truth is, none of us can play psychologist to ourselves. As my business partner always reminds clients: you can't see yourself from the outside if you're on the inside. And no, you are not the exception. There are none.

> What I learned in the depths of my own self-honesty crisis is that we need coaches to help us see the blind spots we've accidentally adopted as parts of our true selves.

What I learned in the depths of my own self-honesty crisis is that we need coaches to help us see the blind spots we've accidentally adopted as parts of our true selves. If the most high-performing athletes in the world have coaches, why would we try to perform at our executive best for the majority of our waking lives without people there to guide us? As a leader, your primary role is to coach those who report to you so they can be empowered in your Waterfall Culture to fulfill the mission of the organization. The entire organization depends on your clarity. In turn, your own coach can help you get the perspective you need to perform at your best. It's like putting your oxygen mask on first before helping others on an airplane.

——— ACTIONS TO CONSIDER ———

1. Get a coach who can continually point out your blind spots and help you identify self-limiting beliefs so they don't accidentally block you from success.

2. Adopt Ray Dalio's rule "If I'm wrong, I want to know about it" by surrounding yourself with smart people and empowering them to disagree with you so you get to the *best* outcome instead of *your* outcome.

3. Post the Johari window in your office and develop a habit of asking yourself of every idea and belief, "Is that actually true?" and "How can I find out?"

Empower Yourself to Empower Others

Some people just aren't ready to face the facts. You might have even identified some self-limiting beliefs in others, realizing that the people around you might have been lying to themselves. You might have even called them out on it. What happened next?

Without the proper framework in place—educating people about what self-limiting beliefs are and why they matter—you're assaulting the very essence of a person's world by telling them that everything they've believed for years might be wrong. When you're confronted with such a radical shift in your worldview, it can feel like experiencing a death . . . the death of your former self. Part of being honest with the self is realizing that each one of us exists on our own spectrum of honesty—and that, as we saw in part one, we all struggle with the truth in ways small and large. In one of the first discussions about what this book could be, my team and I agreed that no one can be forced to be honest; it must come from within.

That said, in the pursuit of making yourself more honest, there's a manner of speaking you can adopt that puts people at ease and helps them understand your perspective rather than forcing it upon them. When I joined the Entrepreneurs' Organization, I became part of a Forum of other founders who serve as my sounding board, board of directors, and overall personal bullshit meter. In Forum, we don't give advice; instead, we only speak from personal experience when suggesting what one might do to improve. Using "I" instead of "you" is a completely disarming language technique that shows others humility and respect. For instance, you might notice that many of these chapters have Actions to Consider and Questions for Honest Reflection. I'm not telling you what to do, because I have no doubt that your situation is unique; instead, I'm asking you to reflect on a few interesting ideas and consider some actions you might take. The difference is subtle but effective.

Every time you tell someone what they should do, their natural response will be to put up their defenses. Watch for "you should" in your daily conversations, and observe what the other person says, does, or feels. Sometimes I can see "you should" land like a linguistic blow to the person's face; other times they'll shift uncomfortably or begin to get defensive in their response. If you watch for it and observe what you're seeing, you might be as horrified as I was to see how important that language is, and how assaulting it can be. This whole idea—the concept of how you humbly interact with others (or don't)—directly relates to how honest you are with yourself. Removing "you should" from your vernacular signifies that you don't tell people what they should do, because you, yourself, don't know. The less we admit to knowing, the more powerful we are. The more we can help light the way for others instead of forcing them down a path that we, ourselves, may not even fully understand, the more effective we will be.

Does it invigorate you to help others succeed? Does it thrill you to open the minds of your colleagues, friends, and family members, so that you can all, together, achieve a business goal or live a more fulfilling life? If so, if you're truly a leader, then consider vulnerably, openly, and honestly sharing your experiences with others. Consider asking them provocative questions that can help them unearth new insights. Consider guiding people with an invitation to be honest instead of commanding that they be more innovative. After earning my badge as "most likely to continue being a jerk" in high school, I can tell you that being a know-it-all doesn't make for an honest self. And I can't fully tell you what does—except that the more I get honest with my own weaknesses and the humbler I become, the more I seem to be able to effectively lead others to greatness.

As you've seen, the path to greatness is the same for leaders as it is for organizations. I've learned to become comfortable consistently killing my old self and reinventing as a better me, like a phoenix from the ashes. And yeah, it hurts like hell to endure that process, but achieving greatness means pushing boundaries way beyond the comfort of the status quo. Our organizations can metamorphose the same way, again and again, to capitalize on the trends that threaten their existence. To that end, introduce honesty to your team. Show them the Johari window. Help them understand what a blind spot is. Seek the truth together. Share experiences. Just talking about these concepts will help identify some roadblocks that no one even thought to consider.

Or don't. Or live in the status quo. But at least be honest with yourself about whether you're going to use brutal honesty to achieve massive success, or not. No matter which one you choose, at least be honest: you have the power to use honesty to change your organization and change your life. Choose wisely.

───── QUESTIONS FOR HONEST REFLECTION ─────

1. How can you adopt an attitude of humility and openness to begin to identify your self-limiting beliefs and biases?
2. How can you invite a coach or consultant to referee your decisions and call you on your bullshit?
3. How can you introduce honesty to your organization, encourage your people to be honest with themselves and with others, and lead by example by embracing "I don't know" and eliminating "you should" from your language?

CHAPTER 15

Effective Honesty for Managers and Frontline Employees

Sometimes people suck. They're so stuck in their own heads that no amount of personal storytelling reaches through their thick biases and self-limiting beliefs to land the epiphanic message. What then? What if you have to move people and organizations who seemingly don't want to change and evolve? What about when you're faced with an egomaniac who thinks it's their way or the highway, even if they're running the organization into the ground? And what happens when no one can get around one powerful individual who's acting like the biggest roadblock of them all?

No book on honesty would be complete unless it admitted that sometimes honesty is a tough dish to serve. Therefore, in this chapter, I'll discuss what is special about operating from within an organization as a manager or frontline employee squeezed from all sides by the institutional imperative, politics, and those most honorable of colleagues who only look out for themselves. (Yes, that was sarcasm there.) As I've noted before, many of these tactics blend together. You can use many of the same techniques whether you're managing down, across, up, or over to clients and prospects.

USING HONESTY AS A STRATEGIC MANAGEMENT TOOL WHETHER YOU'RE MANAGING UP, DOWN, OR ACROSS THE ORGANIZATION

When it comes to using honesty within an organization, there are two truths we must consider. Truth number one is that we can create organizational honesty through a wide variety of approaches. We've seen in this book a myriad of examples of how every leader has a different way to go about using honesty in the organization, from Bethenny Frankel's *I don't know* and Dan Hesse's *focus on the long term* to Jay Farner's *I don't care who's right, only what's right* and Dalio's insistence on *radically transparent feedback*. However, while there are myriad approaches, they won't all work equally well *in your situation*. That leads us to truth number two, which is that you must tailor your approach according to your individual culture. What works at Sprint might be seen as tiptoeing around the issue at Bridgewater, while the radical transparency of Bridgewater might possibly get you fired at Sprint. You need to find what works for your organization.

So how do you come up with an approach that is ideal for your culture? Although your specific solution will vary, there are three guidelines and related set of actions that may help you, as a manager or frontline employee, make change happen within your organization. These guidelines will help you formulate an approach that will yield effective results within most cultures. The three guidelines are (1) do what you can within your own team, (2) assemble and use coalitions of support wisely, and (3) use data, and if that fails, use more data.

Guideline 1: Do What You Can Within Your Own Team

Jay Farner is a big fan of doing what you can as a leader within your own team. "Just worry about yourself, initially, and create that momentum," he recommended to me when I asked about his tips for creating change within an organization. "I'm envious of a leader leading fifty to a hundred people because it's so actionable inside of that world—they can make such a huge difference and do it fairly quickly and turn around later and see the difference they've made." In turn, Farner asserts, the success you create inside your group can help inspire people across the organization to change as well, as long as you thoughtfully show your results using objective data and without stepping on the toes of your colleagues and bosses.

To that end, successfully driving change in your team means understanding how to balance individual vs. group mentalities. True, this takes a bit of political mastery, but let's be honest: *our efforts go nowhere without the people—the right people—to back us up*. That means spending time understanding what's going on with the people around you and what motivates them, so you can start to figure out how to move them by dangling carrots rather than by hitting them with sticks.

Sometimes, those carrots include asking people to consider if they're really living up to the organization's values. Sometimes it's that simple: the organization has decent values, it's just that they're not enforced because no one's reminding the team why their culture code is important. As Dan Hesse shared, "How we live our values" should always underpin the conversation you have with the members of your team individually and together.

> "I'm envious of a leader leading fifty to a hundred people because it's so actionable inside of that world—they can make such a huge difference and do it fairly quickly, and turn around later and see the difference they've made."—Jay Farner

Other times, your culture doesn't have values, or has crappy values, or no one really thinks about the identity of the organization, and the result is a free-for-all where *what* you do supersedes *who* you are. In that case, you have lots of options here, and you may want to start by getting to know the people around you—again, managers, direct reports, bosses, etc.—to begin to understand their personal goals, biases, and assumptions. You'll need to get honest about the people around you if you're going to make any headway, especially in a politicized work environment. Be honest: Are you taking into account the core values and the values hierarchies of the people you need to impress or persuade? So often, we act without deeply understanding the beliefs and interests of the people on the other side of the table—in this case, likely your peers or your bosses, who may think very differently than you do. Honestly assessing others will greatly assist you in designing an action plan to make your organization more honest and your team more innovative.

Build strong relationships throughout your team so you get to truly know people. Become known as the person crusading for what's true, and build on that reputation. You might be surprised how quickly you can rally others around the ideal of honesty. If you hope to extract superior performance from your team, you must, as Martin Whittaker reminded me, "appeal to better motives and incentives—that is, 'there's something in it for us'—and present a positive business case on how we can look at this in a different way."

> Be honest: Are you taking into account the core values and the values hierarchies of the people you need to impress or persuade?

Even so, changing your current culture to a high-performing one will take time— enough time to form new habits of asking better questions, eliminating assumptions, saying yes before no, and dislodging the institutional imperative. Russell Weiner emphasized that one reason companies drift into obscurity is that leaders think simply returning to their core business and halting non-core projects is an honest assessment. It's not that easy, though. "You can't go to a therapist one time and you're solved," Weiner pointed out. "It's not going to come to you in a three-hour brainstorming session. It's going to be hours and hours of discovery and reflection and refinement." When you get stuck, bring in an outside perspective so you earn the benefit of Pietersen's "outside-in" philosophy. The pursuit of honesty is about creating industry-dominating success. It's not easy, but the Hourglass of Honesty is the framework you can count on as a dedicated manager who wants to create meaningful change from within your own department.

Share this book or the concepts in it with your teammates. As Buffett noted, get people "alert to the problem," and become the expert on strategic honesty within your own team. If you can't seem to get your comrades excited about asking what's true in order to find new opportunities, consider the possibility that your message might be spot-on but you're simply not the right messenger. Seeing this about yourself requires an enormous amount of self-reflection and honesty, but that critical realization could make all the difference. Is there a colleague who is better suited to deliver your assessment? What about your boss? Or a small group? This is where understanding your target audience is key—not only *what* they need to hear but also *who* can make them most receptive to hearing it.

> "You can't go to a therapist one time and you're solved. It's not going to come to you in a three-hour brainstorming session. It's going to be hours and hours of discovery and reflection and refinement."
> —Russell Weiner

Guideline 2: Assemble and Use Coalitions of Support Wisely

At some point you're going to need to make a case for honesty to either your peers, bosses, or direct reports. If so, consider assembling a coalition. What does this look like? As Rohit Malik, one of the architects behind Columbia Business School's honor code, specifies, "Form a committee of those [you] consider to be high-integrity leaders and work with those people to create programs, workshops," and brainstorming sessions specifically designed to mine honest insights. Employees who bring a united front to the decision-maker are harder to ignore, particularly if they make a strong, data-backed case for what they believe in and if what's being proposed is truly for the good of the organization.

——————— **ACTIONS TO CONSIDER** ———————

1. Build relationships on the basis of honest principles so you can earn the trust of your team. Ask them questions to get at their biases, beliefs, and motivations. Share your beliefs about honesty with them in return, and make honesty a critical part of every discussion, asking, "Is that true?" and "How do we know?"
2. Map out which people you would need—in every direction of the hierarchy—to help you execute honest change. Include (and be honest about) their motives, beliefs, and the relative support you can expect from them.
3. Become an expert on strategic honesty, but also ensure that you're the right messenger to introduce these concepts to the rest of your organization. Bring in team members to help land your message if that's what it takes to get through to your colleagues.

Remember Russell Weiner's assertion that brainstorming won't yield true insights if the session only unearths opinions instead of facts, so lean on data to make the case for you.

Before we examine what a coalition is and how to create one, I'll provide a word of caution: *don't be a victim of your own zeal.* Sending around secret email chains and meeting in dark corridors during lunch is definitely not the way to go about convincing higher-ups to act on your ideas. In addition, outright whistle-blowing or getting on your soapbox is usually a poor choice for change management, so avoid going to the press or your Twitter account; instead, look at what motivates the company, whether it's profits, investors, other stakeholders, etc., and use those intrinsic motivations as reasons to come together for the benefit of the organization. In the pursuit of honesty and transparency, begin this process by putting an agenda item on the next company meeting and speaking transparently about your vision for strategic honesty, as Ray Dalio requires at Bridgewater. Then, follow through with a request to put together a coalition with the sole purpose of discovering ways to use strategic honesty to achieve the organization's most important goals. Make sure you frame your coalition request correctly, *as a team with the sole mission of achieving the organization's goals.*

If you get the green light, it's time to pick your team. We are searching for truth, remember, not conformity (which is the great killer of truth in many instances). Therefore, diversity is key—and, more specifically, a diverse group of individuals who all believe that honesty will positively transform your organization and who *disagree* about exactly how to do it. There will be people in your organization who are interested in ways to break out of the status quo and improve performance; find them and recruit them. As Ray Dalio reminds us, we must listen carefully to people who disagree with us so that we "replace the joy of being proven right . . . with the joy of learning what is true." Consider bringing in an outside referee who can keep the group honest, productive, and asking the right outside-in questions. As an outside consultant I've seen the benefits of being able to serve two critical roles: first, to help a group achieve the stated goal by serving as an independent guide, and second, to be a scapegoat that allows employees to push responsibility for success on the outsider, so the team gets all the upside credit with far less downside risk.

> Employees who bring a united front to the decision-maker are harder to ignore, particularly if they make a strong, data-backed case for what they believe in and if what's being proposed is truly for the good of the organization.

Your coalition will go further, and faster, than you could on your own. After studying which tactics worked best to create organizational change, researchers Susan J. Ashford and James R. Detert found that "building a coalition generates organization buy-in more quickly and on a larger scale as more people contribute energy and resources."[1] The authors reiterated that diversity is key. As they wrote in the *Harvard Business Review*, "One person might have access to important data . . . and another might have a personal relationship with one of the top managers you're trying to persuade." The most successful leaders in their study involved a diverse group of colleagues in pitching their concepts, because the network effect gave the group access to resources and relationships that made the whole buy-in process easier.

I'll be the first to admit that the last thing I want is for people on my payroll to be sitting around "discussing innovation" at 3 PM on a Tuesday while pressing projects go untouched. Therefore, your coalition must produce actionable results, and on a timetable. Come up with a plan, perhaps first focusing on open-ended brainstorms that run through the Hourglass of Honesty, the Flawed Diamond, and Waterfall Culture, to see where opportunities exist to become more nimble, innovative, and effective. Introduce the Johari window and start to explore what might be in the organization's and the leaders' blind spots. Then create a list of opportunities that exist along with potential actions that different departments can take. This is not about highlighting problems; it's about illuminating opportunities along with some associated solutions (i.e., *action*). If your bosses want to create a high-performing, industry-leading organization, this shouldn't be a tough sell. If they don't . . . then there's always Monster.com.

Guideline 3: Use Data, and If That Fails, Use More Data

To really get your organization moving, take action. Start small, with accessible hypotheses and tests. Gather data—especially from customers, just as Russell Weiner did at Domino's. It's worth noting that Weiner asked his *current customers* what they thought about his pizza, and they told him how to fix it. Often I get questions about doing external marketing research. To be honest, I'm not a huge fan. The reason I'm not a fan is that anyone can say they *might* buy a product. Can you imagine basing an entire business strategy on the feedback of people who *might* be your customers? But when you open your wallet and *buy*, that's a powerful vote, and—as Weiner pointed out—it's the

─────── **ACTIONS TO CONSIDER** ───────

1. If you're trying to push change through an organization with several layers, use a coalition of support to strengthen your argument.
2. Build your coalition openly, honestly, and transparently as a change agent pursuing opportunities for growth within your organization.
3. Embrace a diverse coalition to ensure you don't lose insights to your collective blind spots, and develop recommended *actions* your organization can take.

only vote that matters. Ask current customers what they think; they're usually more than happy to be put in charge of how you might make positive changes.

While capturing perspectives and data within your organization, you may also want to benchmark your findings with other, competitive organizations, as Martin Whittaker provides with the JUST 100. When managing up in particular, rankings of peers frequently matter to corporate executives who fear losing to competitors (remember Buffett's imperative and consider exploiting that weakness). As the former CEO of Sprint, Dan Hesse, said, "You *can* make a case—you could go to the numbers and take a look at the companies [with] a culture of honesty and truth . . . who have higher returns on equity and sustained better business performance" to show to your bosses. You can also show binders full of cases where market caps have been destroyed by dishonesty, like in the cases of Wells Fargo, VW, and Facebook when the Cambridge Analytica data scandal broke. "If you could speak to me in the language of improving our performance," Hesse said, "you would have an impact" in convincing the CEO to make strategic changes. That institutional imperative is strong, and you may ironically be able to use it to your advantage in the beginning stages of transformation.

Once again, don't bring problems; bring solutions. I'll add to that: don't *be* a problem. Making the case for organizational change to your boss while she's right in the middle of preparing for her next board meeting is probably an ill-fated idea. Executives, boards, leaders of all kinds are people, too, so some sensitivity is in order here. Remember the feed-forward framing technique for gently nudging people along to the benefit of all. With a scientific, data-driven method in hand, and the right persuasive tactics, you'll be able to make a proper case to effectively communicate to those in charge when the time is right.

——— ACTIONS TO CONSIDER ———

1. Lean on objective data whenever possible—in the absence of facts, only opinion and politics are available to decision-makers.
2. Use benchmarks to make a solid, objective case for making change in your organization so your colleagues, managers, and direct reports can see *why* using honesty is important.
3. Be sensitive to timing in terms of conveying the insights you've gleaned from the data so you don't accidentally crush your chances before you can even get started . . . and be sensitive to the egos who pay you every two weeks.

A special note to those who are managing up. Convincing those above you that they need to change may seem impossible. It isn't, but it does take some attention to empathy and detail. Without expertise, consensus, and evidence, most arguments will fall on the deaf ears of a manager who has an entire set of rules, initiatives, and worries floating around her head at any given time. But if you can use principles of honesty to create a culture of innovation within your own team, you'll be well on your way to creating change in your organization (guideline one). If you can recruit the assistance of those around you by finding like-minded colleagues and asking more honest questions, you can start to build momentum with a coalition (guideline two). And if you can speak in the language of the leader and present data-backed examples where honesty has succeeded, you can "present those examples in a compelling way such that there's a Return On Honesty," as Rohit Malik suggested (guideline three). Take it back to the basics, in the language the leaders understand, and use the frameworks and stories in this book to back you up. Then you might have a chance to create the same game-changing results as many of the leaders in this book, who all stand behind you.

GETTING BRUTALLY HONEST IN A PLACE WHERE DISHONESTY THRIVES

We've looked at some ways that managers can bring about honest change in their workplaces. Trouble is, in today's world, we aren't exactly inundated with the benefits of virtue and principle. Instead, as Rohit Malik pointed out, many leaders see "example after example of individuals and organizations that do not follow high integrity and yet are still able to succeed in the marketplace." As long as that's true, honesty only looks like a nice-to-have option instead of a must-have opportunity. But if you believe that a world with ultimate transparency is fast approaching, then you might also believe that any leader wanting long-term, sustainable success will have to embrace honesty and integrity at some point. And in a world with instantaneous information, "some point" looms closer as transparency increases.

Plus, remember that the power of honesty touches all the elements your organization cares about—not in the long term, but *right now*. When it comes to using strategic honesty within your organization, the implications of the case studies in this book touch recruiting, human resources, operations, finance, sales, marketing, and more. Marching into your CEO's office with a picket line is likely not the way, but gently reminding your organization that it needs to recruit better talent, innovate ahead of its competition, and increase profits makes you the type of thoughtful leader that every organization should want. Making change is tough but not impossible. Alexander McCobin, CEO of Conscious Capitalism, said it best: "Being honest and calling out dishonesty is often a lot easier than people make it out to be in their own heads."

> There may come a time when you decide you're done beating your head against a wall and you don't want to go down with the ship you're on. That's a tough call, and nothing saddens me more than seeing enlightened individuals stuck in companies that can't get out of their own way.

All that said, there may come a time when you decide you're done shouting about honesty through a megaphone while no one listens, and you don't want to go down with the ship you're on. That's a tough call, and nothing saddens me more than seeing enlightened individuals stuck in companies that can't get out of their own way. Millennials especially have less and less patience for old-fashioned ways of doing business when we can work remotely from Bali in between yoga sessions. Cliché, but why not? Sometimes the answer is in Rohit Malik's advice when you realize the organization you work for will never embrace honesty: "Find a new organization to work for." Or, in Russell Weiner's words, "The beauty of data is it can help you turn around the brand or get out of a company you probably don't want to work for. If the upper management doesn't want to make a fact-based decision, then you probably don't want to work there—and you win either way."

───── QUESTIONS FOR HONEST REFLECTION ─────

1. When might be the right time to introduce your organization to strategic honesty? How can you present honesty to all your colleagues so they see the benefits?
2. How can you set an example by using honesty within your own team and developing a mini-culture of innovation that produces better insights and results?
3. How can you think and act more politically in your organization—including discovering what your colleagues think and feel, assembling coalitions of support, and making data-backed arguments to adopt honesty in your own organization?

— CONCLUSION —

Why did I write a book about honesty?

I stick my neck out for honesty at my own peril. We live in a time when everyone's living their own truth, when objective facts have fallen victim to alternative ones, and outright deceit has carried CEOs to massive paychecks and politicians to Washington. Folks will come out of the woodwork to spot inaccuracies and untruths in this book and rub them in my face. And that's OK. I'm ready for it. You'll be right to point out my fallacies, and I'm proud to know enough to be thankful for what you'll teach me. Cynics will read this tome and assume I must be too naive to understand how the world *really* works. I vividly remember the advice of a senior banker early in my career: "Say what you have to say to get the client half-pregnant, and then it's harder for them to back out." I shuddered then, and I shudder now to think of what people have done in the name of making money. Which brings us back to why I wrote this book. In a word: *sustainability*.

I believe that in a world made increasingly transparent by technology, deceit is not a sustainable way to earn success—personally or professionally. Along with JUST Capital, I believe that with more information, consumers will make different choices, choices that will reward the honest. I believe that capitalism as we know it must evolve if it's going to survive our growing wealth gap, and that all corporations will soon be incentivized to be noble stewards of society rather than profiteers from it.

I believe that we're experiencing the beginning of the end of some of the biggest concerns in our community, and that we'll soon see more equitable resolutions on issues like gender inequality, race relations, and a whole host of others that should have been eradicated long ago. I believe that the people around us grow more cynical by the second, and that objective truth will be the only way to restore trust. I believe that deceit, not ineptitude, is what holds most leaders and organizations back from greatness, because I've seen it over and over and over again in the conference rooms of Fortune 500 companies and start-ups alike. And I believe that we all have some serious self-exploration to do along with a grave responsibility to set aside our egos and entitled attitudes and step off our social media soapboxes. If we don't, we'll only grow further apart.

It doesn't have to be that way. Charlotte McCourt wrote that some of her cookies taste like crap, and people showed their respect for her doing so by buying nearly thirty thousand boxes of cookies. J. Patrick Doyle went on national TV to say his pizza sucks, everybody knows it, and he's going to do something about it. Shareholders went nuts, lifting his stock by 3,268 percent. Dan Hesse at Sprint took a page out of Buffett's long-term playbook and tore the guts out of his own company so it would survive. His customers thanked him with their approving patronage, awarding Sprint with the highest customer satisfaction ratings in the American Customer Satisfaction Index and lifting Sprint's stock roughly 30 percent more than the S&P 500. The Ritz-Carlton told its customers to get in line behind its employees, because its employees must come first. Not only did their customers return year after year to fuel a global expansion but also fifty thousand executives worldwide flocked to get The Ritz's leadership training. Ray Dalio invited his team to tell him he was wrong so that he could ensure he never would be. Being the world's biggest hedge fund would seem to indicate that his strategy has paid off. Let's not forget Quicken Loans, who stole the mortgage market from larger incumbents by inviting its employees to ask dumb questions and then giving them the leeway to answer those questions with action. And then there's Bethenny Frankel, who went from broke thirtysomething to Real Housewife to millionaire entrepreneur by completely owning the fact that *she didn't fucking know*.

I believe all these success stories come back to one common core: honesty. That's why I wrote a book about it. I spent years observing greatness and failure in the business world and wondering where the root cause was, and I found the core challenge in honesty—about what's going on in the community, in others, and in the self. Yet we've spent pages and pages together without a clear definition of what honesty even is. I've twisted it into many forms, from straight-up truth-telling, to treating others with psychological respect, to diving into your blind spot, to unearthing innovative ideas and taking bold action. Kind of convenient for me, right? But hopefully you're developing a sense of what honesty is and what it definitely is not.

WHAT IS HONESTY?

For Russell Weiner, honesty means *doing*, not saying. "You're not really honest unless you change," he explained. For Jay Farner, honesty means *transparency*. "Bringing transparency to anything is what makes the difference," he said. "People will see it and that will inspire them to want to work at your organization when they see you're genuine and authentic and trusting."

Dan Hesse defines it as "integrity . . . that's what honesty in business means to me . . . we had it in our culture, and one thing we've learned—not only through studies but over the years—is really successful companies have strong cultures. Honesty and integrity are really important, and customers thrive on it."

For Rohit Malik, honesty means *authenticity*. "That you mean what you say," he clarified, "and when you tell somebody something, [it's] a commitment when you give someone your word." Malik also identifies honesty as "being really authentic with who you really are, with your employees, your customers, your shareholders, and to not overmarket yourself to be someone you're not."

For Alexander McCobin, honesty is simply telling the *truth*. "In practice," he offered, "that [means] being truthful about the situation that a business or person is in, being vulnerable to admit when there are mistakes or things that are not going well, and also not deceiving oneself." For Ray Dalio, honesty means "saying what you think: the opposite of duality. Being forthright, honest, and accurate; describing things as you really see them [and] as they really are."

Honesty is all those things—along with the canary in the gold mine of our moral compass and the sinking feeling we get when we're even slightly off-course in our lives and businesses. To me, an honest business leader is someone who acknowledges the good news and the bad news and everything in between. It's about being brutally honest about what's going on with your customers—what problems they have and what solutions they crave. It's about designing a business that takes care of all constituents, facilitates growth and change, and helps empower people to innovate. It's about giving and taking feedback without offense; listening to the diverse perspectives of others; and considering that, as Ray Dalio says, we're all just dumb humans needing to open our primitive minds and learn a whole lot more. Living honestly means properly assessing the people around us, getting honest about what it takes to motivate and inspire them, and being unafraid to make changes to ensure we surround ourselves with the right people. It also means not succumbing to Warren Buffett's institutional imperative, and understanding that if we don't innovate, we might just cease to exist at all.

HONESTY: A PROFITABLE BUSINESS MODEL

The Heart Attack Grill, founded by Jon Basso, purposely serves burgers, fries, and other foods high in fat, sugar, and cholesterol. In fact, the *8,000-calorie* "bypass" burger is a favorite, as are the "flatliner fries" cooked in pure lard. The entire Las Vegas–based restaurant is themed like a hospital; customers wear hospital gowns, the waitstaff are "nurses," and customer orders are called "prescriptions."[1] Customers can also weigh in if they want to prove that they're over 350 pounds, because if they are, they eat for free.

Despite our country's current health movement, the Heart Attack Grill is thriving—earning not only patrons and fans but also media coverage for its outlandish commitment to harming its own customers. And yet, this is a classic case of caveat emptor—buyer beware—and customers can't *not* be aware of what they're getting into.

A moral hazard? Maybe. Dishonest? I don't think so. All around us, dishonesty tempts us with miracle diets and fake shed restaurants. But the Heart Attack Grill isn't one of those; instead, it shows us how powerful honesty can be in business. For better or worse, the Heart Attack Grill shows us that being honest, transparent, and authentic, even when the honest truth is harmful, can indeed produce profits. *Should it* is another ethical matter entirely, plus there's the issue of whether killing the customers who support your business is good business in the first place.

But at least the Heart Attack Grill is honest about its burgers and fries; which other fast-food restaurant can claim as much?

Perhaps Theranos founder Elizabeth Holmes and Vice Media's Shane Smith preferred dishonesty because somehow they considered it simpler: just create your own reality, blindly follow it, and don't bother dealing with the nuances of honesty at all. They certainly show that living your own truth can work—for a time, and until the truth catches up with you (which is surely why that phrase exists). But I suspect the Heart Attack Grill will survive for the long term, with nothing to hide, because the truth is that it's actually simpler to just be honest. In the face of such open candidness, what can we say about the Heart Attack Grill that it hasn't already said about itself? Indeed, brutal honesty has the power to render attacks powerless.

YOUR NEXT STEP IS HONESTLY UP TO YOU

Reminders to be honest exist everywhere—in our vernacular when we say, "to be honest . . . ," in our mottoes and mission statements, in our legends and stories (who doesn't know Pinocchio?), and in every Hallmark holiday movie that advises us to find our true selves. In high school at Milton Academy, I was reminded daily: *Dare To Be True*. At Brandeis as an undergrad, I read the seal declaring *Truth Even Unto Its Innermost Parts*. Thanks in part to Rohit Malik, Columbia Business School *again* reminded me to adhere to truth. The damn concept followed me around everywhere. I thought it was a throwaway. Didn't everyone know to be honest? Don't we learn that as kids? And in true Peter fashion, I was wrong. Despite the fact that honesty permeates our language, our stories, our religions, our institutes of higher learning, and more, it doesn't always infiltrate real life, to our own detriment. When you look at the life you've created, have you been honest with yourself? When you open up your corporate policies, is honesty *really* one of them? If not, isn't that ironic if we're to believe that honesty is, in fact, the best policy of all?

Very soon, honesty will be a prerequisite to greatness, because honesty is sustainable—both in your organization and in yourself. How long can your organization survive with roadblocks and blind spots and the institutional imperative? How long can you live being out of alignment with who you really are? Being honest is just so much easier than inventing ways around the truth, don't you think?

Unfortunately, dishonesty disguises itself as honesty all too often, frequently in our own heads and ubiquitously in the business world. We conjure a thought, or take an action, and then rationalize what we've done to protect our delicate egos from admitting that we've made a mistake. On the scale of a business, those protective instincts compound into terrible consequences that pollute both our world and our ethics. We humans fight an uphill battle with what is true, but I hope you'll agree that honesty not only gives you a strategic tool to create spectacular results in your life and business; it also represents the future of commerce in an increasingly transparent world that won't tolerate deceit for much longer.

At least, as a millennial, that's my hope. It's a brave new world with lots more choices than we've ever had before, brought to us by lots more information than anyone had ever thought possible. During this seismic time, it behooves us to realize that we, as both business leaders and consumers, all want the same happiness, success, and safety. It's just that the world is moving faster. It's only getting worse or only getting better, depending on how you look at innovation and technology. Soon, wearable and even implanted technology will become the norm, and that will set off an entirely new and uncharted ecosystem of business in which we merely think of an item we need and it arrives on our door-step within an hour. When our minds ask for the best products from the most reputable companies, will yours make the short list?

Right now, in this fascinating infancy of information ubiquity, organizations have an opportunity to recognize what is different and what is the same, and to reorganize themselves toward a future that will reward transparency and bravery and render meaningless secrecy and fear. There is a formula to success; there is a constant about the nature of how humans understand reality, interact, and trust each other. Don't delay. Now is the time for change, because preparing now is the only sound business strategy that makes any sense in a world moving at this speed.

Here's the best part: you have the ultimate power to use brutal honesty to achieve massive success. You, as a business leader, are a con-stant source of morals, values, and decision-making acumen. You have the power to help your brand evolve and innovate, and to inspire your colleagues to embrace honesty, too. You have a responsibility to hon-estly get to know yourself, accept yourself, and love yourself. In fact, in coaching leaders, growing companies, and helping clients innovate and grow, I've seen that few people truly understand, accept, and love who they are. As *New York Times* best-selling author Lewis Howes once told me, "Everything negative usually stems from people not understanding who they are. They're judging themselves and other people. We haven't learned the art and skill of falling in love with who we are. And that is the biggest struggle."

Indeed, it's tough out there in the world. In our modern times, it seems like everything needs to be overhauled. With environmental dam-age and fake accounts and falsified emissions reports and deliberately addictive medications, our business world kind of sucks sometimes. Our politics suck all the time. Occasionally, the ego-driven attitudes of our ungrateful, entitled friends, family members, and colleagues suck, too. But you don't have to suck. You can just be honest. Honestly you. If you're not going to embrace your honest self, you'll never give others the chance to embrace the true you, either. And when that happens, everybody loses.

You get fifty million choices to make every day, and I can only hope you'll make some of them more honest. But no matter what you do, just remember to accept the fact that your actions are the bread crumb trail that tells you who you are. And at the end of the day, when you're creeping along the hallways of eldercare with your walker and cane, I hope you can look back and think, *Well, at least I was honest.*

Confucius, perhaps the greatest executive leader who never was, knew the truth: "To know that we know what we know, and that we do not know what we do not know, that is true knowledge."[2] Honesty with the self is perhaps the most difficult level of honesty, but it takes being honest on three levels to achieve the industry-dominating results of the greatest leaders of our time:

First, you must be brutally honest about the world around you, the industry around you, and the environment in which you live and work.

Second, within that context, you must be honest with and about the others around you so you can find and inspire the right people to help you achieve your biggest goals and live your most fulfilling life.

Third, you must be honest with yourself about who you really are, what you really want, and what it will take to get there.

When you get into honest alignment, you'll inevitably accept your *real* dreams, fears, desires, and goals. When you do that, you'll rearrange your life by embracing the people who will join your fight and help you achieve greatness. That's how industry-dominating results happen; not through sheer will or supreme intellect but by embracing honesty as a strategic tool to bend your world toward you and *thrive.*

In a life with no guarantees, we *all* have the choice to embrace honesty and allow fortune to favor us—the bold—for who we really are.

Will you join us?

GET THE WORKBOOK

Would you like to lead your team through the exercise of using strategic honesty? Go to peterkozodoy.com/honesty to get the free workbook that can help your team unearth new insights by getting honest with and about your community, your others, and yourselves.

APPENDIX

List of Core Values for Your Values Hierarchy

The following is a list of five hundred personal values, in alphabetical order, to help you create your values hierarchy.[1] This list is by no means exhaustive, and I encourage you to Google phrases like "core values" and "common adjectives" to ensure you get the ones that feel right to you. The idea is to narrow this list down to twenty or thirty, and then to six to ten final values. Then put them in order from most important to least important, thinking critically about when you might put one value over another. Of course, some situations might disrupt your hierarchy, but at least it will be there to guide you and help you understand why you might be feeling a certain way or why you might be inclined to take a certain action.

Above and beyond
Acceptance
Accessibility
Accomplishment
Accountability
Accuracy
Accurate
Achievement
Activity
Adaptability
Adventure
Adventurous
Affection
Affective
Aggressive
Aggressiveness
Agility
Alert
Alertness
Altruism
Ambition
Amusement
Anti-bureaucratic
Anticipate
Anticipation
Anti-corporate
Appreciation
Approachability
Approachable
Assertive
Assertiveness
Attention to detail
Attentive
Attentiveness
Availability

Available
Awareness
Balance
Beauty
Being the best
Belonging
Best
Best people
Bold
Boldness
Bravery
Brilliance
Brilliant
Calm
Calmness
Candor
Capability
Capable
Careful
Carefulness
Caring
Certainty
Challenge
Change
Character
Charity
Cheerful
Citizenship
Clean
Cleanliness
Clear
Clear-minded
Clever
Clients
Collaboration

Comfort
Commitment
Common sense
Communication
Community
Compassion
Competence
Competency
Competition
Competitive
Completion
Composure
Comprehensive
Concentration
Concern for others
Confidence
Confidential
Confidentiality
Conformity
Connection
Consciousness
Consistency
Content
Contentment
Continuity
Continuous
    improvement
Contribution
Control
Conviction
Cooperation
Coordination
Cordiality
Correct
Courage

Courtesy
Craftiness
Craftsmanship
Creation
Creative
Creativity
Credibility
Cunning
Curiosity
Customer focus
Customer satisfaction
Customer service
Customers
Daring
Decency
Decisive
Decisiveness
Dedication
Delight
Democratic
Dependability
Depth
Determination
Determined
Development
Devotion
Devout
Different
Differentiation
Dignity
Diligence
Direct
Directness
Discipline
Discovery

Discretion
Diversity
Dominance
Down-to-earth
Dreaming
Drive
Duty
Eagerness
Ease of use
Economy
Education
Effective
Effectiveness
Efficiency
Efficient
Elegance
Empathy
Employees
Empower
Empowering
Encouragement
Endurance
Energy
Engagement
Enjoyment
Entertainment
Enthusiasm
Entrepreneurship
Environment
Equality
Equitable
Ethical
Exceed expectations
Excellence
Excitement

Exciting
Exhilarating
Exuberance
Experience
Expertise
Exploration
Explore
Expressive
Extrovert
Fairness
Faith
Faithfulness
Family
Family atmosphere
Famous
Fashion
Fast
Fearless
Ferocious
Fidelity
Fierce
Firm
Fitness
Flair
Flexibility
Flexible
Fluency
Focus
Focus on future
Foresight
Formal
Fortitude
Freedom
Fresh
Fresh ideas

Friendly	Impartial	Lively
Friendship	Impious	Local
Frugality	Improvement	Logic
Fun	Independence	Longevity
Generosity	Individuality	Love
Genius	Industry	Loyalty
Giving	Informal	Mastery
Global	Innovation	Maturity
Goodness	Innovative	Maximizing
Goodwill	Inquisitive	Maximum utilization
Gratitude	Insight	Meaning
Great	Insightful	Meekness
Greatness	Inspiration	Mellow
Growth	Integrity	Members
Guidance	Intelligence	Merit
Happiness	Intensity	Meritocracy
Hard work	International	Meticulous
Harmony	Intuition	Mindful
Health	Intuitive	Moderation
Heart	Invention	Modesty
Helpful	Investing	Motivation
Heroism	Investment	Mystery
History	Inviting	Neatness
Holiness	Irreverence	Nerve
Honesty	Irreverent	No bureaucracy
Honor	Joy	Obedience
Hope	Justice	Open
Hopeful	Kindness	Open-minded
Hospitality	Knowledge	Openness
Humble	Leadership	Optimism
Humility	Learning	Order
Humor	Legal	Organization
Hygiene	Levelheaded	Original
Imagination	Liberty	Originality
Impact	Listening	Outrageous

Partnership	Prepared	Resolve
Passion	Preservation	Resourceful
Patience	Pride	Resourcefulness
Patient-centered	Privacy	Respect
Patient-focused	Proactive	Respect for others
Patients	Proactively	Respect for the
Patient satisfaction	Productivity	individual
Patriotism	Profane	Responsibility
Peace	Professionalism	Responsiveness
People	Profitability	Rest
Perception	Profits	Restraint
Perceptive	Progress	Results
Perfection	Prosperity	Results-oriented
Performance	Prudence	Reverence
Perseverance	Punctuality	Rigor
Persistence	Purity	Risk
Personal development	Pursue	Risk-taking
Personal growth	Pursuit	Rule of law
Persuasive	Quality	Sacrifice
Philanthropy	Quality of work	Safety
Play	Rational	Sanitary
Playfulness	Real	Satisfaction
Pleasantness	Realistic	Security
Poise	Reason	Self-awareness
Polish	Recognition	Self-control
Popularity	Recreation	Self-directed
Positive	Refined	Selfless
Potency	Reflection	Self motivation
Potential	Relationships	Self-reliance
Power	Relaxation	Self responsibility
Powerful	Reliability	Sense of humor
Practical	Reliable	Sensitivity
Pragmatic	Resilience	Serenity
Precise	Resolute	Serious
Precision	Resolution	Service

Shared prosperity	Sustainability	Universal
Sharing	Sympathy	Useful
Shrewd	Synergy	Utility
Significance	Systemization	Valor
Silence	Talent	Value
Silliness	Teamwork	Value creation
Simplicity	Temperance	Variety
Sincerity	Thankful	Victorious
Skill	Thorough	Victory
Skillfulness	Thoughtful	Vigor
Smart	Timeliness	Virtue
Solitude	Timely	Vision
Speed	Tolerance	Vital
Spirit	Tough	Vitality
Spirituality	Toughness	Warmth
Spontaneous	Traditional	Watchful
Stability	Training	Watchfulness
Standardization	Tranquility	Wealth
Status	Transparency	Welcoming
Stealth	Trust	Willfulness
Stewardship	Trustworthy	Winning
Strength	Truth	Wisdom
Structure	Understanding	Wonder
Succeed	Unflappable	Worldwide
Success	Unique	Work/Life balance
Support	Uniqueness	
Surprise	Unity	

NOTES

INTRODUCTION

1. As of 1994; John Antioco took over in 1997. Erik Devaney, "Netflix vs Blockbuster – 3 Key Takeaways," *Drift* (blog), July 6, 2017, accessed March 7, 2019, https://www.drift.com/blog/netflix-vs-blockbuster.
2. Valued according to its sale to Viacom Inc. Christopher Harress, "The Sad End Of Blockbuster Video: The Onetime $5 Billion Company Is Being Liquidated As Competition From Online Giants Netflix And Hulu Prove All Too Much For The Iconic Brand," *International Business Times*, December 5, 2013, accessed February 1, 2020, https://www.ibtimes.com/sad-end-blockbuster-video-onetime-5-billion-company-being-liquidated-competition-1496962.
3. "Blockbuster LLC," Wikipedia, accessed March 31, 2019, https://en.wikipedia.org/wiki/Blockbuster_LLC.
4. Greg Sandoval, "Former Blockbuster CEO tells his side of Netflix story," CNET, May 25, 2011, accessed March 7, 2019, https://www.cnet.com/news/former-blockbuster-ceo-tells-his-side-of-netflix-story.
5. Greg Satell, "The Myth of the Moron CEO," *Forbes*, August 1, 2013, accessed February 1, 2020, https://www.forbes.com/sites/gregsatell/2013/08/01/the-myth-of-the-moron-ceo/#686a76082c58.
6. Ibid.
7. Julia Pyper, "A Conversation with David Crane on Getting Fired From NRG and What's Next for His Energy Plans," Green Tech Media, April 29, 2016, accessed January 12, 2019, https://www.greentechmedia.com/articles/read/a-conversation-with-david-crane#gs.rYrvUJs.
8. Compares Sprint's closing stock price (NYSE:S) to both the S&P 500 Index closing price and the Vanguard Communications Services ETF (NYSE:VOX) closing price in the period between January 2, 2009, and July 31, 2014.
9. Niccolo Machiavelli, *The Prince,* Project Gutenberg e-book, chapter 18: https://www.gutenberg.org/files/1232/1232-h/1232-h.htm.
10. "Bertrand Russell Quotes." BrainyQuote.com, accessed February 2, 2020, https://www.brainyquote.com/quotes/bertrand_russell_384629.

CHAPTER 1: FRAUD IS OUR FAULT

1. "Theranos," Wikipedia, accessed February 2, 2020, https://en.wikipedia.org/wiki/Theranos.
2. "A Theranos Timeline," *New York Times*, July 9, 2016, accessed January 12, 2019, https://www.nytimes.com/2016/07/09/business/theranos-elizabeth-holmes-timeline.html.
3. Virginia Heffernan, "Elizabeth Holmes Downfall Has Been Explained Deeply—By Men," *Wired*, July 19, 2018, accessed January 12, 2019, https://www.wired.com/story/elizabeth-holmes-downfall-has-been-explained-deeplyby-men.
4. Ibid.
5. Reeves Wiedeman, "A Company Built on a Bluff," *New York* magazine, June 10, 2018, accessed January 12, 2019, http://nymag.com/intelligencer/2018/06/inside-vice-media-shane-smith.html.
6. Ibid.
7. Ibid.
8. Emily Steel, "At Vice, Cutting-Edge Media and Allegations of Old-School Sexual Harassment," *New York Times*, December 23, 2017, accessed January 12, 2019, https://www.nytimes.com/2017/12/23/business/media/vice-sexual-harassment.html.
9. Ibid.
10. Wiedeman, "A Company Built on a Bluff."
11. Keach Hagey, "Vice Just Had a Big Revenue Miss, and Investors Are Getting Antsy," *Wall Street Journal*, February 7, 2018, accessed January 12, 2019, https://www.wsj.com/articles/vice-media-confronts-tv-woes-amid-leadership-troubles-1518003121.
12. Siddharth Venkataramakrishnan, "Vice Media writes down value of international arm," *Financial Times*, January 6, 2020, accessed February 2, 2020, https://www.ft.com/content/992644be-30b2-11ea-9703-eea0cae3f0de.
13. "It's Lit, a guide to what teens think is cool," Google, accessed January 12, 2019, https://storage.googleapis.com/think/docs/its-lit.pdf
14. Wiedeman, "A Company Built on a Bluff."
15. Alex Sherman, "Vice's $400 million deal for Refinery29 illustrates the pointlessness of private valuations," *CNBC*, October 3, 2019, accessed February 2, 2020, https://www.cnbc.com/2019/10/03/vices-400-million-deal-for-refinery29-illustrates-the-pointlessness-of-private-valuations.html.
16. You can read the entire story here, ironically on Vice's website, which hopefully serves to prove my point: Oobah Butler, "I Made My Shed the Top-Rated Restaurant on TripAdvisor," *Vice*, December 7, 2017, accessed January 12, 2019, https://www.vice.com/en_us/article/434gqw/i-made-my-shed-the-top-rated-restaurant-on-tripadvisor.

CHAPTER 2: THE COMPLICATED STORY OF WHY WE LIE

1. William Wan and Sarah Kaplan, "Why Liars Lie: What science tells us about deception," *Washington Post*, August 24, 2018, accessed March 16, 2019, https://

www.washingtonpost.com/news/speaking-of-science/wp/2018/08/24/why
-liars-lie-what-science-tells-us-about-false-statements.

2. "Was 2018 The Year Of The Influential Consumer?" *Nielsen*, December 17, 2018, accessed February 2, 2020, https://www.nielsen.com/us/en/insights/article /2018/was-2018-the-year-of-the-influential-sustainable-consumer/.

3. Conscious Capitalism, Inc. Board of Directors, Conscious Capitalism, accessed January 12, 2019, https://www.consciouscapitalism.org/boardofdirectors.

4. "Guiding principles," *Rotary*, accessed February 9, 2020, https://my.rotary.org /en/guiding-principles.

CHAPTER 3: GIVING POWER TO THE PEOPLE WILL MAKE YOU RICH

1. Maggie McGrath, "Inside The 2020 Just 100: How We Rank America's Best Corporate Actors," *Forbes*, November 12, 2019, accessed February 2, 2020, https:// www.forbes.com/sites/maggiemcgrath/2019/11/12/inside-the-2020-just-100 -how-we-rank-americas-best-corporate-actors/#3f702c5f5bc4.

2. "JUST Capital and Forbes Announce Partnership to Collaborate on Research Based on Corporate Behavior," *Forbes*, November 4, 2016, accessed January 12, 2019, https://www.forbes.com/sites/forbespr/2016/11/04/just-capital-and-forbes -announce-partnership-to-collaborate-on-research-based-on-corporate-behavior /#26f257183a76.

3. "The JUST 100," YouTube video, 1:45, posted by Just Capital, December 14, 2017, accessed January 12, 2019, https://youtu.be/btr_6b9fhdM.

4. "From Insight to Action—JUST Capital's 2018 Survey Results & Roadmap for Corporate America," JUST Capital, October 2018, accessed January 12, 2019, https://justcapital.com/wp-content/uploads/2018/10/JUSTCapital_Survey Report_10252018.pdf.

5. "New Survey Reveals 75% of Millennials Expect Employers to Take a Stand on Social Issues," Glassdoor, September 25, 2017, accessed February 14, 2020, https://www.glassdoor.com/blog/corporate-social-responsibility/.

CHAPTER 4: THE HOURGLASS OF HONESTY

1. Mark Manson, "Personal growth is merely the process of learning to lie to oneself less," Instagram, February 8, 2020, accessed February 9, 2020, https://www .instagram.com/p/B8T2MgAAg_c/.

2. "Steve Jobs' Vision of the World," YouTube video, 0:45, posted by Gocarlo, November 19, 2011. https://youtu.be/UvEiSa6_EPA.

3. "'You've got to find what you love,' Jobs Says," *Stanford News*, June 14, 2005, accessed January 12, 2019, https://news.stanford.edu/2005/06/14/jobs -061505.

CHAPTER 5: SALES: THE HONEST-TO-GOODNESS TECHNIQUE FOR EXPLOSIVE SALES

1. Martin Whittaker, "Snap Back to Reality for CEOs on Corporate Purpose," LinkedIn, October 3, 2019, accessed October 4, 2019, https://www.linkedin.com/pulse/snap-back-reality-ceos-corporate-purpose-martin-whittaker.
2. Mike Rowe, "Truth in Advertising," January 26, 2017, accessed February 2, 2020, https://mikerowe.com/2017/01/truth-in-advertising.
3. A copy of the original email was forwarded to me by Sean McCourt.
4. Mike Rowe, Facebook post, February 16, 2017, accessed February 2, 2020, https://www.facebook.com/TheRealMikeRowe/posts/time-to-close-the-loop-on-charlotte-mccourts-great-american-girl-scout-cookie-ca/1439024296107709.

CHAPTER 6: MARKETING: THE UNDENIABLE POWER OF COURAGEOUS CANDOR

1. "Domino's—Show Us Your Pizza," YouTube video, 0:30, posted by MU Franchising, February 17, 2011, https://www.youtube.com/watch?v=Aqy8mAs-Izk.
2. Comparing Domino's Pizza (DPZ) closing stock prices from January 4, 2010 to June 22, 2018, to the S&P 500 (SPX) closing prices on the same dates. DPZ's total stock return was nearly twenty-three times larger than the SPX's total return over that period.
3. "Domino's DXP VR," YouTube video, 1:47, posted by "Domino's Pizza," July 18, 2016, https://www.youtube.com/watch?v=6m5QdrMELIQ.

CHAPTER 7: FINANCE: INVESTING LIKE BUFFETT IN LONG-TERM HONESTY

1. Fred Imbert, "Warren Buffett Likes Quarterly Earnings Reports from Companies but Not Guidance," CNBC, August 30, 2018, accessed March 16, 2019, https://www.cnbc.com/2018/08/30/warren-buffett-i-like-quarterly-reports-from-companies-but-not-guidance.html.
2. Verizon Communications Annual Report Form 10-K for the Fiscal Year ended December 31, 2008, accessed March 17, 2019, http://verizon.api.edgar-online.com/EFX_dll/EdgarPro.dll?FetchFilingHTML1?SessionID=s_w3U3CGBeUgXx5&ID=6435582.
3. Special thanks to Trevor S. Harris, Professor of Accounting at Columbia Business School, for providing guidance on this example.
4. "Sprint is most improved company in customer satisfaction – Fact Sheet," Sprint, May 21, 2013, accessed February 3, 2020, https://newsroom.sprint.com/sprint-is-most-improved-company-in-customer-satisfaction-fact-sheet.htm.
5. "Sprint Is First Among Major Wireless Carriers for Customer Satisfaction," Sprint, May 15, 2012, accessed February 3, 2020, https://newsroom.sprint.com/sprint-is-first-among-major-wireless-carriers-for-customer-satisfaction.htm.

6. Donald Trump, Twitter post, August 17, 2018, 4:30 a.m., https://twitter.com /realdonaldtrump/status/1030416679069777921.

CHAPTER 8: MANAGEMENT: HOW AUDACIOUS AUTHENTICITY BUILT AN EMPIRE

1. "The Ritz-Carlton Hotel Company," Wikipedia, accessed January 12, 2019, https://en.wikipedia.org/wiki/The_Ritz-Carlton_Hotel_Company.
2. "The Ritz-Carlton Gold Standards," The Ritz-Carlton, accessed January 12, 2019, http://www.ritzcarlton.com/en/about/gold-standards.
3. "What It Takes to Work Here: Ritz-Carlton Hotels," Minyanville, accessed January 12, 2019, https://web.archive.org/web/20190630055514/http:/www .minyanville.com/special-features/articles/ritz-carlton-ritz-jobs-jobs-ritz/6/15 /2010/id/28530.
4. Megan Wells, "Turnover and Retention Rates for Hotels and the Hospitality Industry," Dailypay, November 13, 2018, accessed January 12, 2019, https://business .dailypay.com/blog/staff-turnover-rates-hotel-motel-hospitality-industry.
5. Katie Kelly Bell, "Former Ritz Carlton President Horst Schulze Talks About the New Frontier In Luxury Hotels," *Forbes*, May 3, 2012, accessed January 12, 2019, https://www.forbes.com/sites/katiebell/2012/05/03/horst-schulze-on-the -new-frontier-in-luxury-hotels/#6f68d29666ef.

CHAPTER 9: COMMUNICATION: HOW HONEST FEEDBACK LED TO BILLION-DOLLAR GREATNESS

1. Ray Dalio, *Principles* (New York: Simon & Schuster, 2017), ix.
2. Dalio, *Principles*, jacket cover.
3. Tae Kim, "Ray Dalio Made $50 Billion for His Clients, Topping List of Biggest Hedge Fund Moneymakers Ever," CNBC, January 26, 2018, accessed January 19, 2019, https://www.cnbc.com/2018/01/26/ray-dalio-made-50-billion-for-his-clients -topping-list-of-biggest-hedge-fund-money-makers-ever.html.
4. Sarah Berger, "This powerful formula helped Ray Dalio build his $18 billion fortune," CNBC, October 11, 2018, accessed February 9, 2020, https://www.cnbc .com/2018/10/11/this-powerful-formula-helped-ray-dalio-build-his-18-billion -fortune.html.
5. Dalio, *Principles*, 34.
6. Dalio, *Principles*, 36.
7. Email correspondence between Dalio and the author, received October 17, 2018.
8. Julia La Roche, "RAY DALIO: It's 'Fantastic' When We Play Conversations We've Recorded Back to Our Employees," *Business Insider*, December 11, 2014, accessed January 12, 2019, https://www.businessinsider.com/bridgewater-records -conversations-2014-12.
9. Richard Feloni, "Ray Dalio Explains Why 25 Percent of Bridgewater Employees Don't Last More Than 18 Months at the Hedge Fund Giant," *Business Insider*,

March 23, 2016, accessed January 12, 2019, https://www.businessinsider.com /biggest-challenges-new-bridgewater-employees-face-2016-3.

10. Bess Levin, "A Sex Scandal at Bridgewater Is Testing Ray Dalio's 'Radical' Philosophy," *Vanity Fair*, November 7, 2017, accessed January 12, 2019, https://www .vanityfair.com/news/2017/11/ray-dalio-greg-jensen-bridgewater.

11. Jacquelyn Smith, "23 Intense Questions You'll Have to Answer If You Want to Work at the World's Largest Hedge Fund," *Business Insider*, April 15, 2016, accessed January 12, 2019, https://www.businessinsider.com/intense-bridgewater-associates -interview-questions-2016-4#why-shouldnt-we-hire-you-manager-candidate-23.

12. Richard Feloni, "Here's Why the World's Largest Hedge Fund Makes Applicants Take 5 Personality Tests Before Sitting Through Hours of Intensive Interviews," *Yahoo! Finance*, August 16, 2016, accessed January 12, 2019, https://finance .yahoo.com/news/heres-why-worlds-largest-hedge-124000146.html.

13. Bess Levin, "Ray Dalio's Master Plan to Make His Hedge Fund Cult Immortal," *Vanity Fair*, August 10, 2017, accessed January 12, 2019, https://www.vanityfair .com/news/2017/08/ray-dalio-bridgewater-charter.

14. Alexandra Stevenson and Matthew Goldstein, "At World's Largest Hedge Fund, Sex, Fear and Video Surveillance," *New York Times*, July 27, 2016, accessed January 12, 2019, https://www.nytimes.com/2016/07/27/business/dealbook/bridgewater -associates-hedge-fund-culture-ray-dalio.html.

15. "Bridgewater Associates Employee Reviews," Indeed, accessed January 12, 2019, https://www.indeed.com/cmp/Bridgewater-Associates/reviews?fcountry =ALL&lang=.

16. Feloni, "Ray Dalio Explains Why 25 Percent of Bridgewater Employees Don't Last More Than 18 Months at the Hedge Fund Giant."

17. Excerpt lightly edited for grammar and punctuation, not for content: "Bridgewater Associates Employee Reviews," Indeed, accessed January 12, 2019, https://www .indeed.com/cmp/Bridgewater-Associates/reviews?fcountry=ALL&lang=.

CHAPTER 10: INNOVATION: SAYING NO TO THE STATUS QUO

1. "Quicken Loans' 1st Quarter Mortgage Volume Solidifies Its Position as America's Largest Residential Lender," Quicken Loans, May 2, 2018, accessed January 19, 2019, https://www.quickenloans.com/press-room/2018/05/02/ quicken-loans-1st-quarter-mortgage-volume-solidifies-position-americas-largest -residential-lender.

2. "Fast Facts," Quicken Loans, accessed February 3, 2020, https://www.quicken loans.com/press-room/fast-facts/.

3. "It's Who We Are—Not What We Do: Ideas Are Supported By Belief | Quicken Loans Culture," YouTube video, 4:24, posted by Quicken Loans, November 8, 2013, https://www.youtube.com/watch?v=X2mnx_Ce7ck.

4. "To the Shareholders of Berkshire Hathaway Inc.," Berkshire Hathaway, accessed January 12, 2019, http://www.berkshirehathaway.com/letters/1998htm.html.

CHAPTER 11: LEADERSHIP: THE UNDERAPPRECIATED QUALITY OF SUPREME IGNORANCE

1. Sections of this chapter originally appear in Peter Kozodoy, "Bethenny Frankel Just Gave Brilliant Advice on How She Went From TV Housewife to 'Shark Tank' Star," Inc.com, October 26, 2017, accessed January 12, 2019, https://www.inc.com/peter-kozodoy/bethenny-frankel-went-from-tv-housewife-to-shark-tank-expert-here-are-her-2-top-pieces-of-advice.html.
2. Dalio, *Principles*, ix.
3. Nate Silver, *The Signal and the Noise: Why So Many Predictions Fail—but Some Don't* (New York: Penguin Books, 2015), 45.
4. "To the Shareholders of Berkshire Hathaway Inc.," Berkshire Hathaway, accessed January 12, 2019, http://www.berkshirehathaway.com/letters/1985.html.
5. Re-created from: "File:Johari window.PNG," Wikipedia, accessed January 12, 2019, https://commons.wikimedia.org/wiki/File:Johari_Window.PNG.
6. Sections of this chapter originally appear in Peter Kozodoy, "Try This Technique 11,000 Leaders Use to Understand Themselves Better," Inc.com, June 14, 2017, accessed January 12, 2019, https://www.inc.com/peter-kozodoy/try-this-technique-11000-leaders-use-to-understand-themselves-better.html.
7. "To the Shareholders of Berkshire Hathaway Inc.," Berkshire Hathaway, accessed January 12, 2019, http://www.berkshirehathaway.com/letters/1983.html.
8. Pietersen's ideals are taken largely from a blog post on his personal website: Willie Pietersen, "Outside-In Thinking; Crucial but Unnatural," WilliePietersen.com, August 13, 2015, accessed January 12, 2019, https://williepietersen.com/outside-in-thinking-crucial-but-unnatural.

CHAPTER 12: HOW TO GET HONEST WITH AND ABOUT YOUR COMMUNITY

1. "To the Shareholders of Berkshire Hathaway Inc.," Berkshire Hathaway, 1989, accessed January 12, 2019, http://www.berkshirehathaway.com/letters/1989.html.
2. James Clear, "How to Start New Habits that Actually Stick," accessed February 4, 2020, https://jamesclear.com/three-steps-habit-change.

CHAPTER 13: HOW TO GET HONEST WITH AND ABOUT YOUR OTHERS

1. "Formula for Change," Wikipedia, accessed November 10, 2019, https://en.wikipedia.org/wiki/Formula_for_change.
2. "Asch Conformity Experiment," YouTube video, 4:10, posted by "eqivideos," December 22, 2007, https://youtu.be/TYIh4MkcfJA.
3. "Conquering a Culture of Indecision," *Harvard Business Review*, accessed January 12, 2019, https://hbr.org/2006/01/conquering-a-culture-of-indecision.

4. Jim Harter, "Employee Engagement on the Rise in the U.S.," Gallup, August 26, 2018, accessed March 31, 2019, https://news.gallup.com/poll/241649 /employee-engagement-rise.aspx.
5. Susan Sorenson, "How Employee Engagement Drives Growth," Gallup, June 20, 2013, accessed October 20, 2019, https://www.gallup.com/workplace/236927 /employee-engagement-drives-growth.aspx.

CHAPTER 14: HOW TO GET HONEST WITH AND ABOUT YOURSELF

1. Sections of this chapter originally appeared on Inc.com: Peter Kozodoy, "The 1 Trick to Knowing Whether A Prospect Will Be A Good (Or Terrible) Client," Inc.com, October 24, 2017, accessed February 18, 2020, https://www.inc.com /peter-kozodoy/what-this-values-exercise-taught-me-about-selecting-right -clients.html.

CHAPTER 15: EFFECTIVE HONESTY FOR MANAGERS AND FRONTLINE EMPLOYEES

1. Susan J. Ashford and James R. Detert, "Get the Boss to Buy In," *Harvard Business Review,* January–February 2015, accessed January 12, 2019, https://hbr .org/2015/01/get-the-boss-to-buy-in.

CONCLUSION

1. See for more information: http://www.heartattackgrill.com.
2. As paraphrased by Henry David Thoreau, in *Walden* (CreateSpace Independent Publishing Platform, 2018), chap 1.

APPENDIX

1. Special thanks to Threads Culture for this excellent list of examples: "Core Values Examples," Threads Culture, accessed November 10, 2019, https://www .threadsculture.com/core-values-examples.

INDEX

— ABOUT THE AUTHOR —

Photo by Riq Dilly

Peter Kozodoy is an *Inc. 5000* serial entrepreneur, TEDx speaker, and business coach who works with organizations and their leaders to help them overcome self-limiting bullsh*t and use honesty to achieve greatness. His articles on leadership and entrepreneurship have appeared in *Forbes, Inc.*, HuffPost, PR Daily, and more. He holds a BA in economics from Brandeis University and an MBA from Columbia Business School, and lives outside New York City with his wife and their spoiled dog. To strike up an honest conversation, visit PeterKozodoy.com.